MEMORY, COMMUNITY, AND ACTIVISM

MEXICAN MIGRATION AND LABOR IN THE PACIFIC NORTHWEST

JERRY GARCIA AND GILBERTO GARCIA
EDITORS

JSRI BOOKS
PUBLISHED BY THE JULIAN SAMORA RESEARCH INSTITUTE
MICHIGAN STATE UNIVERSITY • EAST LANSING, MICHIGAN

Cover Design by Danny Layne, JSRI
Book Layout & Design by Danny Layne, JSRI

Visit the Julian Samora Research Institute online at:
http://www.jsri.msu.edu

Visit Michigan State University Press online at:
http://www.msu.edu/msupress

TABLE OF CONTENTS

MEMORY, COMMUNITY, AND ACTIVISM:
MEXICAN MIGRATION AND LABOR IN THE PACIFIC NORTHWEST

TABLE OF CONTENTS

Dedicated To

Para Betty Kumiko Samulitis, nunca me olvidaré de nuestro
tiempo junto en Japón y su inspiración sobre los años...
con amor...

Jerry Garcia

Para mi esposa Dora, que participo en el nacimiento de este libro,
aguantando horas de soledad, cuando mi mente se perdia,
en el tema de mis investigaciones...

Gilberto Garcia

ACKNOWLEDGEMENTS

The conceptualization of this book goes back at least a decade when I first began collaborating with my longtime mentor Gilberto Garcia as a graduate student at Eastern Washington University. His mentorship sparked my intellectual curiosity on the Mexican diaspora in the Pacific Northwest, so my first words of thanks go to him for his mentoring and friendship. The completion of any book, an edited one in particular, is the culmination of many people working together. Unlike the genesis of other anthologies where conferences are held, participants are invited, and the best of the best get chosen for publication, my coeditor and I were faced with a daunting task of simply finding first-rate authors doing rigorous scholarship on Mexicans in the Pacific Northwest. As we note in the introduction and conclusion of this book, scholarship on this region remains underdeveloped and authors scarce. Nevertheless, over a period of two years we were able to identify scholars doing original and new scholarship on Mexicans in the Northwest. The various contributors deserve our sincere appreciation. They wrote their respective chapters with creativity and professionalism. More importantly, they showed great patience and trust when this project took longer than expected to complete.

I also want to thank Dionicio Valdés, Director of Julian Samora Research Institute (JSRI) at Michigan State University, for seeing the contributions this book makes to the field of Chicana/o Studies and for agreeing to publish this book under their new Latino series publications. We would also like to give a word of thanks to Danny Layne at the JSRI who provided excellent technical expertise on the design of the book and its layout. We are also grateful to the anonymous reviewers for the JSRI who provided critical and insightful suggestions to improve the volume.

ACKNOWLEDGEMENTS

A note of thanks and appreciation to Raul Garcia for his help in searching the special collections and archives at the University of Washington for the chapter on Chicana/o Studies Directions in the Northwest. Gilberto Garcia wants to thank Dr. Lawrence Briggs, Associate Dean of Graduate Studies and Adjunct Professor in the History Department at Eastern Washington University, for reading previous drafts of his research on Othello, Wash., and for his suggestions on the chapter on the Catholic Church. We would also like to thank Pacific Northwest Chicano artist Daniel Desiga for allowing us to use his artwork for the book cover. Daniel's artwork visually expresses much of what is conveyed in this volume of work. A word of thanks to Andrejs Plakans, Chair, History Department at Iowa State University for his support in my (J. Garcia) research endeavors. Lastly, to Janis Holmberg, the copyeditor, who helped bring to completion our project with her professionalism, insights, and suggestions on eleven separate chapters. Hopefully, this anthology will be an inspiration to young scholars who want to follow in our footsteps in recording the history of the Mexicano/Chicano community in the Northwest.

¡Mil Gracias!

Jerry Garcia and Gilberto Garcia
Editors

The cover art reflects portions of a 100-foot mural "El Sarape" that was created by artist Daniel DeSiga in August 2001. It is the sixtieth mural in Toppenish, Wash., and the first to depict Mexican Bracero workers during World War II.

INTRODUCTION

Beyond the Spanish Moment: Mexicans in the Pacific Northwest

Jerry Garcia

Overview

The movement of Mexicans into the Pacific Northwest has a long and varied history,[1] intertwined with the Spanish explorations beginning in the sixteenth century, continuing through the colonial period, followed by the migration of Mexicans in the nineteenth century and the settling out patterns of twentieth-century ethnic Mexicans. One central question regarding the experience of Mexicans in the Northwest is how do we approach their movement and arrival to this region? Are the Mexicans coming to the Northwest traditional immigrants into the region similar to their Euro-American counterparts? Is examining Mexican immigration and migration from the regional perspective too confining? Should we connect the movement of present-day Mexicans to the Northwest as simply another link in the chain that goes back to the Spanish explorations? On the one hand, Spanish-speaking people predate the arrival of English- speaking immigrants to the Pacific Northwest; on the other, the arrival of English and American explorers and immigrants supplanted this "Spanish moment." Nevertheless, the Spanish chapter of Pacific Northwest history has left an undeniable legacy on the region's history and landscape that provides a sense of continuity for ethnic Mexicans.

Currently, the region made up of Idaho, Oregon, and Washington has one of the oldest and most consistent streams of ethnic Mexicans in the country. The modern movement and settling out of Mexicans in the Northwest began in the early twentieth century, but as some essays in this collection will attest, the movement of Spanish-speaking individuals began long before this period. Thus, *Memory, Community, and Activism* will examine

1

the movement of Spanish-speaking individuals into the Pacific Northwest dating back to the colonial period and into the modern era when ethnic Mexicans began to emerge in large numbers and became permanent fixtures in the region. Furthermore, the essays in this volume provide new material on Mexican culture and agricultural labor in Pacific Northwest.

In general, Mexican immigration to the Pacific Northwest follows some of the same contours of the national pattern. For example, the impact of the Mexican Revolution reverberated well into the Northwest. With thousands of Mexicans being pushed and pulled into the United States by the turbulent period of the Revolution, jobs along the border region became scarce and competitive. This in turn created an expansion of the Mexican diaspora that reached into many points including the Pacific Northwest (see Chapter Three, "The Racialization of Mexican and Japanese Labor in the Pacific Northwest"). Furthermore, the first organized importation of Mexicans in 1917–1922 reached as far north as the Alaskan fisheries. Despite this movement of Mexicans into the Northwest during the early twentieth century, it is clear that well-established Mexican communities did not emerge until after the 1920s, when agricultural production expanded and recruitment of Mexican labor intensified. This expansion was due in part to the development of dams and canals that brought irrigation to such places as the Yakima, Willamette, and Snake River Valleys. Many of the first arrivals during this period were foreign-born Mexicans. For example, one source puts the Mexican population in Idaho at fewer than one hundred at the beginning of the twentieth century, but one thousand by 1920.[2]

The upheaval of the 1930s and the subsequent large-scale deportation drives that affected Mexicans in other regions also shaped the experience of Mexicans in the Northwest. Many Mexicans in the region were encouraged to leave and a policy of "whites only apply" developed because of the scarcity of work. In 1930 Washington reported 562 persons born in Mexico or having parents born in Mexico; Oregon, 1,568; and Idaho, 1,278.[3]

INTRODUCTION

However, by the beginning of the 1940s the Mexican American population of the Pacific Northwest stood at 6,400.[4]

This population increased considerably during and after World War II. For instance, as the United States entered World War II the immigration restrictions in place a decade earlier eased as the war caused labor shortages throughout the American West. Thus, the Pacific Northwest became the beneficiary of thousands of imported Mexican braceros from approximately 1943 to 1947. Although the bracero program all but ended for the region by 1947, one exception is the braceros brought in as a result of the Korean War in 1951 when some braceros were recruited into small regions of the Northwest such as the Columbia Basin in Washington.[5]

Although the Mexican braceros left an undeniable mark on the overall agricultural history of the region, it would be the post–World War II period that ushered in new movements of ethnic Mexicans into the region.

The immediate post–World War II movement of ethnic Mexicans into the Northwest was, by and large, U.S. citizens of Mexican ancestry coming from south Texas, the Midwest, Rocky Mountain region, and to a lesser extent California. Irrigation once again played an important role during this era. For example, completed in 1942, Grand Coulee Dam in Washington State focused on electricity to aid the war effort, but postwar production prioritized irrigation through the development and completion of the Columbia Basin Irrigation Project. Water first reached the Columbia Basin region in 1952 and in the subsequent decades over 500,000 acres have come under production. The large number of labor-intensive crops put into production ensured a steady stream of laborers into the region. During the late twentieth century the Pacific Northwest also received an untold number of undocumented Mexican immigrants. By 1970 the combined Mexican population of Idaho, Oregon, and Washington reached 55,221.[6]

When the 1986 Immigration Reform and Control Act (IRCA) was being discussed and eventually implemented thousands of Mexicans in the Northwest came forward for amnesty. Although IRCA had a short-term effect in deterring the movement of undocumented Mexicans into the United States, by the 1990s this clandestine movement had picked up once again. The agricultural and service industries of the Pacific Northwest have been beneficiaries of documented and undocumented workers since the end of World War II.

A Contemporary Demographic Profile

Scholarship on Mexican immigration to the United States remains a vibrant industry. However, as with other topics within the field of Chicana/o studies, the majority of the literature examines the movement of Mexicans into the southwestern region of the United States. As mentioned earlier, the Pacific Northwest has been host to the movement of colonial Spanish-speaking people and ethnic Mexican immigrants flowing out of Mexico and various regions of the United States during most of the twentieth century. These movements have profoundly shaped the late twentieth- century and early twenty-first century demographics of the Pacific Northwest and have affected the overall trend at the national level. Similar to their predecessors, today's Mexican immigrants and Mexican American migrants travel to the fertile valleys of Idaho, Oregon, and Washington, which continue to require a large labor force for their respective industries. Despite this contemporary period having been marked by an expanding ethnic Mexican population base and viable communities created throughout the region, the history of this group continues to be neglected.

The release of the 2000 Census and 2003 estimates demonstrates a continued increase in the Latino[7] population of the Northwest. Furthermore, as in the past, individuals of Mexican descent form the majority of this population. For example, at the national level the Mexican population recorded a 52.9 percent increase, the highest of any Latino group. Put another way, Mexicans increased nationally from 13.5 million to 20.6 million people from 1990–2000; and census estimates for July 2003 note an increase in the Mexican diaspora from 20.6 million in 2000 to 25.2 million by 2003. In addition, an examination of Mexican population growth from 1990 to 2000 indicates significant increases well above the national average in Idaho, 92 percent; Oregon, 144 percent; and Washington, 106 percent. A significant demographic feature of this increase is the large Mexican population in the Pacific Northwest in comparison to other Latino groups (Graph 1).

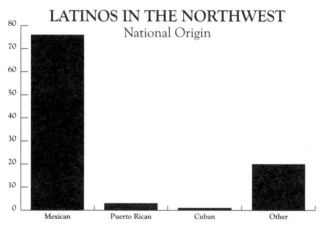

Graph 1. *Percent Distribution of the Population by Type: 2000*

According to the 2000 U.S. Census, each of the Northwest states ranked in the top ten in regard to percentage increase of Hispanics[8] and recorded a total Mexican population of 623,920, with the state of Washington having the tenth largest in the nation.[9] Although a large number of ethnic Mexicans immigrated and migrated to the Northwest for opportunities in the agricultural sector, they also gravitated toward urban and nonagricultural labor markets of the Northwest. In fact, as in other regions of the country, the overall Latino population resides in the urban areas of the region because of several attractions: growing opportunities in the service industries, businesses started by Mexican entrepreneurs taking advantage of and catering to the expanding Latino market, and family networks and chain migration that continue to pull Mexican immigrants to the region. In sum, the growth of the Mexican population in the Northwest during the past fifteen years can be attributed to Mexican immigration, Mexican American migration, and high fecundity.

Memories of the Pacific Northwest

Over the last century the expression *El Norte,* literally meaning "the north," often translated as "going north" into the United States from Mexico, has been extended as the Mexican diaspora moved beyond the confines of the Southwest. In fact, some might even argue, the frontier, *la frontera,* no longer exists in the Southwest, but in all likelihood has moved to regions beyond it. If we are to believe that landscapes, places, and spaces make a difference in our lives, then certainly, ethnic Mexicans residing outside of the Southwest occupy the new *el norte* and *frontera* and clearly provide a link for a national experience shared by all Mexicans living in the United States.

Furthermore, the axioms mentioned above have evolved into the metaphorical for those longing for a better life whether that is in the Southwest, Midwest, or Pacific Northwest. For example, in the 1983 Gregory Nava film *El Norte* the two protagonists, Rosa and Enrique, dream of fleeing the war-torn country of Guatemala and coming to the United States. Their vision of safety and sanctuary is the U.S.-Mexican border region. Although Rosa and Enrique eventually make it to the United States, however, the image they saw depicted in magazines where everyone lives in brand new homes and drives shiny new cars is quickly shattered by the reality of their status as undocumented immigrants and a society indifferent to the struggles of the working class. Nonetheless, going to *El Norte* came to represent, at least symbolically, a new beginning for those attempting to escape repression, hardship, and a state of economic stagnation.[10] For example, Arreola and Curtis state:

> In the minds of many Mexicans, certainly in the minds of *los fronterizos* as the border Mexicans are called, *la frontera* is often equated with prosperity and economic opportunity.[11]

And similar to Central Americans or Mexican immigrants who longed for a change in their lives, a parallel exists for ethnic Mexicans who left the U.S-Mexican border region and traveled to the Pacific Northwest. For the approximately one million Mexicans who have journeyed to the Northwest during the twentieth century, the region represents an extended *Norte,* but historically attached to what is considered Greater Mexico or that region that now represents the American Southwest.

Thus, similar to Rosa and Enrique, Mexican migrants from the Southwest who felt trapped, socially oppressed, and economically stagnant also envisioned a different life, but one north of the U.S.-Mexican border. For example, my parents first fled Mexico and then the southern border region of Arizona and Texas. Over the years I have discussed this movement not only with my parents, but also with relatives and other Mexicans living in the Northwest. A common theme emanating from these interviews was the wish to flee the Southwest for a better life in the Northwest. The reality of fleeing for my grandparents and their sons and daughters (my father) was a better wage and a sense of relief from the intense racism and discrimination of the Southwest, Texas in particular. In sum, my parents and individuals like them came to the Northwest for a better future for their children. However, like Rosa and Enrique, my family soon came to realize that one could not flee from the realities of being Mexican or different in a region dominated by Euro American ethos or the struggles of a migrant background.[12] I was born and raised in the Pacific Northwest after

7

my father's initial immigration into the United States and his eventual migration to the state of Washington in the early 1950s (see Fig. 1.1). My mother, after spending her first five years in Arizona, has lived in Washington continuously since 1945. My memories as a migrant child are filled with the cold winters of North Central Washington, the basalt cliffs carved out by Columbia River that flows near my hometown, and the isolation that came with being one of a handful of Mexicans in a community dominated by

Fig. 1.1 Garcia Family, Immigration photograph early 1950s. Front Ruben D. Garcia, Natalia Garcia, Juan Garcia, back, Roberto D. Garcia (photo Courtesy of the Garcia Family Collection).

descendants of German immigrants. My consciousness is embedded with images of my father laboring in the sugar beet harvest wearing several layers of clothes to protect him from the biting wind and the blowing snow and of my mother coming home with a layer of dust on her clothing from working in the windswept fields of the Columbia Basin during an early spring. As a child, our family maneuvered not through international boundaries via the border towns of McAllen-Reynosa, Eagle Pass-Piedras Negras, or El Paso-Ciudad Juarez, but into ports of entry such as Blaine-Rock, Oroville-Osoyoos, or across the Strait of Juan de Fuca from Neah Bay, Clallam Bay, or Port Angeles into Victoria, British Columbia. I often recall periods when our family entered these various ports for salmon fishing expeditions (see Fig. 1.2). As a second generation Chicano, the space and place that defines my lived experiences is not the U.S.-Mexican border, but the northern polity separated at the forty-ninth parallel or more commonly known as the U.S.-Canadian border. Similar to the topography of the Pacific

Northwest, the experiences of Mexicans in the United States are not monolithic or based on a singular existence, but fluid and changing.

Fig. 1.2. Ruben D. Garcia (author's father) with a 35lb. King Salmon near Quincy, Wash., 1968 (photo Courtesy of the Garcia Family Collection).

While attending K-12 in Quincy, Wash., ethnic relations revolved around the Anglo-Mexican paradigm; or put another way, Anglos and Mexicans were the only ethnic groups in my community with the exception of a couple of Japanese-American families. More importantly, issues of race and race relations centered on these two groups. My indoctrination into the prevailing paradigm on Pacific Northwest history began with my primary education, which included the historical significance of the English explorers into the Northwest and the Euro American movement into the region, but learned little in regard to the impact of the Spanish explorers or the contributions Mexicans have made to the history of the Pacific Northwest. In fact, I did not learn about the fifty thousand braceros that came to the Pacific Northwest during World War II until I started graduate school in the early 1990s!

Like most students, I was required to take Pacific Northwest and Washington State history in high school, which romanticized such individuals as Captains Cook and Gray, or dwelled on the exploits of fur trappers and traders, and extolled the Lewis and Clark overland expedition. This followed a discussion on the movement of white immigrants into the Northwest and the benevolence of 1840s missionaries such as Marcus and Narcissa Whitman. Although these European and U.S. forebears are important to the region's history, conspicuously absent from these narratives was any discussion of the explorations of the Spanish in

9

the Pacific Northwest, which predates those of the English and American. Nor was their any dialogue on the Mexican vaqueros (cowboys) who ventured to the Pacific Northwest in the early nineteenth century to train white settlers on the art and science of mule packing. In essence, what I experienced as a child and adolescent in the Washington State educational system is what other historians have labeled "a Tunerian celebration of the hardy, heroic people who explored and settled the Northwest frontier..."[13] As will be illustrated later in this book, a strong Mexican presence began to emerge in the region by the early twentieth century and surged as agriculture expanded throughout the Northwest and other opportunities opened up for ethnic Mexicans.

Throughout most of the twentieth century the agricultural zones of the Pacific Northwest relied heavily on the labor of Mexicans, including mine as child that not only assisted the development of the region but also provided an extraordinary amount wealth unequally distributed.[14] For example, while attending middle school an Anglo girl was allowed to share with the class a photocopy of a check for one million dollars her uncle had received from the sugar and potato growers association. My mother and father were paid $2.75 per hour to help cultivate and harvest those crops (see Fig. 1.3). The embarrassment and anger I felt for such a disparity in the distribution in wealth remains a vivid childhood memory. More importantly, that image is a stark reminder not only that the contributions of Mexicans in the Northwest have been neglected, but also that often Mexican laborers did not enjoy the fruits of their labor. In the end, my hometown and the Northwest in general became a magnet for immigrant and migrant labor due to the offer of year-round employment in agriculture for individuals such as my father and mother.

Fig. 1.3. Garcia family weeding sugar beets, Jay Petersen Farms 1970s, Quincy, Wash. From L-R, Santos Villegas, Rene Villegas, Felicitas Garcia (author's Tia), Roberto Garcia, Jr. (author's Primo), Isabel Muñoz (author's Tia), Gloria Garcia (author's mother), Ruben Garcia, Jr. (author's brother), back standing, Rosalinda Garcia, (author's Prima). Photo Courtesy of the Garcia Family Collection.

Creating Space for Chicanas/os in the Pacific Northwest

Although the presence of Mexicans in the Northwest dates to the colonial period, scholarship on their presence and contributions to the region remain underdeveloped. Studies on Mexicans in this region are sporadic at best and neglected at worst. Easily attributed to the lack of experts in the field, such neglect more importantly reflects the tendency of Pacific Northwest historians to downplay the role of Spanish explorers and the movement of Mexicans into the Northwest by the nineteenth century and their unmistakable contributions to Pacific Northwest history. For instance, the Spanish were the first Europeans to explore the Pacific Northwest.[15] Although many historians point to Juan Perez's voyage of 1774 as the first by a European to reach the Northwest coastline, David J. Weber points to the 1542–1543 exploration of Juan Rodriguez Cabrillo, which took him to forty-two degrees latitude or the California-Oregon boundary.[16] To further illustrate the Mexican presence during this period many of those early Spanish explorers were Mexican-born Spanish subjects.[17] Nonetheless, these important historical events rank secondary to the exploits of such individuals as Englishmen Captain James Cook or the American explorer Captain Robert Gray, credited with the discovery of the Columbia River. This pattern of indifference and neglect continues through the twentieth century. For instance, in a high school history textbook on Washington State the author is bold enough to write,

> …Mexican Americans have long worked in agricultural fields. But for the most part, the labor force has consisted of white Americans and immigrants eager to move into an uncrowded area in search of jobs and opportunity. Rarely have there been too few people to work in fields or factories or in construction.[18]

The above quote is similar to previous decades when local, regional, and national histories centered on white Americans and the voice of groups such as Mexicans were either marginalized or simply forgotten. A cursory examination of the handful of historical narratives written on the Mexican experience in the Pacific Northwest provides evidence of Mexican labor arriving in significant numbers by the 1920s and by World War II it was considered an indispensable labor force in the region. Furthermore, a long legacy of subordination in the U.S. socioeconomic structure, one that favored whites over nonwhites, ensured that very few Mexicans joined the land-owning elites of the Pacific Northwest. In fact, in *Racial Fault Lines* Tomás Almaguer provides an excellent analysis of how Mexicans in California had been divested of over fourteen million acres by the dawn of the twentieth century by the new Euro American capitalist structure that relegated many Mexicans to the lower levels of the economic system.[19]

This legacy of economic subordination continued throughout the twentieth century and spread to other regions. By the end of the twentieth century, Mexicans had become the backbone of the agricultural labor force sustaining the agricultural industry and those communities in which they resided. Yet, historians of the Pacific Northwest have written the region's history to coincide with the arrival of English explorers as its foundation and the movement of Lewis and Clark as the moment that civilization, law, order, and development abruptly appeared in the region. This of course excludes the important contributions of the region's first settlers, Native Americans as well as the legacy and link between the Spanish exploration of the Northwest and the current Mexican presence.

Furthermore, as I was writing my master's thesis in 1993, I detected that the scholarship on the Chicano experience and culture in the United State focused primarily on the Southwest with almost no links to other regions of the United States. Because I was born and raised in the Pacific Northwest and continued to witness the increasing number of Mexicans moving into the region, it became clear to me that the Chicano experience extended beyond the Southwest (see Fig. 1.4 Pinata Party for Y. Garcia). Nevertheless, the dominant paradigms that govern Pacific Northwest history and Chicana/o Studies have neglected this diaspora. My observations regarding the exclusion of Chicanos from other geographic regions within the field of Chicana/o Studies is not unique. Gilbert Cardenas has been advocating for the inclusion of Midwest Chicanos into the dominant Chicana/o Studies paradigm since at least 1975. One of Cardenas' central arguments against a southwest centric regional identity said:

...that it was an "imposed" identity, a form of
colonial domination. Among the first to demarcate
the territories stolen from Mexico as "Southwest"
were the non-Chicano victors and their descendant
historians and social scientists.[20]

Although a large and impressive body of research on the
Chicano experience in the Midwest has emerged since that period,
Cardenas' overall vision of a national Chicana/o model remains
unfulfilled. Similar to the Midwest, the general scholarship on
Pacific Northwest history is implicated in this pattern of exclusion
for having said little about the contributions of Mexicans to the
region. Thus, the motivation in assembling this collection of essays

*Fig. 1.4. Piñata Party for Yolanda Garcia (author's sister), Quincy, Wash., 1965 (photo
Courtesy of the Garcia Family Collection).*

is to address what we consider shortcomings in the field of Chicana/o Studies and Pacific Northwest history.

In the case of Pacific Northwest history, we argue that many historians practice a form of "empire building," or a creation myth of history that depicts English explorers and white settlers as the first arrivals to the Pacific Northwest. As historian Donald Worster wrote in "Two Faces West: The Development Myth in Canada and the United States,"

> Development thus became a compelling international myth about the growth of nation-states. By myth, I mean simply that it told a popular story about origins and destiny, one progressing from primitive life to civilization, from the simple to the complex, from an inferior colonial dependency to nation-state maturity...[21]

Even noted historian Carlos Schwantes devotes only two paragraphs to "Hispanics" in his book titled *The Pacific Northwest: An Interpretive History*. However, explorers, missionaries, and captains of industry receive chapter-length discussions. In short, two prominent movements have hindered the voice of Mexicans in the Pacific Northwest and their history. First, the Eurocentric perspective of the Pacific Northwest history has monopolized and marginalized the voices of the "other" or those ethnic groups considered marginal or unimportant to the region's history, such as Mexicans.

Second, the field of Chicana/o Studies continues to use the Southwest paradigm as its *modus operandi* in explaining the Chicano experience for all people of Mexican ancestry in the United States. The premise for this paradigm is based on a "collective memory of conquest and the U.S.-Mexican border providing the formation and maintenance of a unique Chicano identity and history."[22] However, as in other regions these key features of "Chicanoness" did not apply to all Mexicans in the

Pacific Northwest. A handful of Chicana/o scholars have argued that regional narratives on the Chicana/o experience neglects the linkages and contributions of those Chicanas/os outside of the Southwest. Nonetheless, Chicana/o scholars continue to emphasize the sacredness of the Southwest. For example, in his article "Southern California Chicano History: Regional Origins and National Critique," Richard Griswold de Castillo argues that Chicano history written from the local and regional perspective is a problem due to its resistance to large conceptualizations.[23] Moreover, de Castillo also states that regional history can be used to conceptualize a national character and as an example uses Frederick Jackson Turner's *Frontier Thesis* that promoted American individualism and democracy based on the region of the American West. To his credit, de Castillo also points to the limitations of Turner's thesis in ignoring non-Euro-Americans.[24] Although de Castillo argues for the equivalent of a Turnerian thesis for Chicanos or an all-encompassing paradigm, he and other scholars of Chicano history have also been dogmatic and rigid in regard to the field. For example, de Castillo claims that Chicano history "as a self-consciously" written record originated in Southern California in the 1970s… and that Southern California has arguably been the cradle of modern Chicano history as a scholarly field of study."[25] However, we argue that de Castillo's as well as other Chicana/o scholars' rationalization for such assertions do not hold up under scrutiny. For example, the claim that Southern California's universities became prime targets for political action and intellectual ferment during the civil rights era, and thus make it unique, also holds true for other regions such as the Pacific Northwest (see Gilberto Garcia's conclusion this volume).[26]

To some within the field of Chicana/o Studies, the idea of expanding the discourse simply means shifting the emphasis to other regions of the Southwest. For example, when Rodolfo Acuña's book *Occupied America: The Chicano's Struggle Toward Liberation* emerged in 1972 it was hailed as placing the Chicano experience at the national level.[27]

INTRODUCTION

Acuña's approach to the general history of Chicanos was innovative from the perspective that he argued that "the conquest of the Southwest created a colonial situation in the traditional sense... with the Mexican land and population being controlled by an imperialistic United States," thus incorporating the newly founded internal colonial model into his work.[28] However, virtually nothing is discussed in regards to Chicanas/os outside of the Southwest. In the fifth edition (2004) of *Occupied America*, Acuña added a new chapter on the pre-Columbian cultures, relegated the internal colonial model to nineteenth-century Chicano history, and made other changes; however, only a total of two pages are devoted to the Northwest in a book over five hundred pages in length and considered by many to be the definitive book on Chicano history![29] As a result, the Southwest centric approach has created a de facto model in which the experience of all Chicanos is measured. As a consequence, *Memory, Community, and Activism: Mexican Migration and Labor in the Pacific Northwest* is a response to the multiple challenges put forth over the past thirty years to create a more inclusive environment within and without the field of Chicana/o Studies. This book has also been created so that the memory of Mexicans in the Pacific Northwest continues to be recorded, to illustrate the development of Mexican communities throughout the region, and most importantly, that Mexicans in this locality have never succumbed to despair, but through activism and determination have overcome their victimization.

About the Book

This volume makes a number of contributions regarding the experience of Mexicans in the Pacific Northwest. One of the main contributions of this volume is the examination of pre–World War II and post-1947 Mexican experience in the Pacific Northwest. Erasmo Gamboa's book on braceros has been the dominant interpretation of Chicano Northwest history, but the period before and after the Bracero Program has not received scholarly attention.

Another contribution underscores the role of women in building communities in the Pacific Northwest. Previous studies have focused on Mexican men with little or no attention to the important role of Mexican women, some who accompanied men on the railroads and sugar beet harvests. This volume includes mujeres who worked in the fields, made homes in the labor camps, organized farmworkers, and built communities in the Catholic Church. Even in those essays that do not focus on women, they are present. For example, Jones and Hodges show how labor contractors provided female prostitutes for male workers and J. Garcia notes how rumors about a white female being assaulted by a male that "looked Mexican" provoked a citywide restriction order.

Another important contribution challenges the Southwest-centric scholarship of Chicana/o Studies. As mentioned earlier, the Pacific Northwest should be viewed as an extended "El Norte" where many Mexicans have planted roots, but whose experiences have been left out of national histories. Even the informants studied within this volume were taking part in redefining "El Norte" for themselves. Carlos Maldonado's essay on labor contractor Julian Ruiz mentions a Tejano family that would call out "Vamonos al Norte" to other families, signaling that time of year when their trek north began to the Pacific Northwest.

More importantly, this volume provides a more comprehensive overview of Chicanos and Chicanas in the Pacific Northwest. First, it moves beyond the state focus studies such Erasmo Gamboa and Carolyn Buan's edited volume, *Nosotros: The Hispanic People in Oregon* (1995); Erasmo Gamboa's *Voces Hispanas: Hispanic Voices of Idaho: Excerpts from the Idaho Hispanic Oral History Project* (1992); and Robert McCarl's edited volume, *Latinos in Idaho: Celebrando Cultura* (2003). Second, it is much stronger than the largely descriptive and encyclopedia-like volume, *The Chicano Experience in the Northwest* first published in 1995 by Carlos Maldonado and Gilberto Garcia. The essays in this volume are well researched and filled with explanatory power. Lastly, this volume, unlike the 1995 anthology, does a better job in addressing issues such as immigration, popular culture, comparative race relations, and religion.

Thus, the research in this volume will allow other scholars to compare the Northwest with other regions and ethnic enclaves. It will place the Mexican diaspora beyond the traditional U.S.-Mexican "borderlands" region and contribute to the development of a national paradigm on the Mexican experience in the United States. Furthermore, this book adds to the overall knowledge of human experience in the American West, and to the history of the agricultural development of the Pacific Northwest that created the foundation for Mexican communities and the recruitment of Mexican labor that continues today. The need for additional research and assessment of questions pertaining to the Mexican origin population of the Pacific Northwest has never been greater.

Endnotes

1. In this essay, the terms *Chicanos* and *Mexican Americans* refers to American citizens of Mexican descent and the term is used interchangeably, regardless of their length of residence in the United States. The term *Mexican immigrants* is used to refer to citizens of Mexico residing in the United States. Although all of these groups historically have recognized important distinctions between and among themselves, all have been subject to varying degrees of prejudice and discrimination in the United States, regardless of their formal citizenship status. Thus, when referring to the combined population of all persons of Mexican ancestry or descent living in the United States, the term ethnic Mexicans is employed. These definitions can be found in David G. Gutiérrez, "Significant to Whom?: Mexican Americans and the History of the American West," *Western Historical Quarterly* 24, no. 4 (November 1993): 520n1.
2. Laurie Mercier and Carole Simon-Smolinski, *Idaho's Ethnic Heritage/Historical Overviews* (Boise: The Idaho EthnicHeritage Project, 1990), as cited in Richard Baker, *Los Dos Mundos: Rural Mexican Americans, Another America* (Logan: Utah State University, 1995), 57.

3. U.S. Distribution of persons born in Mexico or having Mexico-born parents, 1930. (U.S. Bureau of Census, *Census of the Population, 1930*).

4. U.S. Census Bureau, *Table D-4 Hispanic Origin (of Any race), for the United States, Regions, Divisions, and States: 1940 and 1970* (Sample Data). Internet Release Date: Sept. 13, 2002.

5. Gilbert Garcia and Jerry Garcia, "Mexican Communities in the Columbia Basin," Unpublished article, 10 (to obtain a copy of this unpublished article please contact either author). See also "Mexicans Arrive for Farm Work," *Columbia Basin Herald*, Washington, May 3, 1951, 1; "Slave Labor refuted by Growers," *Columbia Basin Herald*, Washington, Dec. 27, 1951. According to these Moses Lake, Wash., newspaper accounts, one hundred Mexicans were flown in from El Paso, Texas, to Larson field in Moses Lake. Employment of the braceros was arranged by the Northwest Farm Labor Association and the state employment service at the request of local farmers. The crew of braceros remained until November 1951.

6. Ibid.

7. In this chapter I use the term Latino only when speaking of the broader U.S. population that traces its descent to the Spanish-speaking, Caribbean, and Latin American worlds.

8. In this chapter I use the term *Hispanic* only when making reference to census data. The United States government currently uses the label *Hispanic* as its nomenclature for all those individuals originating from the Spanish-speaking Caribbean and from Latin America.

9. Census 2000 PHC-T-10. Hispanic or Latino Origin for the United States, Regions, Divisions, States, and for Puerto Rico: 2000. Table 1–13, Hispanic or Latino Origin for Idaho; Table 1–38 Hispanic or Latino Origin for Oregon; Table 1–48 Hispanic or Latino Origin for Washington. U.S. Census Bureau, Census 2000, Summary File and unpublished data. Internet Release date: Oct. 22, 2001. The total population of Mexicans in Idaho was 79,324; in Oregon, 214,662; and in Washington , 329,934.

10. *El Norte*, Directed by Gregory Nava and written by Anna Thomas and Gregory Nava, Cinecom Pictures, 1983.

11. Daniel D. Arreola and James R. Curtis. *The Mexican Border Cities: Landscape Anatomy and Place Personality*. Tucson: University of Arizona Press, 1993), 218.

12. For a longer discussion on the movement of my family and other Mexicans into North Central Washington see my master's thesis "A History of a Chicano/Mexicano Community in the Pacific Northwest Quincy, Wash., 1948–1993," Eastern Washington University, 1993; "A Chicana in Northern Aztlan: An Oral History of Dora Sanchez Trevino," *Frontiers: A Journal of Women Studies* 19, no. 2 (1998); "The Measure of a Cock: Mexican Cockfighting, Masculinity, and Culture in Chon Noreiga," I AM AZTLAN:

The Personal Essay in Chicano Studies (Los Angeles: University of California Chicano Research Center, 2004).

13. Susan H. Armitage, "From the Inside Out: Rewriting Regional History," *Frontiers: A Journal of Women Studies* 22, no. 3 (2001): 34.

14. These zones include the Yakima Valley, Willamette Valley, Snake River Valley, Mt. Vernon region, and the Columbia Basin.

15. Carlos Schwantes, *The Pacific Northwest: An Interpretive History* (Lincoln: University of Nebraska Press, 1989), 23. According to Schwantes the Spanish explorer Juan Perez was the first European to visit the area of Nootka Sound in 1774.

16. David J. Weber, "The Spanish Moment in the Pacific Northwest," in Paul Hirt, Ed., *Terra Pacifica: People and Place in the Northwest States and Western Canada.* (Pullman, Wash.: Washington State University Press, 1998), 4–5.

17. Ibid., 3.

18. Charles LeWarne, *Washington State* (Seattle: University of Washington Press, 1993), 281.

19. Tomás Almaguer. *Racial Fault Lines: The Historical Origins of White Supremacy in California* (Berkeley: University of California Press, 1994), 47.

20. Gilbert Cardenas, "Who are the Midwestern Chicanos: Implications for Chicano Studies," *Aztlan: A Journal of Chicano Studies* 7, no. 2 (Summer 1976): 141–52.

21. Donald Worster, "Two Faces West: The Development Myth in Canada and the United States," in *Terra Pacifica: People and Place in the Northwest States and Western Canada,* ed. Paul Hirt (Pullman, Wash.: Washington State University Press, 1998), 73.

22. Refugio Rochín and Dennis N. Valdes, *Voices of a New History: Chicana/o History* (East Lansing: Julian Samora Research Institute, Michigan State University Press), 2000, 115–16.

23. Richard Griswold de Castillo, "Southern California Chicano History: Regional Origins and National Critique," *Aztlan: A Journal of Chicano Studies* 19, no. 1 (Spring 1988–1990): 109–24.

24. Ibid., 117.

25. Ibid., 109.

26. Ibid., 111–12.

27. Rodolfo Acuña, *Occupied America: The Chicano's Struggle Toward Liberation* (San Francisco: Canfield Press, a Department of Harper and Row Publishers, Inc., 1972).

28. Ibid., 3.

29. Rodolfo Acuña. *Occupied America: A History of Chicanos,* 5th ed. (New York: Pearson Longham, 2004).

Northwest and the Conquest of the Americas: Chicana/o Roots of Cultural Hybridity and Presence

Ramon Sanchez

The dominant interpretive history of the Pacific Northwest presents an isolated region whose main currents eventually coincide with the course of development in the United States. Two events seem to dominate this perspective. One is Captain James Cook's 1778 voyage, which sought the Pacific entrance to the Northwest Passage. As historian Carlos Schwantes observes, although Captain Cook's expedition was not the first to reach the Pacific Northwest, it brought the region into close association with Europe.[1] The second event, the Lewis and Clark Expedition (1804–1806) that came to be seen as the dividing line between the old and the new region, was expressed by the Lewis and Clark Exposition of 1905.[2]

However, this dominant historical perspective excludes an important point: the region now called the Pacific Northwest not only existed prior to Captain Cook's voyage and the Lewis and Clark expedition, but also includes an evolving cultural hybridization begun by the Spanish that is very much a part of the region today. It is that hybridization process that needs to be examined in the context of the motives that brought the Europeans to the Americas.

Three major motives of the European conquest of the Americas were to gain wealth, expand an empire, and spread Christianity. Beginning with the enterprise of Christopher Columbus, the conquerors' goal of increased riches in the Americas fueled radical political and economic consequences and changed cultural dynamics. Thus, a Bakhtinian approach that takes into account voices that reflect ideological and cultural perspectives in conquest narratives can assist in examining two goals that were part of the motive to gain wealth: finding the golden city and the route to Asia. An examination of these goals, significant symbols in intertextual and extratextual narrative exchanges and influences, can reveal the imperial conquering process and impart insight into the conquest of the Americas, specifically the region now known as the Pacific Northwest.[3]

From the European perspective, the encounter between Europe and the Americas is a war of conquest of a land and its people. A very interesting point, though, is how this unfamiliar world is dealt with. Even though they do not know this alien land and people of the Americas, they make them known through narratives that give meaning to and take away the alien nature of this experience. European narratives are imposed on the unknown to make this utterly different world not only known but also to allow the claim that they already knew this world. So, for instance, the tales of golden cities and Amazons present a world in familiar patterns that give meaning to their actions.

Of course, the Americas and its people were truly unknown to the Europeans, who made the unknown known through different narrative impositions. The desire to gain wealth with its enticements of golden cities and routes to Asia offered a way for European conquerors to know a place without actually knowing it. For example, Columbus reached the Americas, but because of Marco Polo's narrative believed that he had reached Asia, a land of riches. Later, Viceroy Mendoza of New Spain sought the seven golden cities in the northern lands of the Americas, cities that had to exist because they came into being in narratives penned in medieval Europe. The Spanish crown instructed its commanders to find the Strait of Anian, the existence of which evolved in part from the need to find the Strait of Malacca that leads to the wealth of Asia. Narrative imposition, a process that makes things known through stories already known, becomes an important manner of dealing with the conqueror's anxiety of an alien land and people, and also allows the conqueror to claim possession of the Americas.

The conqueror's narrative impositions assist him in the conquest of the Americas, as well as in the establishment of new boundaries of status and of race/ethnic group privilege and segregation. Such accounts assist in building an imperial structure that attempts to get the conquered to become cultural mimics of the empire. At the same time, cultural hybridity [the mixing or composing of cultures] arises and by its very existence forces questions about legitimacy, justice, and power.

Cultural hybridity must not be romanticized. Instead, one must recognize its importance in understanding the Americas since 1492. A product of the European conquest and an unintended outcome of the European invasion of the Americas, cultural hybridity ironically often confers both desirable and undesirable outcomes. For example, the conqueror who successfully imposes his imperial endeavor by using hybridity as a deindianization process can find his goal undermined when Gonzalo Guerrero fights on the Native Americans' side against the Spanish. Thus, cultural hybridity ensures the contradictions of the conqueror's world.

The gaining of wealth in the Americas, for instance, through enticements of golden cities and routes to Asia keeps the process of cultural mixing going, for it assures the coming of Europeans as conquerors who attempt to impose their cultural/social structure on the Native Americans and others struggling against that imposition. The power and privilege of the European conqueror depends on a dualistic and unjust inclusion/exclusion structure: in the conquest of the Americas, it means that people of color are excluded and exploited. Although cultural hybridity can be used by the conqueror to reinforce the power/privilege cultural divide, there is no doubt that for the European conqueror the rise of hybridity inevitably challenges his assumed rights and privileges as it challenges supposedly fixed imperial cultural boundaries. That is why hybridity is quickly categorized as an illegitimate existence for persons labeled by it (for example, through racist policies).

RAMON SANCHEZ

The Spanish conqueror's master/servant imperial dichotomy with its strict cult of purity and fixed boundaries attempts to freeze social structures into two connecting but not interacting parts, a dichotomy that clearly supports inequality by separating people and cultures into superior and inferior. In this social framework, hybridity is condemned as being denigrating, as leading to marginalization, or as being without social significance. However, hybridity is not simply the combining of two different and equal parts. It is not the best or worst of two halves coming together. The development of hybridity in the Americas represents an asymmetrical and multipronged conquering process involving the uneven mixing of diverse elements in an evolving process. Even groups considered culturally homogenized are not. One must remember, for instance, that the Spanish community is not homogeneous and that Native American communities are also not socially and politically and even at times culturally homogeneous. In addition, since the European conquest of the Americas brought other groups such as African slaves into the mix, it cannot be viewed in black and white terms as a simple cultural dualism.

As exemplified by Spanish imperialism, European imperialism plays a major part in changing the Americas. It attempts to establish a culturally/socially homogeneous structure, an imperial cultural homogeneity with a strong racist element. All groups caught up in the conquest adapt, accommodate, and resist, resulting in different levels and expressions of hybridity. The enticements of golden cities and routes to Asia fuel the process of mixing in the Americas as the Spanish conqueror persists in imposing a standardized cultural/social structure on a diverse cultural/social people from the Americas, Europe, and other places.

The expeditionary members representing the Spanish conquerors who expected to gain wealth pulled the Pacific Northwest into a history of empire building that promised great profit and caused a major cross-cultural clash. Clearly, the Northwest region is neither culturally nor socially isolated from the

European conquest, and the Northwest does not acquire a "real" history only when the Lewis and Clark expedition appears. An examination of important conquest texts presents a Northwest region shaped by the European conquerors' desire to gain wealth, clearly connecting the region to the cultural dynamics that changed the Americas once the European invasion began. In the narrative voices of the conqueror, one recognizes the significance of the Spanish impact on the development of a cultural hybridity (*mestizaje* being an aspect of it) in the Americas.

Important Spanish narratives related to the taking of the Americas contain voices that reveal the desire for wealth by the conquerors that affected the Northwest along with the rest of the Americas. An examination of these voices of conquest reveals a subjugation process that destroys what is there but also creates everywhere an unintended hybrid reality that leads people to physical and cultural adaptation, accommodation, and resistance. It also allows one to see how other endeavors such as the Lewis and Clark expedition are very much a part of a conquering movement rooted in Europe that significantly changed everything in the Americas despite containing many misperceptions. The Spanish conquest led to fragmentation and reordering of social borders, the imposition of ethnic/race and cultural hierarchies, privileges based on race, economic inequality and narrative impositions, social/cultural contradictions, boundary crossings and challenges, demands for social and economic justice, narrative syncretism, hybrid consciousness, and the development of the people known as Chicanos, defined as United States citizens of Mexican cultural heritage. The conquest of the Americas is an unbroken cultural process very much a component of the Northwest today.

Man is a social animal surrounded by cultural ideologies that affect his view of the world.[4] The narratives of the Spanish conquerors attempt to work out the difficult problem of dealing with the unknown land and people of the Americas as the conquering enterprise provides a powerful and useful manner of knowing the world they maneuver in. Penetrating the Americas, the Spanish conqueror imposed golden cities from European narratives of the land and the certainty of sea routes to Asia, giving them validity, for his cultural framework makes clear their expected existence. Consequently, the conqueror's expectation of gaining wealth gives meaning to the expeditions and enterprises that enter the Americas at multiple points by turning the events into ways of confirming truth known in advance: voices speak of cities of gold and routes to Cathay, voices that confer meaning and at the same time justify action. The taking of the Northwest region is part of a conquering enterprise renaming, transforming, and appropriating a world that already exists but with alien names, a world conquerors claim to already know and confirm by canceling and erasing the native name.[5]

The unknown is made known by fitting it into a preestablished narrative. This way of knowing an unknown is exemplified by Christopher Columbus' interpretation of Marco Polo's *Il milione*; Columbus reaches the unknown Americas, but "knows" he has reached the Indies as expected from interpreting Marco Polo.[6] The Spanish conquerors repeat this process, fitting the Americas into a known grid. Historiographer Edmundo O'Gorman argues:

> In the history of humankind, nothing has been produced *ex nihilo*. Each new phenomenon, whether mechanical contrivance or mental concept, is the product of its past. Parturition may be by accident or design, but in either case the new thing will have been prepared for and will have to be understood within the context of that preparation. And if some new thing, happened upon by accident, should indeed be wholly new, unexpected, and unlooked for, it will be forced to fit a previous conceptual mold, yielding its own nature to the human imperative to account for the unknown always in terms of the known. The Americas were not so

much discovered as invented, the Admiral
[Columbus] to the end of his days professing that
he had discovered the "Indies."[7]

Hernán Cortés told Moctezuma's emissary: "Send me gold, for
me and my companions have a sickness of the heart, an illness
that can be cured with gold."[8] According to translator López de
Gómara, these words give voice to the conqueror's expectation of
gaining wealth, in this case, the search for the *golden city*. The
other expectation was to find the *route*, also referred to as the
strait or passage to Asia, whose cities were said to possess gold and
other wealth. These two goals compelled the conquerors to reach
the wealth of Asia, still a Western obsession today.

Cortés is important in beginning the penetration northward
that would lead to the conquest of the Northwest. From New
Spain, he sent expeditions north. Although he did not seek divine
signs that the lands of wealth were in that territory, he was
nonetheless influenced by the expectations associated with gaining
riches. So he investigated to the north for the existence of lands *of*
wealth and routes *to* wealth. Cortés had no choice but to use the
cultural values at hand that validate the conquering process.[9] This
is a way of making the American land and its people known and a
way to communicate the conquering process to people involved in
the imperial endeavor as Cortés did in addressing the Emperor in
his fourth letter.

Once Cortés conquered the Aztecs, he sent expeditions north
in search of the Amazon kingdoms touted to possess much gold in
an ancient Greek narrative imposed on the land.[10]

When he started out from Cuba (before rebelling against
Governor Velázquez), a part of his instructions was to search for
the golden Amazon kingdoms. Consequently, Cortés stated in his
fourth letter to the Emperor that he would discover a rich land, an
island inhabited by women, and a strait that would lead to Asia.[11]
Thus, a series of expeditions proceeded further and further north
along the Pacific Ocean, setting the stage for the taking of the

Northwest region. In 1533, Cortés sent an expedition north along the West Coast; in 1535, he led an expedition to the peninsula of Baja California; and in 1539, he directed an expedition sailing north to the head of the Gulf of California. In the process of these endeavors—as well as the other conquering enterprises— hybridization occurs and the area now known as the Northwest begins to be known in the same manner as the rest of the Americas. This process of the mixing of races and meeting of cultures creates a cultural hybridization with problematic interconnections for imperialism.

The conquering expeditions continued to confront a land and people totally alien to the Europeans. In the process of taking the land, the conquerors made the unknown known by naming and transforming everything into familiar tales that reassured them by replacing the great alienness of the Americas with what was already known by the struggling conqueror. The narrative relocation to the Americas of the islands of wealth from *Amadís de Gaula* and the medieval tales of seven cities of wealth was a way of making the land known. Marco Polo's *Il milione*, known in English as the *Travels of Marco Polo*, made known the East and was used to make known the Americas.

The Spanish conquering process pushed cultural hybridity, which turns out to be polyglot, multivoiced, and multicultural. But the Spanish conqueror finds meaning in this asymmetrical process by the twin goals legitimized by the Spanish Crown: finding the golden city and the route to Asia. The narratives placed the alien in a known narrative frame, thus enabling the Spanish conqueror to expect golden cities in the Americas. Thus, the narrative of álvar Núñez Cabeza de Vaca, one of the few survivors of the failed Pámfilo de Narváez expedition (1527–37), spoke of cities of great wealth, one being in the north.[12] Fray Marcos (of the reconnaissance expedition of 1539) entered the northern lands seeking the city of wealth mentioned by Cabeza de Vaca, and Fray Marcos claimed to catch a glimpse of a great city thought to be one of seven cities of gold.[13]

Such narratives led to Francisco Vásquez de Coronado's 1540 enterprise to the north, searching for Cíbola (seven cities of gold) and golden Quivira.[14]

The Sebastian Vizcaino expedition (1602–03) had as part of its maritime reconnaissance objectives the search for Quivira and a strait supposedly north of Cabo Mendocino. These objectives became an aspect of the Vizcaino expedition because in 1597 Hernando de los Rios Coronel outlined two possible sea routes to Asia. One route meant going through the Strait of Anian. The other one was "sailing by way of New Mexico," for Coronel stated that information from others indicated that "the two seas are close together in that place," which led him to request that the Crown pacify New Mexico in order to make navigation from there easy.[15] By 1573, the euphemism *pacify* was used to mean conquest. Juan de Oñate made his way into New Mexico in 1598 to conquer, settle, and survey the coastline of New Mexico and to establish harbors. Captain Gerónimo Marqués, under the command of Oñate, reported his belief that Quivira was in New Mexico and that the entrance to the Strait of Anian led to a river running to Quivira.[16] Thus, the conquering drive northward continued with the Crown as the audience that legitimized the conquest.

The Northwest region like the rest of the Americas eventually felt the European economic penetration, political subordination, and renaming of the land. The Northwest was in part perceived, as Columbus perceived the Americas, as a region outlying the Great Khan's empire.[17] It was approached by conquerors seeking the golden city and the strait to the east. In the process, they took possession of lands, people, and kingdoms. They legitimized their taking of the land because they already knew the land. However, this process cannot hide the dynamics of hybridity that arose from the conquest, for the conquering process itself created new hybrid cultural references and eventually hybrid cultures unintended or unforeseen by the conquerors.

The drastic native population losses, the imposition of European culture on native Americans, and the bringing of African slaves to the Americas culminated in creating cultural hybridity in everyone. Wherever the Spanish entered, they destroyed what was there and changed peoples and systems, including themselves. They inadvertently contributed to a cultural reality of hybridity. Cultural crossings, mixings, and syntheses with their social repercussions are at the heart of the emerging American experience of hybridity. The conquering expeditions not only altered Native American people and culture but also led and transplanted people of different backgrounds further and further north.

The conquerors' words—like all words, not neutral—were part of the forced social changes on an environment they were trying to possess.[18]

The conqueror's words carry with them imperialist and racist notions affecting all social relationships; their words are very much part of the conquering process exemplified by the tie between master/slave and master/serf conditions to racist relationships. The conquerors were trying to assimilate human elements defined as inferior and a possible contaminant to the privileged Europeans in general.

The conquering process caused Native Americans to either die from overwork because of fatigue, malnutrition, and/or the lack of immunity to European diseases or to run away or rebel against their conquers. The result was that over and over again the native people and their cultures were wiped out or radically altered. Hybridity arose from the violence of the conquest, a colonial imposition, and obligatory assimilation, but the hybridity that evolved was not the outcome that the conqueror sought. The conquest, no matter what the members of an imperialist power desired, was creating evolving hybrid cultures whose very presence, although not acknowledged as valid, was forcing the recognition of new possible relationships that inevitably challenged the imperial enterprise. Indeed, one attempt to control, define, and know new elements resulted in the identification of hybrid people by labels and categories created by a racist social structure that in part reflects Indian, African, and European mixtures such as *mestizos, mulatos, castizos, tresalbos, lobos*, and others. However, since Europeans, Native Americans, and Africans were part of this new evolving cultural hybridity, the conquest itself in the end created a land and people who could not be known by freezing them into the narrative constructs that were used in the first place to know the Americas.

Behind the narrative symbols of the golden city and the route to Asia were economic interests that drove the exploitation of the Americas. For instance, in the Spanish case, the network of credit fueling the conquest of the Americas ran from local agents and entrepreneurs to royal officials and rich *encomenderos* in the Antilles and across the Atlantic to commercial interests in Seville and the great banking houses of Genoa and Augsburg.[19] The conquering discourse is embedded in an exploitative context defining economic relationships that demand grand profits. All of the Americas are to the conqueror, and the exploitative network behind him, but a resource to be utilized for maximum gain without regard to those who are there or the subordinate transplanted people.

In their search for gain, the Spaniards saw the Pacific Ocean (also called the South Sea) and wondered whether the northern part of America was an extension of Asia or a separate land mass. The riches of Cathay, golden cities, and a strait to Asia stimulated the northern movement, and so the northern part of the South Sea became the object of the search.

Between 1529 and 1536, Nuño de Guzmán moved northward in search of wealth in part articulated by the tale of a province of Amazon women in a land of gold. In 1542, during a maritime expedition to the north, Rodriguez Cabrillo found no golden city but appeared to reach part of what is today Oregon. However, the desire to find a strait such as the elusive Strait of Anian that would cut across the American continent remained strong and rumors of such a passage continued. In 1550, Balthazar Obregon made known the tale of Juan Juaréz, who supposedly sailed from the Atlantic to the Pacific Ocean, confirming great Indian settlements along the way. By 1562, a strait across the northern American continent was appearing on maps. The tale of Juan de Fuca (published in 1625), tells that he supposedly sailed to the Northwest in 1592 and found the strait and a land rich in gold and other wealth. In 1602, Lieutenant Martín Aguilar, under Vizcaino, was dispatched north in the frigate *Tres Reyes* in search of Quivira and the Strait of Anian, and the ship's chronicler's account notes the entrance to the Strait of Anian.

The López de Legazpi 1565 voyage discovered an eastern return route from the Philippines to Alta California, thus making possible a trade route to and from Asia and the Americas. For some time, this trans-Pacific trade and the Spanish crown's contention that the Pacific Ocean was its exclusive domain, which other powers appeared not to challenge, made expeditions to the Northwest unattractive.

However, the Spanish crown seriously renewed its interest in the Northwest when it grew concerned about losing its grip in the region. The realization that the Russian Empire was encroaching— and later the British and United States—into what the Spanish crown considered Spain's domain along with the fear of losing the "strait" to another power began anew Spain's expeditions to the region. In these tales, texts, reports, letters, and maps, the cultural dynamics that altered the Americas, as represented by the strait, make themselves visible by claiming and showing a location for the passageway that gives impetus to it and the conquest. The narratives that helped fuel the conquest of the Americas from the beginning make themselves felt in the Northwest through the expeditions that penetrate the region and create cultural hybridity.

The Spanish crown's expeditions of 1774, 1775, and 1779 originated from New Spain; their resources, its crews (but for officers in general), and support came from New Spain. The 1774

Juan Perez expedition sailed all the way north to what appears to be today Queen Charlotte Islands and traded with the natives near the tip of Nootka Island; the 1775 Bruno de Hezeta and Juan Francisco de la Bodega y Quadra expedition sailed along the coast of present-day Washington State and reached the coast of present-day Alaska; the 1779 Ignacio de Artega and Bodega y Quadra expedition made contact with the Tlingit natives, and they expanded their exploration of the Alaskan coast.[20] At that time, the Spanish crown concluded that the Russian danger lacked substance, found no sign of a Northwest Passage, and reported a few regional resources worth exploiting.[21] However, the 1788 Martinez and Gonzaleo López expedition changed this perception by chronicling a Russian establishment, a lucrative trade in sea otter pelts, and the threat of other European powers interested in and searching for an inter-oceanic passage in the region.

In 1789, Martinez occupied Nootka Sound; in 1790 a Spanish settlement and fortification on Vancouver Island consisted of a priest, medical doctor, some livestock, and eighty soldiers. This company of *Voluntarios de Cataluña* was sent to strengthen the settlement, but illness incapacitated or killed many and desertions further reduced their number. Twenty soldiers of *la Compañía Fija de San Blas*, raised in New Spain, took the place of the *Cataluña* volunteers from 1774–75. Because of a political agreement the Europeans made at the Nootka Convention of 1790, the Nootka outpost survived only from 1790–1795.[22]

In 1791 the first part of Malaspina-Bustamante expedition sailed north. As presented to the Spanish crown, its two objectives were: "one public... gathering of curiosities (artifacts) [and]... all the geographical and historical part... the other confidential which will be directed to political studies."[23] In 1791, the Crown ordered the expedition to search for the Northwest Passage. The voices of the political-scientific narratives of this expedition do not exist in a vacuum; they reflect the European dream of gaining Asian wealth associated with golden cities.

The first Malaspina expedition left Acapulco in 1791 and eventually reached Mulgrave Sound to search for the Strait of Anian.[24] When they did not find it, they proceeded to Prince Williams Sound, and even to present-day Valdez, Alaska, and visited the Spanish settlement at Nootka. The goal of the second expedition in 1792 was to search for the inter-oceanic strait in the Strait of Juan de Fuca.[25]

Although the Nootka Convention of 1790 showed the political and military limits of the Spanish Crown, it did not remove the motives of conquest. The competition between European powers and then also the Untied States led to ritual acts of possession of the Northwest over and over again, with the Spanish Crown claiming a spiritual conquest and insisting that Native Americans would do much better as Spanish vassals than as vassals to a native king or to a non-Spanish monarch. The Spanish Crown asserted their right to the territory and saw Asian wealth connected to it. Although the Malaspina expedition failed to find the inter-oceanic passage, the dream of Asian wealth and of cities of gold continued.

As a by-product of the search for the Northwest Passage, sea otter pelts were traded in Chinese markets, but the environmental impact of excessive economic exploitation had nearly exterminated the animals by 1794. The concomitant European and Native American cultural encounters created an evolving multifaceted cultural blending that forced rearticulations of power and privilege for all.

Part of the conquering process brought crews of Europeans, *mestizos*, southern Indians, blacks, and *mulatos* to the Northwest region. Some stayed because of work in the area and some because they deserted or had no choice because they suffered a shipwreck or similar calamity. For instance, Juan Perez in 1774 wrote of having met natives with blue eyes and white skin; native tribes, such as the Quileute, have tales of Spaniards settling with them; and years later in 1806 the Lewis and Clark expedition encountered a red-haired Indian in what is now Oregon. These indicators are only one aspect of an asymmetrical and multipronged cultural process of hybridity involving diverse elements in a continuing cultural mixing that affects all parties and is the profound tale of the Americas.

Lewis and Clark arrived in the Northwest not as representatives of a new force that shaped the region but as an extension of economic and political motives to conquer that began with Columbus and continue to play a part in an evolving hybrid culture. What is now known as the Northwest of the United States has long been seen as having an episodic, segmented, unconnected history, especially in connection to Chicanos. At times, the area is presented as having arrived at some historical and cultural stage that has already played itself out in the rest of the United States. But, in fact, the Northwest has been the product of a conquering cultural history, one that is not episodic, segmented, and unconnected to the conquering forces that reshaped the Americas, nor to the narratives that gave meaning to the conquest. The conquest of the Americas with its *entradas* (openings), destructions, assimilations, subordinations, and revalidations all lead to bloody and painful births of hybrid peoples and cultures. No European, no Native American, no one entangled in this process remains unchanged.

Focusing on the desire to gain wealth in Spanish conquest narratives makes one aware of important historical cross-cultural reverberations coming from the conquest that clearly affect the Pacific Northwest to this day. Hybridity is part of the historical development of the Northwest, part of the boundary shifts and identity remixings of its evolution. The Chicano population came to the Northwest over time as soldiers, trappers, mule packers, ranch hands, settlers, agricultural workers, and railroad workers. They came drawn by a process begun in 1492. They came with the legacy of a world-shattering conquest. They came as a clearly designated culturally evolving hybrid community. They became part of an interdiscursive process that began with the conquest of the Americas by Spanish imperialism, a process that inevitably demands the fulfillment of the social ideals of equality and freedom.

Chicanos today make up a significant portion of the Northwest population. For instance, the 2000 United States Census Bureau reports the Chicano population of three Northwest states in numbers and percent of the total, as follows: Washington, 329,934 and 5.59 percent; Oregon, 214,662 and 6.27 percent; and Idaho, 79,324 and 6.13 percent. As the twenty-first century progresses, this population continues to grow. However, it is not simply the population size that makes the Chicanos an important group of people to study. It is their significance as embodiments of cultural hybridity, a reality that historically marginalized that community. All people in the Americas embody the historical cultural hybridity, but Chicanos have always been specifically identified as hybrids—an ethnic group with a hybrid culture and language. This designation is their lot because of their historical circumstances. Consequently, because of those circumstances, the Chicano community inescapably—and especially in the twenty-first century—is involved in the struggle to fulfill the ideals of equality and freedom. The issue, therefore, is not whether or not hybridity exists, for it unquestionably has existed since at least 1492, but whether or not the cultural interpretation of this cross-cultural transformation will lead to an open and creative fulfillment of a humanizing process.

The Chicano population of the Northwest region today is not only a product of the imperialistic political, economic, cultural dynamics of the past but is very much involved in the struggle against the conquest's lingering injustices and current incarnations. The conqueror, as exemplified by Cortés' desire for wealth, heads an enterprise that validates an oppressive and exploitive process. So Cortés requests from the natives confirmation of wealth in the American region he has penetrated by handing a helmet to an emissary of Moctezuma and requesting that he fill it with gold. Asked why, Cortés replies, "I wish to know if the gold of this land is like the one we get from our rivers."[26] He wishes confirmation of wealth that he will take. This, of course, already establishes the view that the conqueror is not in the Americas just to extort gold but to subjugate.[27] The cataclysmic clash between Europe and America is set, and the conquest of the Americas and its colonial legacy continues to affect all people of the Americas, including those of the Northwest region of the United States.

Endnotes

1. Carlos Schwantes, *The Pacific Northwest: An Interpretive History* (Lincoln: University of Nebraska Press, 1989), 21–24.
2. Schwantes, 216–17.
3. Mikhail Bakhtin, *Speech Genres and Other Late Essays*, ed. Caryl Emerson and Michael Holquist, trans. Vern W. McGee (Austin: University of Texas Press, 1986), 162–63.
4. Mikhail Bakhtin and Medvedev Pavel, *The Formal Method in Literary Scholarship*, trans. Albert J. Wehrle (Cambridge: Harvard University Press, 1985),14.
5. Stephen Greenblatt, *Marvelous Possessions: The Wonder of the New World* (Chicago: The University of Chicago Press, 1991), 82–83.
6. Christopher Columbus, *The Four Voyages of Columbus*, ed. and trans. J. M. Cohen (New York: Penguin Books, 1969), 51.
7. Frederick Turner, Beyond Geography: The Western Spirit against the Wilderness (New Brunswick: Rutgers University Press, 1992), 144.
8. As translated by Francisco López de Gómara, *Historia General de las Indias*, seg. Parte (Barcelona: Ediciones Orbis, S.A., 1985), 48.
9. Mikhail Bakhtin, *Toward a Philosophy of the Act*, ed. Vadim Liapunov and Michael Holquist, trans. Vadim Liapunov (Austin: University of Texas Press, 1993), 35.
10. Irving A. Leonard, *Book of the Brave* (Berkeley: University of California Press, 1992), 36.
11. Hernán Cortés, *Letters from Mexico*, trans. Anthony Pagden (New Haven: Yale University Press), 1986, 298–301.
12. Cabeza de Vaca, álvar Núñez, *La Relación* (Zamora: Agustin de Paz & Juan Picardo, 1542, sigs. G1r, G1v, H7r, H7v.
13. Beatriz Pastor Bodmer, *The Armature of Conquest: Spanish Accounts of the Discovery of America, 1492–1589*, Trans. Lydia Longstreth Hunt (Stanford: Stanford University Press, 1992), 110–11.

14. George P. Hammond, "The Search for the Fabulous in the Settlement of the Southwest," In *New Spain's Far Northern Frontier: Essays on Spain in the American West 1540-1821*, ed. David J. Weber (Albuquerque: University of New Mexico Press, 1979), 21–22.

15. Henry R. Wagner, *Spanish Voyages to the Northwest Coast of America in the Sixteenth Century* (Amsterdam: N. Israel, 1966), 176–78.

16. Wagner, 267.

17. Columbus, 7–72.

18. Mikhail Bakhtin, *The Dialogic Imagination: Four Essays*, ed. Michael Holquist, trans. Caryl Emerson and Michael Holquist (Austin: University of Texas Press, 1981), 293.

19. J.H. Elliot, *Imperial Spain 1469–1716* (New York: A Meridian Book, 1963), 30.

20. Christian I. Archer, "The Political and Military Context of the Spanish Advance into the Pacific Northwest," in *Spain and the Northwest Pacific Coast*, ed. Robin Inglis (Vancouver: Vancouver Maritime Museum Society, 1992), 11–12.

21. Ibid., 13.

22. Ibid., 14–15; René Chartrand, "The Soldiers of Nootka: Spanish Colonial Troops at the End of the 18th Century," in *Spain and the Northwest Pacific Coast*, ed. Robin Inglis (Vancouver: Vancouver Maritime Museum Society, 1992), 112–13, 115.

23. María Dolores Higueras Rodríguez and María Luisa Martín-Merás, "The Malaspina Expedition on the Northwest Coast of North America in 1791 [And 1792]," in *Spain and the Northwest Pacific Coast*, ed. Robin Inglis (Vancouver: Vancouver Maritime Museum Society, 1992), 183.

24. Catherine Poupeney Hart, "Malaspina at Port Mulgrave," in *Spain and the Northwest Pacific Coast*, ed. Robin Inglis (Vancouver: Vancouver Maritime Museum Society, 1992), 78.

25. Donald Cutter, "The Malaspina Expedition and Its Place in the History of the Pacific Northwest," in *Spain and the Northwest Pacific Coast*, ed. Robin Inglis (Vancouver: Vancouver Maritime Museum Society, 1992), 3.

26. Bernal Díaz del Castillo, *Historia Verdadera de la Conquista de la Nueva España* (Madrid: Editorial Espasa-Calpe, S.A., 1992), 104.

27. Tzevetan Todorov, *The Conquest of America*, trans. Richard Howard (New York: Harper Perennial, 1984), 99.

A Long Struggle:
Mexican Farmworkers in Idaho, 1918–1935

Errol D. Jones and Kathleen R. Hodges

On Mar. 27, 2002, student activist and farmworker Leo
Morales watched Idaho's Governor, Dirk Kempthorne, sign Senate
Bill No. 1289—the Farm Labor Contractor Registration and
Bonding Act—into law. "Defeated in 1995, 2000, and 2001, the
bill picks up where the farmworker minimum wage struggle left
off," Morales wrote in an *Idaho Statesman* guest editorial. The new
piece of legislation would address "the problem of farmworkers
being cheated out of wages by unscrupulous farm labor
contractors."[1] The minimum wage struggle to which Morales
referred in his editorial had been won the year before after bitter,
hard-fought battles waged over the course of four years. The
minimum wage law that went into effect Jan. 1, 2002, extended
the federal minimum wage (at the time, $5.15 per hour) to
farmworkers in Idaho. There were exceptions—children younger
than sixteen working with their parents during harvests, workers
on cattle and sheep ranches, and seasonal harvesters living locally
and spending less than thirteen weeks in farm labor. However,
advocates of the bill estimated that about 95 percent of the state's
farmworkers, most of Mexican heritage, would be covered. While
labor activists (like Leo Morales, Adán Ramírez of Idaho
Community Action Network, and Humberto Fuentes, then
director of the Idaho Migrant Council), celebrated with Gov.
Kempthorne as he signed the minimum wage bill into law at a
Wilder farm labor housing complex on Mar. 22, 2001, they stressed
the need for all farmworkers to be included.[2]

The fact that these two pieces of legislation took so long in
coming and were won only after acrimonious and contentious
political struggle suggests that the history of farm labor in Idaho
has been marked by more confrontation than harmony. It was not

until 1996 that farmworker advocates succeeded in passing a law extending workers compensation coverage to farm labor. Agriculture was one of the state's largest industries during most of the twentieth century, and though farmworkers of Mexican descent played a crucial role in Idaho's agricultural economy, that role has often been disparaged or ignored. Workers have faced both indifference and active prejudice. Idaho had exempted workers in agriculture from employment compensation insurance when the law was originally enacted in 1917. As late as 1994, Idaho and Nevada were the only western states that failed to cover agricultural laborers under workers compensation. According to a booklet published in Boise by the Farmworker Resource Committee, farm work had "the highest death rate and the third highest injury rate of any occupation in the country."[3] For Idaho not to cover its farmworkers was discriminatory and unfair. Between 1917 and 1995 there were eight unsuccessful attempts to remove the exemption from the law books. Finally, Idaho Legal Aid threatened a lawsuit based on denial of equal protection for the mostly Mexican farmworkers. Javier Tellez Juárez, an uninsured worker who lost both arms and a leg in a farm accident, campaigned for the legislation. Republican Gov. Phil Batt threw his full support behind the reform, and the Legislature narrowly voted to remove the exemption. On Mar. 12, 1996, Gov. Batt signed the bill into law.[4] This followed an earlier victory for agricultural workers when the State Legislature in 1981 made it mandatory that farmers provide their employees with portable toilets in the fields.

The progressive changes and victories won by Idaho's farmworkers have only come about as a result of significant economic adjustments in Idaho's economy that brought an influx of people no longer dependent upon agriculture for their livelihood. Although Idaho's agricultural interests were still able to wield considerable political power in the beginning of the twenty-first century, they no longer dominated as they had during the previous one hundred years. In the 1920s and 1930s farmers and their business allies commanded such economic and political power that they recruited labor for planting and harvests from other states and from other countries, with little or no legal restraint on how they treated workers. Many of these workers were either Mexican nationals or Mexican Americans migrating from other states, and few established institutions rendered them support or protection. For the most part, migrant laborers found themselves at the mercy of farmers, food processors, and labor contractors. Limited by language, operating in an unfamiliar culture and at times in a hostile environment, workers were expected by their hosts to arrive when needed, do the work they were told for the lowest amount of pay, and move on when the job was done. If housing was inadequate to nonexistent, if working conditions were difficult if not unbearable, if food was scarce and prohibitively expensive, if compensation was less than earlier agreed upon, what recourse did the migrant have, especially if the migrant was not a citizen of the United States, but a Mexican national?

Mexican migrant labor proved to be a tremendous asset to the American economy, costing little but contributing much. Mexican workers arrived ready to work, the costs of rearing, educating, feeding, and clothing them borne by the laborers themselves or by programs inside Mexico. U.S. political leaders and employers were well aware that immigrant labor provided them with what amounted to a subsidy. The *New York Journal of Commerce* noted as early as 1886, "Men, like cows, are expensive to raise, and a gift of either should be gladly received. And a man can be put to more valuable use than a cow!"[5] In addition, migrants spent some, if not all, of their hard-earned money on goods and services in the communities where they lived and worked, further contributing to the economy.

A series of events between 1918 and 1935 illustrates the difficulties faced by Mexican nationals working in Idaho's fields, and the economic relationships between large produce companies, farmers, and migrant laborers. The story also offers a glimpse into the operations of the Mexican government through its Salt Lake City consulate and suggests that, for Mexican nationals at least, the consulate was the only institution to which they could turn when they felt their rights were being abused. The emergence of a *huelga* (strike) in the pea fields around the Teton County seat of Driggs demonstrates how the state government of Idaho responded to the urgings of local farmers, and to the needs of out-of-state agribusinesses whose interests were compromised by farmworkers' demands for better pay and decent treatment. The strike and circumstances leading up to it show that the experiences of migrant laborers in Idaho differed little from what they endured in other states at about the same time, except that, rather than negotiate a settlement between migrant workers and employers, Idaho's governor rushed to declare martial law, sending in the National Guard to end the strike. Finally, these events show that Mexican workers did not passively endure unfair and abusive treatment, but fought back with whatever means were at their disposal.

During the first few decades of the twentieth century southern Idaho underwent a significant agricultural transformation. Massive government irrigation projects enabled farmers and developers to turn the waters of the mighty Snake River out upon sage-covered flood plains, and the desert yielded marketable crops of potatoes, sugar beets, and other agricultural produce. Working in tandem with developers, the railroads sought to expand their markets by bringing settlers to the desert and shipping their crops to market. For those familiar with Idaho's history this is a well-known and often told story, and needs no elaboration here.[6] Unfortunately, what is missing from Idaho's history is any extensive coverage of the contributions made by Mexican nationals and Mexican American workers during this formative period.[7]

In fact, publications from earlier decades were misleading and omitted the presence of Mexicans in the labor force completely. A 1944 *National Geographic* article titled "Idaho Made the Desert Bloom" by then U.S. Senator from Idaho D. Worth Clark extolled the virtues of Idaho's agricultural success. But only once in forty-one pages did the senator mention that Mexicans had been involved in that effort when he wrote that in 1943 Mexicans and Jamaicans were brought to Idaho "to help harvest 'spuds.'" Numerous photographs illustrate Clark's narrative but none show Mexicans at work in the fields. Instead, staged photos show pretty girls in high-heeled sandals harvesting hops and picking fruit. The reality for Idaho at this time had to be otherwise, owing to the role it played in World War II as a supplier of natural resources and foodstuffs. It may be expecting too much of Senator Clark to probe deeply into Idaho's labor history, but he made almost no mention of the thousands of Mexican nationals and Mexican Americans working in agricultural, railroad, and mining industries at the time he wrote the article. By that time several thousand Mexican nationals had been brought to the state as a part of the *bracero* agreement between the United States and Mexico. For Idaho's leaders and for many of its citizens at the time, Mexicans seemed to have been an invisible people.[8] With a few exceptions, that is still the case.

An explanation for this omission in Idaho's history can be attributed, in part, to racism, a distinguishing feature of American society at the time. The prevalent attitude among Idaho's dominant class was that the influx of Mexicans into the state was temporary and isolated in certain sectors of the economy like agriculture and the railroads, and that when Mexican workers completed their tasks they would move on. Farmers and businessmen were reluctant to admit that some of their wealth and power resulted from exploiting a cheap, docile, and transient labor force, or to assume any responsibility for poor working conditions. Moreover, Idaho's historians had paid scant attention to the twentieth century, instead focusing on a version of Idaho's nineteenth century territorial and mining history that glorified the perils and exploits of Anglo pioneers.[9] However, people of Mexican descent have lived in Idaho since the 1860s, and Mexican workers have been recruited in significant numbers since World War I. In

Mexico, during the paternalistic, authoritarian regime of Porfirio Díaz (1876–1910), many who disagreed with the internal order crossed the border into the United States. People in the working and peasant classes found it increasingly difficult to live in Mexico. As their income stagnated or declined, government policies caused prices of basic foodstuffs to rise, forcing those who could to bolt for the border. They hoped to find better jobs and a better life, often promised to them by labor recruiters sent south by U.S. companies. During the next two decades, as revolution convulsed their country, Mexicans at the lower end of the income scale continued to seek survival opportunities across the border in the United States.

Mexico's great rebellion with its violence and turmoil coincided with a period of rapid economic growth in Idaho and in the Pacific Northwest. As the United States government facilitated the construction of irrigation projects, farms replaced sagebrush with row crops and towns sprang up along the Snake River plain. More railroad and farm jobs were available than Idaho's small population could fill. The United States' entrance into the world war in 1917 opened up further opportunities for Mexican labor. Not only did wartime conscription increase the need for workers, but also the Immigration Act of 1917 imposed a head tax and literacy test that effectively restricted immigration from eastern and southern Europe. The law applied to all immigrants, but on May 23, 1917, at the urging of western and southwestern entrepreneurs, the government specifically exempted Mexican agricultural workers from the law's requirements. Under industry pressure the exemption was extended to Mexicans working in railroad, mining, and industrial sectors. Assurances from the government that Mexicans would not be drafted helped to keep the immigrants flowing northward.[10] In the 1920s when Congress adopted a quota system to determine numbers of immigrants allowed into the United States southern and eastern European immigration continued to dwindle. Mexican immigration remained high throughout the decade. Labor recruiters brought Mexicans and Mexican Americans to Idaho from northern Mexico, from the border region, and from Utah, Colorado, New Mexico, and California. They put them to work on the railroads and in the recently developed potato and sugar beet fields.

The numbers of Mexicans migrating to Idaho are difficult to determine and sketchy at best. The 1920 census revealed that 1,215 Idaho residents had been born in Mexico. Unfortunately, the census did not indicate ethnic background, so we do not know how many Idaho residents may have been of Mexican heritage although born in the United States.[11] Nor do we know how many Mexicans were recruited for seasonal work in Idaho but missed by census takers and counted only haphazardly by the companies that recruited them. We can only guess at their numbers based on newspaper accounts, consular reports, government documents, and anecdotal materials. For example, in 1918 the Mexican Consul General in San Francisco wrote to Idaho Gov. Moses Alexander that he had received numerous complaints from "a great number of laborers brought from Mexico by several sugar companies to work in their beet fields in your State."[12] Although the Mexican Consul General did not note how many Mexicans were at work in Idaho at the time, local newspaper accounts of hundreds of Mexicans arriving to work in the potato and beet fields indicate that many more were working at one time or another in the state than census figures revealed. In the published works on Idaho history these people are invisible, despite the fact that seasonally they were an important factor in the state's economic growth. To paraphrase one Kansas beet grower in the 1920s, the sugar beet industry owed its development and prosperity to Mexican labor. It is clear that Idaho's railroads and its agricultural base could not have been built without these invisible people.[13]

Sometime in the early fall of 1918 Mexicans working in the beet fields of southern Idaho complained to the Mexican Consul about working conditions. In a letter dated Oct. 1, the consul requested Idaho's Gov. Moses Alexander to investigate the allegations of abuse and to ensure that "conditions may be duly improved where necessary…" The consul listed a number of areas of concern. Housing, in general, "is alleged to be insufficient for the total number of families, and that which does exist is in so bad a condition as to render it entirely improper to live in, and… caused the regretful death of several children." Further, the consul contended, "the wages have not been paid as offered to the men before they embarked at the border… In many instances certain improper discounts have been made, such as the transportation expenses, which as per the contract were to be paid by the employer…" after the worker had worked for three months. Moreover, the consul reported, the contracts stipulated that the men were to be returned to "the point from whence they came…but as yet they remain in the fields, without pay, food nor shelter." These alleged violations of worker contracts notwithstanding, the Mexican official went on to say that, "in several cases where some of the men appealed to the company for the improvement of their distressful situation, or tried to secure employment elsewhere, they were fined and imprisoned, being subjected at the time of arrest to outrageous insults and abuses."[14]

Wasting no time, Gov. Alexander directed William J. A. McVety, one half of Idaho's two-man Labor Commission, to visit the sugar factories. McVety was to go to Twin Falls, Paul, Blackfoot, and Lincoln in the southern and southeastern part of the state to determine if the consul's charges were true and to report back to the governor "at the earliest possible date." He jotted down a handwritten list of contacts on the back of the governor's letter, including sugar company employees in several southeastern Idaho towns, as well as "Raymond Noble, Mexican, runs Pool Hall & Restaurant Idaho Falls" and "Pocatello—J. U. Chacon, Labor Scout for district." He complied with the governor's request, visiting all of the above sites as well as some other places where he could obtain reliable information, and submitted his report on Oct. 24, 1918. Beyond the report itself, no detailed record of his trip exists. We do not know if he talked directly to workers. If he did, it is unlikely that he was able to speak to them in Spanish, but judging from his list of contacts, he certainly met people who could translate for him. McVety himself came from an educated but blue-collar background, working as foreman in the print shop of the *Idaho Daily Statesman*, the state's largest and longest-running daily newspaper. Though being a labor commissioner was apparently not a full-time job (Boise city directories listed his occupation as print shop foreman during all of his seven-year stint on the commission, from 1915 through 1922), this was not McVety's first official trip. He had already traveled to northern Idaho to investigate the lumber industry in the wake of Industrial Workers of the World (IWW) strikes. In that instance, he recommended that the lumbermen join the Idaho Federation of Labor instead of allying themselves with the more radical Wobblies.[15]

On his trip to southern Idaho, the commissioner investigated working conditions quite thoroughly, but again made a rather conservative recommendation. In the Twin Falls area, encompassing Burley and Paul, Amalgamated Sugar Company employed about two hundred Mexicans, none of whom came under prior contract with the company. In fact, "no Mexican laborers have been shipped into this district under bond for over two years," McVety wrote. Rather they came to the area voluntarily, made individual agreements with the farmers, and worked as field hands. The commissioner found satisfaction among the workers and "no complaints were brought to light."[16] Unfortunately, such was not the case in the southeastern district of Idaho Falls, Shelley and Blackfoot. Here, "complaints were numerous regarding their accounts [wage agreements], living quarters and about winter clothing." McVety estimated that about fifteen hundred Mexican laborers, including five hundred women, "many of whom work in the field," had been brought to the area "through a special agreement between the Utah-Idaho Sugar Company and the Government of the United States." The contract held the sugar company responsible for the workers, to guarantee them work, to return them to Mexico when the contract expired, and to "report to the immigration authorities any laborer, who does not live up to the contract." The commissioner's observations led him to the belief that "too much is left to the supervision of the Sugar Company. They are all powerful under the existing contract. It savors of paternalism." Acknowledging the absolute necessity of Mexican labor to the sugar beet industry, McVety warned the governor that if the industry were to survive in the future, "it depends largely upon how the laborers fare under the present contracts." From his observations they were not faring very well.[17]

McVety's report did not make it clear if the sugar companies worked through an intermediary labor boss as Utah Copper Company did in its Bingham, Utah, mines or the Canadian Pacific Railroad did in its construction operations. Chacon, the "labor scout" may have been such a labor boss, but the record is unclear. In other industries such as mining and railroads, companies relied upon labor contractors to hire and fire workers and to deal with the other labor-related issues of transportation, food, lodging, and even medical needs. For those services, workers paid the contractor a portion of their wages. While filling some needs, the system also lent itself to numerous abuses. As we shall see, such labor contractors were ensconced in other areas of Idaho agriculture, but hiring practices may have worked differently in the sugar industry.[18] McVety did verify a number of the problems that the Mexican consul had brought to the governor's attention in his letter of Oct. 1. One of those was the issue of wages. McVety did not think that the company was trying to cheat the workers out of their pay. Rather, he believed that misunderstanding emerged owing to the workers' inability to understand the contracts and the failure of the company to provide workers with proper explanations of U.S. law and customs. However, company deductions for hospital fees were excessive, especially when workers were expected to pay doctors' fees themselves. Many of the misunderstandings that arose from language and the interpretations of the contracts could be remedied if these matters were "handled by a qualified state representative or one delegated by the Sugar Company for that special purpose."[19]

In general, McVety found the housing to be bad. (An interview with Felicitas Pérez García confirms McVety's first impression. When she and her husband arrived in Shelley around 1910, there was not enough housing for workers. They were forced to build their own house with discarded boards scavenged from a nearby lumber mill. Pérez García made curtains from flour sacks and a mattress from corn sacks stuffed with grass, and constructed an outdoor oven by digging a hole in the ground.)[20] McVety, however, was encouraged that the company was building "adobe houses, such as the Mexicans desire, and is also lining with lumber and building paper, the inside of their present portable houses, which will make them comfortable for winter weather." He also noted that the company would give the workers a strip of land near the permanent houses that could be used to raise gardens. However, he found that sanitation and living conditions could be better if the company put such a responsibility "in the hands of one person who shall exercise a general control over the laborers in their mode of living, teaching them the necessity of sanitation, fumigation, social living conditions and prevent the overcrowding of houses." Many of the problems in McVety's view could be alleviated if workers had a person to whom they could take their complaints regarding accounts, credits, transportation deductions, or other issues arising between them and the company. "There are numerous complaints by the laborers regarding their accounts and it would seem that a great deal of dissatisfaction and suspicion could be allayed if the Sugar Company would issue monthly statements to each person, rendering them in a manner easily digested by the laborers."[21] It is clear from his report that McVety thought an ombudsman type position would benefit workers and the company, but the position should be held either by someone within the company or in government service, not by a worker or union spokesman. The suggestion itself was paternalistic.

The commissioner found untrue the allegations that workers' appeals to the company about unsatisfactory conditions or attempts to find employment elsewhere were met by fines, imprisonment, and other abuses. On the contrary, he claimed that the sugar company had an agreement with the railroad "to use all their spare men, and the men can also hire themselves to individual farmers, as some have already done." In fact, many men had gone to work for area farmers picking potatoes or threshing wheat to the "detriment of the Company's work." Nonetheless, no matter where they worked, there was dissatisfaction with the confusion that arose over wages, credits, and fees deducted from wages, especially where these were not clearly explained to the workers. This was a shame, McVety noted, because "the Mexican laborers, as a rule, are a good working, trusting class. Their labor is essential at present to southern Idaho, and it should be someone's duty to maintain a supervision over them other than the Sugar Company."[22]

It does not appear that McVety's suggestion to create an advocate position at the state government level was given serious consideration. Throughout the decade of the 1920s, more and more Mexican Americans and Mexican nationals migrated into the state, and as they did a pattern of discrimination and human rights abuses began to manifest itself. Newspapers during the decade reflected negative attitudes about Mexicans in general. News items that appeared in the *Twin Falls Daily News* in the summer of 1924 show a clear bias against people of Mexican heritage. For example, after the theft of some clothes from a laundry company and the discovery of a cache of marijuana, Twin Falls police arrested a Mexican and charged him with the crime. In describing the affair the newspaper noted that the "dope, smoked chiefly by Mexicans… affect[s] the smoker to such an extent that they go temporarily and dangerously insane…" The city's Chief of Police P.O. Herriman believed the Mexican had been smoking this "dope" and concluded that "every Mexican who can not show some visible means of support will be arrested for vagrancy and run out of the city."[23] The next day the same newspaper carried the headline "Three Mexicans Now in City Jail as a Result of Campaign to Rid Twin Falls of Idle Foreigners." The article informed readers that "idle Mexicans" had been causing the police a "great deal of trouble" for a period of six months.[24] The three Mexicans were charged with smoking "dope," stealing laundry and a suitcase, and were sentenced to serve thirty days each in the county jail.[25]

Before the end of World War I and throughout the 1920s many railroad companies hired Mexican immigrants ("traqueros" in Spanglish) to help build and maintain the rail system in the western United States. When unable to find work on the railroads, Mexicans looked for work in the fields and vice-versa. By 1929 these track workers of Mexican descent made up nearly 60 percent of the section crews employed in Idaho by the Union Pacific, Northern Pacific, Oregon Short Line, and Great Northern railroads. "Indeed," wrote Erasmo Gamboa, from its regional headquarters in Pocatello, the Union Pacific "assigned Mexican section and extra gang crews throughout southern Idaho."[26]

In southeastern Idaho, the city of Pocatello emerged as the center of the rail transport industry for the rest of the state. The impact of the railroad on Pocatello's economy was immense and remained the dominant factor in the community until long after World War II. According to Gamboa, "Life in Pocatello revolved around the Union Pacific railroad yard." Prior to World War I, the Union Pacific generally hired laborers of Chinese, Native American, Greek, and Italian backgrounds. The imposition of federal restrictions on eastern European and Mediterranean immigrants after World War I led to "a surge in the employment of Mexicans and African Americans."[27] Arriving Mexican workers joined an already ethnically diverse city where jobs were plentiful, and most of the newcomers went to work for the Union Pacific Railroad. The Union Pacific yard and depot defined the social geography of the city. To the east and south sides of the railyard lived Mexican, Greek, Italian, and black American families, to the north and west resided families from the dominant culture, many of whom worked for the railroad or held other occupations. Within the east side, Mexicans gravitated toward a barrio they called "*la sección*" predominantly composed of Mexican section crews and their families. Thrown together in this ethnically diverse section of the city, comprised of Greeks, Italians, Poles, Mexicans, Chinese, and American blacks, it appears that "there was little conflict."[28] Despite the racial and ethnic prejudice that pervaded Pocatello's society, the railroad culture of the time had "an increased propensity to keep non-whites and some immigrant groups lower in the job hierarchy." Barred from the unions and the brotherhoods, Mexicans found that few of the good jobs were open to them and had to settle mostly for "rear-bench levels of maintenance employment."[29]

As a permanent Mexican population took root in the 1920s and began to grow in the railroad town, the presence of Mexican agricultural workers became notable in other regions of eastern Idaho. From consular records filed by the Mexican Consul at Salt Lake City, a picture emerges of an active, permanent, and vibrant community of Mexican nationals in Idaho Falls. Ten years after the Consul General had asked Gov. Alexander to investigate Mexican worker dissatisfaction with the Utah-Idaho Sugar Company practices in eastern Idaho, Carlos M. Gaxiola, Mexican Consul in Salt Lake City, traveled to Idaho Falls to investigate similar complaints.[30] Responding to a long list of allegations sent him by twenty-five families hired by the company in El Paso, Texas, four years previously, Consul Gaxiola met with company representative Edson Isaac Porter.[31] Porter, who had joined the company in 1919 as an interpreter and labor recruiter, assured the consul that his firm was desirous to "do justice" in the matter, and even paid the consul's expenses while he conducted his investigation. Gaxiola also met with Juan Reyes, representing the Mexican families, to hear their grievances. He assured Reyes that he would take the matter of their complaints to the general manager of the company and that he was confident of a satisfactory resolution.[32]

This meeting resulted in promises from the company that the consul conveyed to Juan Reyes in a letter dated Sept. 25, 1928. Company practice was to hire workers and then send them out to various privately owned farms where workers would weed, thin, and irrigate the beets. In the fall they would return for the harvest. Gaxiola told Reyes that in the future it would be wise to "suspend contracts with Mexican labor contractors that have proven impracticable and disadvantageous for them," and to make contracts with the company that listed "well defined" obligations for the workers and for the farmers to whom they were sent. Gaxiola said that he had secured a verbal promise from Utah-Idaho Sugar Company officials that the workers would receive a signed copy of the contract in Spanish. The firm also agreed that workers would be dealt with seriously and correctly regardless of class, color or race. Gaxiola recommended the company print numbered payment receipts in quadruplicate: a copy for the worker, another for the farmer, a third for the foreman in charge, and the fourth for the company files. Receipts would show how much workers were to be paid, how much they actually received, and how much was credited to their account. At the end of each month each worker would receive a statement showing what was in his account, how much was deducted, and for what purpose deductions were made. The consul told Reyes that the company had agreed that workers should have complete freedom to seek credit wherever available without penalty or company interference, as well as the right to buy goods wherever they could obtain the best prices. Unfortunately, Gaxiola concluded that he could do little about contracts and agreements made earlier between the workers and the company. The origin of their complaints dated from years earlier when contracts with the company were not clear, varied from time to time and worker to worker, and made the situation impossible for the consul and the Mexican government to resolve. He expressed his confidence that soon things would change and that Reyes and his fellow workers would have the opportunity to enter into better, more advantageous contracts based on the agreements he had worked out with company officials.[33] Apparently consular intervention on behalf of Mexican workers contracted by Utah-Idaho Sugar Company resulted in more favorable treatment, at least for the next ten years, as no complaints could be found in the Salt Lake City Consulate files for the decade of the 1930s.

This was not the case, however, with another agribusiness that moved into Idaho in the 1920s and began to hire large numbers of Mexicans and other migrant labor to harvest produce. San Diego Fruit and Produce, a California company, had been licensed to operate in Idaho since Oct. 5, 1923. Company operations in Idaho centered on the production of fresh peas that the company contracted with private farmers to grow for them in various parts of the state. Sometimes the company rented land or bought it and planted it in peas. As harvest time varied from place to place depending upon the elevation of the farms, the company arranged to bring migrant pea pickers to the fields. Using 30-pound hampers, workers picked the peas, sent them to nearby packinghouses located on rail sidings where they were sorted, packed into crates, and loaded into specially manufactured refrigeration cars[34] that were then packed with blocks of ice from an adjacent icehouse. In this way, fresh peas could be rushed from the fields where they were grown for markets as far away as the east coast of the United States. The company's activities in Idaho stretched from Teton County on the Wyoming border to Canyon County on the Oregon border. In the western part of the state, San Diego Fruit and Produce had been planting and harvesting peas at Parma since 1926. In 1931, the harvest came early and the company rushed in a small army of several hundred pickers who within seven weeks harvested enough peas to fill 125 boxcars destined for New York City markets. The estimated payroll for that harvest was between $3,000 and $4,000 per day.[35]

For the workers picking peas it was a backbreaking way to earn a living. Stooped over the whole time, pickers dragged along a basket or "hamper" into which they tossed each pea pod. "Pea vines are habitually non-cooperative," wrote an Idaho journalist.

> They prefer to lay as flat on the ground as possible. Pea pods like to hide. They bury themselves into the ground at the bottom of the plant. When the harvest is in progress, it is a sight worth seeing. It is not uncommon for more than 500 pea pickers to be at work in one field. The pickers are of all ages and descriptions. Some are fast, others slow. Some squat on the ground and hitch themselves along the row. Others straddle the plants, point their noses at the ground and lumber down the rows like ungainly apes.[36]

From the vantage point of an observer the work seemed to have its lighter moments. There were periods of laughter and fun. "The pea field," continued our journalist,

> has a social atmosphere all of its own and the steady run of conversation and cat-calls makes up in volume what it lacks in learnedness. Oldsters discuss their rheumatism and the present condition of their backs. Younger pickers talk of schools, girl friends, automobiles. Entire families will work together and for them it will be old home week all day long. There usually is some fighting and a good supply of arguments.[37]

Pay for a day of bent-over picking under an unforgiving sun varied according to the skill and speed of the picker. In 1930, as the Great Depression began, companies paid between 1¢ and 1.5¢ per pound, but it was not uncommon for them to offer much less, so that by 1935 they were paying a little more than .5¢ per pound. There was always contention over pay between pickers and the companies, at times reaching the level of riots in the fields and pitched battles between workers who accepted company proffered rates and those who didn't.[38] Workers often thought the companies tried to cheat them by offering a bonus if certain conditions were met, but then on payday they informed the pickers that they had not met their obligations to receive the bonus.

In Teton County, the pickers were predominantly Mexican and company operations soon came to attract the attention of the Mexican consul in Salt Lake City. Teton County, so named for the majestic Teton Mountains that loom over its well-watered, lush valleys, sits at an elevation of 6,100 feet or higher. As early as the 1880s Mormon settlers arrived in the valley and took up farming. One student of the area's history observed that "the Mormon community, once a closed society, remained provincial by the twenties, but it had accommodated itself to the times. Mormon policy urged all aspects of economic development: agriculture, mining, manufacturing, transportation, and marketing."[39]

Upon its arrival in 1912, the railroad was received with open arms and "enterprising men engaged themselves in a wide variety of economic endeavors." The area always had a group of "wide awake" businessmen who were "ever ready to boost any laudable enterprise." F.C. Madsen, editor of the *Teton Valley News*, expressed views shared by most Mormon residents: "They admired plain, hardworking, successful people, but preferred to get rid of the 'faddist' social worker, 'so-called health boards,' welfare bureaus for children, and a 'dozen and one such incubi drawing fat salaries at taxpayers' expense.'"[40] The railroad opened the valley to commercial agriculture and to the activities of the San Diego Fruit and Produce Company and other commercial agricultural concerns that found the high mountain valleys ideal for planting green peas. Needing a large labor force that could be concentrated in the fields at harvest time, the companies brought in migrant workers when the peas were ready to pick (see Fig. 2.1). Migrants

Fig. 2.1. Mexican Peapicking Crew Teton Valley, Idaho, 1930s (photo Courtesy, Valley of the Tetons Public Library, Victor, Idaho).

seem to have come from many places such as Utah, California, and other surrounding states. But evidence indicates that by the end of the 1920s there was a rather large population of Mexican nationals and their families living permanently in Idaho Falls, a distance of about seventy miles over gravel roads from Driggs, the seat of Teton County. In the spring around the Idaho Falls area people would be able to find work with the sugar companies and sugar beet farmers once the beets needed weeding and thinning, and also weeding young potato plants. By July as the beet and potato fields needed less attention these workers joined other migrants to the Teton Valley as the pea harvest got underway.

While precise numbers are not available for Mexicans living in Idaho Falls or in Pocatello fifty miles to the south, Mexican consular reports reveal that the consul in Salt Lake City deemed the population significant enough that he should establish in both cities *comisiones honoríficas*. In August 1931 Consul Raúl Domínguez dispatched his Vice-Consul Elías Colunga to Pocatello and Idaho Falls to establish commissions to serve as extensions of the consulate in those areas.[41] The Mexican government "considered the *comisión* an extremely important component of its general consular policies." A prime function of the *comisión* was to extend the protection of the Mexican government through its consular service to Mexican nationals dispersed throughout the U.S.[42]

In his important study of Mexican consuls and labor organizing in the United States, Gilbert G. Gonzalez summarizes the duties of the *comisiones* as follows: to keep "alive and constant the memory and love of Mexico... [to] remind Mexicans of their duty to the Fatherland... [and to] serve as a connector between Mexicans in each of the small localities and [the] consulate." To accomplish these goals the *comisiones* tried to Mexicanize the children of immigrants by establishing primary schools. They also organized charities for the needy and festivals for Mexican holidays, as well as registered births to Mexican citizens, and took care of legal documents of citizenship. Finally, they were charged with taking an annual census of Mexican residents in the district. In other words, these were not independent voluntary organizations of Mexican citizens who wanted to maintain and foster their culture; they were official extensions of the consulate, and hence of the Mexican government. "It was an honor for a *colónia* to be selected as a site for a *comisión*; a *comisión* conferred a sense of importance and commanded respect."[43]

Charged with the task of setting up *comisiones* in the two southeastern Idaho communities, Vice-Consul Colunga set off on Aug. 27, 1931. He also had a second purpose for his trip to Idaho. The consulate had received complaints the year before from Mexican citizens engaged in the pea harvest in the Teton Valley. They alleged that San Diego Fruit and Produce Company had reneged on its promise to pay them the agreed amount for their work. Over the course of about two years the dispute over pay, allegations of mistreatment, deplorable housing, expensive food, and other problems would engage the time and energies of the staff of the Salt Lake City consulate, the consul general in San Francisco, the San Diego consul, the produce company and its agent in Driggs, and lawyers in Idaho Falls who represented the

Mexican workers.[44] Although the pay issue eventually was settled in the workers' favor, most of these problems, especially abuses by labor contractors hired by the company, continued to plague laborers until they struck the company in July 1935.

For the Teton Valley pea harvest in the summer of 1930, Glen Hubbel, San Diego Fruit and Produce Company's Idaho area manager, made arrangements with a contractor named Joe Rodríguez to supply the pickers for that year. On Sept. 1 the company discharged some of these workers who then contended that the company "failed, neglected and refused to pay them in accordance with the terms of [their] agreement." Instead of paying 1.5¢ the company only paid them 1¢ per pound. The workers hired an Idaho Falls lawyer and filed suit in the Teton County District Court, designating Henry Moreno and Zacarías García as assignees for themselves and thirty-five other Mexicans. Born in Chihuahua, Mexico, on Nov. 22, 1901, Moreno came to the United States when he was four years old and had never returned to his native land. For health reasons he migrated to Idaho in early 1930, settled in Idaho Falls, and worked in the beet and potato fields before joining the pea harvesters in Driggs. García had been born in Zacatecas, Mexico, on June 5, 1905, and in 1918 moved to Lincoln, near Idaho Falls, where he remained. He too worked in the beet and potato fields and at the Utah-Idaho Sugar Company mill at Lincoln. With Moreno he gravitated to Driggs for the pea harvest.[45]

At issue in this case was the amount workers were to be paid for each pound of peas picked. The workers insisted it was 1.5¢ per pound and the company claimed they had agreed on 1¢. In reality, both sums were correct. Company officials had adopted a payment system that they hoped would ensure them a reliable labor force throughout the entire harvest, even as the season advanced and fewer peas could be picked in a day compared to what the fields yielded at the outset. For this reason, the company set the price at 1¢ per pound with the promise of a .5¢ bonus if the workers' services were deemed satisfactory and if the worker remained in service until the harvest was over. If, however, the worker quit, or his services "should be unsatisfactory to the [company] and he should be discharged from service," the worker would "forfeit the .5¢ per pound." Company lawyers alleged that Moreno, García, and the thirty-five others had worked only a portion of the harvest and that when they did show up they were "lazy and indolent, and permitted large quantities of peas to lie and rot on the ground" causing the company to suffer "damage in the sum of $1,500..."[46]

As the case waited before district court, workers must have taken their complaints to the Mexican consul (at that time Enrique Ferreira) who received a letter from someone in the management of San Diego Fruit and Produce explaining that the case was before the court, "where the matter should be judged." Nevertheless, the unknown author of the letter claimed that the labor contractor, Joe Rodríguez of Pocatello, had paid all the workers in accord with their earlier agreement. Although company officials "always fulfilled their promises in order to avoid any difficulty," the writer believed that they were dealing with "a group that loved to create these kinds of differences." Hundreds of Mexicans, the correspondent asserted, worked for the company without registering any complaints.[47]

In a report he filed in early February 1931, Vice Consul Elías Colunga noted that some of the Mexicans had stopped working two or three days before ending the harvest season owing to illness or other forced reasons. The company used that as an excuse not to pay the bonus. The company, he informed Foreign Relations, makes payments based on the reports filed by the labor contractor and the company's "revisador" (inspector) about what each worker picked. He noted that his office had interceded in the past on behalf of the workers and had gotten satisfaction for some of them from the company. This had not been the case for Moreno, García, and the thirty-five others, whose case would be heard June 8, 1931, in district court. The labor contractor Joe Rodríguez, Colunga had been told by various Mexicans, had an "understanding" with the company's revisador and the manager,

Glen Hubbel, that allowed Rodríguez to sell "whisky and marijuana to the Mexicans and provide them with prostitutes." Rodríguez also had a "company store" ("*tienda de raya*") that he set up during the harvest and from which he sold food and other items, deducting the cost from the workers' pay. These kinds of arrangements were common throughout the West at this time where produce companies, railroads, and mining operations that used seasonal workers relied on contractors or agents to supply them with laborers on a temporary basis.[48]

The new Mexican consul in Salt Lake City, Raúl Domínguez received a telegram from workers under contract to San Diego Fruit and Produce Company in Driggs that the company refused to pay them the previously agreed sum of 1.5¢ per pound. Instead the company paid them only .75¢ and they were "indignant." Domínguez thought it prudent to send the vice consul to the area to report back to him about the situation.[49]

After traveling to Pocatello and Idaho Falls, where he set up the before-mentioned *comisiones*, Colunga arrived in Driggs on Aug. 27, 1931. He went immediately to the labor camps to interview as many as possible of the five hundred Mexicans involved in the late summer pea harvest. There, he encountered an agitated and armed camp at Driggs. Company employees and local authorities, as well as "some of our compatriots were armed (portan armas)."[50] The situation was deemed so serious that even Mexico's ambassador to the United States asked to be kept current on the problems in Driggs.[51] In the five-page report filed upon his return, Colunga described conditions at the labor camp located about four miles east of Driggs just inside the Wyoming state line at a place called Alta, but known to the locals as "Pratt Ward." Even by Depression Era standards, living conditions for the workers at this camp were wretched. "All the dwellings," he wrote, "with the exception of some tents, are rude huts (jacales) made of the branches of quaking aspens that, as the leaves dry, offer little protection against the sun, wind or rain." Sanitation presented grave dangers for public health. Privies were located next to the shacks and the smell was awful. Privy walls were made from old wood planks, some with six-inch gaps affording little privacy. The toilets were holes in the ground only a half-meter deep from the seat. The company took no measures to make the place safe or more hygienic. Colunga was so shocked by what he saw that he took Glen Hubbel to the camp to show him how bad it was. Hubbel agreed that the situation was not good, but said that next year it would be better when the company relocated the camp to a new site closer to the pea fields. Workers doubted this. The camp had been there since the company began its Teton Basin operations. Colunga did not address the problem of food or its preparation other than to point out that it was scarce and of poor quality. The new labor contractor who had replaced Joe Rodríguez,

Arcádio Carranza, charged $1.10 per day per person to supply the single men with food. Even had workers been able to obtain food elsewhere, the camp's remoteness made it almost impossible (see Fig. 2.2 and 2.3). With the most skilled workers making less than $5.00 per day this was an excessive charge.[52]

Fig. 2.2. Migrant Labor Camp, Driggs, Idaho, 1931. Photo by Mexican Vice-Consul Elías Colunga. Photo Courtesy, Archivo Histórico de la Secretaría de Relaciones Exteriores (AHSRE File No. IV-193-22, Mexico).

As he delved into the world of the pea pickers Colunga learned that worker anger focused on Arcádio Carranza, a labor contractor who had traveled around California and Idaho recruiting workers with the promise of $1.25 for every hundred pounds of peas picked. Workers would receive a bonus on top of that if they worked everyday until the harvest was in. Upon arrival in Driggs, they discovered that the pay was really 75¢ per hundred pounds plus a bonus of 31¢ per hundred pounds if they finished the harvest. When the vice-consul confronted him with this, Carranza claimed that he told recruits that they would get 75¢ per hundred pounds and another 27¢ as a bonus. There was no signed contract with these workers, he said, only one between him and the company granting him 8¢ for every hundred pounds picked by each worker he recruited. Unfortunately, he could not show the contract to Colunga since he had left it in California. Hubbel confirmed the price offered to the workers, but thought Carranza received only 2¢ per hundred pounds picked by each worker. He too claimed his copy of the contract was in California. Wondering if a discrepancy existed between what Carranza offered the Mexican workers and what he offered U.S. workers, the vice consul questioned some of the latter and learned that they understood that they too would get $1.25 per hundred pounds, but they mentioned no bonus.[53]

Fig. 2.3. Migrant Labor Camp, Driggs, Idaho, 1931. Photo by Mexican Vice-Consul Elías Colunga. Photo Courtesy, Archivo Histórico de la Secretaría de Relaciones Exteriores (AHSRE File No. IV-193-22, Mexico).

Next, Colunga persuaded some of the Mexican pickers to go to a notary and swear under oath that they had been offered the higher rate by an official company representative. With notarized statements in hand, he dashed off a telegram to company headquarters in San Diego asking officials to tell him how much workers were to be paid. They responded that wage arrangements were worked out between the site manager and labor contractor, but that they would try to find out for him. Accompanied by five Mexican workers, Colunga went back to Hubbel and showed him the telegram the company had sent him. The manager exploded in anger. He was the boss, he said. No one ordered him around. Moreover, he did not care what the company said. Standing his ground, Colunga asked Hubbel to show him the contract he had with Carranza, whereupon, Hubbel ordered Colunga out of his office, exclaiming that neither he nor twenty other Mexican consuls would see it.[54]

Back in the camp, Colunga's interviews revealed that Carranza had taken over the same rackets that Rodríquez operated before him. He ran card games out of the only wooden structure at the camp, a bunkhouse of sorts where some of the men slept on straw on the floor. Carranza employed a "banker" who collected 20 percent of the winnings that were then divided between the banker, Carranza, and Hubbel. Workers who started up card games on their own were warned against it, and ran the risk of being fired. Colunga's Mexican informants also believed that Carranza controlled the sale of whisky and beer. Colunga concluded, "Mexican workers spend what little they earn." Once the harvest was finished in early to mid-September the "Mexicans leave the camp voluntarily or by force." Many would head for Idaho Falls where they went to work in the sugar beet fields until the end of October.[55] Having obtained as much information as he could, Colunga went back to Idaho Falls where he conferred with the lawyers handling the pay dispute for Moreno and García that had been postponed until October. He then returned to Salt Lake City to write his report.

Based on the information Colunga brought back from his visit to Idaho, Mexican Consul Domínguez informed his superiors in Mexico City that he had filed an official complaint with San Diego Fruit and Produce Company at its headquarters in San Diego and had urged management to fire Carranza and Hubbel. He reminded Foreign Relations of the wage dispute between Mexican workers and the same company the year before and expressed his belief that the company would spend more money in court costs than if it had paid the workers what they were originally due. In his view the present dispute would wind up in court as well and he thought the workers would win their case. In his report, Domínguez attached eight photos taken by Vice-Consul Colunga at the Driggs camp. He pointed out that they clearly showed the poor conditions for the workers, and that copies of the photos had been turned over to Idaho authorities in the hope that they would pressure the company to provide better housing and more hygienic facilities for their workers. Apparently the photos and solicitations had little effect on Idaho officials as the labor camps remained the same for some time thereafter. (Not until taken over by the Farm Security Administration in the early 1940s did conditions in Teton Basin work camps improve. A decade later in a report on labor camps at Driggs and Victor, the FSA noted that the harvest of 1941 was the first time the camp ever had decent housing. "Previous sanitation, order, morale has been most deplorable.")[56]

In a conciliatory gesture, motivated perhaps by wanting to avoid another worker-initiated lawsuit, the company offered to work through the Salt Lake City consulate to resolve the problems Vice-Consul Colunga had investigated. With Colunga doing the negotiating for the workers, and with the help of the Mexican consulate in San Diego, company management agreed to pay each worker $1.06 per hundred pounds of peas picked. Colunga also won a concession that the company would pay an additional $1.00 per hundred pounds for the last six days of the harvest. The deal was for all workers, not just the Mexicans. Consul Domínguez wrote his counterpart in San Diego recapping the past events, Colunga's investigation, and the workers' complaints. He urged his San Diego colleague to approach the company with a list of suggestions that, if adopted, would help alleviate problems in the future. While many of the suggestions were similar to those offered to the Utah-Idaho Sugar Company in 1918, many specifically addressed the abuses characteristic of the way in which San Diego Fruit and Produce and other agribusinesses operated at the time.

Consul Domínguez' first suggestion was to offer each worker a written contract stating exactly how much the company would pay and the terms of bonuses if any. In event of disputes a third party could check worker contracts and pay receipts with company records. Contracts should be in English and Spanish, in duplicate, one for the employee and the other for the company. Using Colunga's ideas for eliminating the problems of keeping workers in the fields as the yields diminished, he suggested that the company raise the price per hundredweight another dollar as an incentive. The company had agreed to do this in their settlement with the disgruntled workers, so why not make it a permanent part of their operation? Although Domínguez did not urge elimination of the contract labor system his other suggestions attacked some of its most notorious abuses: the sale of liquor in the camp, contractor-run card games, and questionable deductions for food from the pay of single workers who should be allowed to procure their meals wherever they chose. Finally, Domínguez urged the company to provide decent worker housing with proper hygienic facilities.[57]

Essentially, the company chose to ignore the problems. W.L. Springstead, president of the firm, wrote to the San Diego consul that the company "will continue to have our harvesting operations handled entirely by contractor, who will be required to be personally responsible for all relations and conditions involving the work of *his employees*, their pay, manner of living, behavior, etc." Moreover, the same bonus system used in the past would continue as it has "proven to be the only way we can feel sure we will have unbroken service as long as necessary..."[58] As time went on, management attempted to place conditions and limitations on the agreement to pay disgruntled workers from the 1931 pea harvest what they had earlier agreed.[59] Nevertheless, during the 1932 harvest the company was willing to pay the salary of a Mexican consular official from Salt Lake City to act as an intermediary between the workers and the company. This seems to have been somewhat successful, at least for that year, as no record indicates that pickers had serious conflicts with the company.[60]

As the Great Depression deepened in the 1930s labor-capital friction increased in many farming regions throughout the United States. Price declines on the produce market combined with unemployment, increased job competition, and wage cuts provoked spontaneous protest movements among agricultural workers. Wage levels of 35¢-50¢ per hour in 1929 fell to around 15¢ by 1933. San Diego Fruit and Produce offered pea pickers only 60¢ per hundred pounds with a 20¢ bonus if they picked to the end of the season.[61] It was a time of economic hardship and suffering for most working people in the United States. Mexicans suffered the additional hardship of being pressured to return to Mexico, whether they had been born there or not. In Idaho the dominant Anglo farmers tended to cast Mexican workers as nonwhite and to give "white" workers preference in hiring. In one incident that occurred in 1932 some thirty or forty "white" workers publicly protested a decision by a Twin Falls sugar beet farmer who let ten "white" workers go and hired nine Mexicans in their place. After meeting with the sheriff, the county commissioner, and the Twin Falls Associated Charities, the beet farmer gave the ten "whites" another chance, declaring, "I would prefer to employ white labor if it can do the work that has to be done."[62]

The summer of 1935 was hot and dry in the Teton Valley. Southeastern Idaho baked in the second year of a severe drought and tensions mounted between farmers of the upper and lower basin over the use of scarce water resources. In that summer Mexican pea-picking crews finally struck. Unfortunately, the Mexican Foreign Relations archives so full of information on the 1931 situation are mute on the strike of 1935. The papers of Idaho's Gov. Ross yield a chronology but no Mexican point of view.

To keep farmers in the area from violent solutions to the water disputes, Gov. C. Ben Ross sent Idaho's Adjutant General, Brigadier General M.G. McConnel to Driggs on Aug. 13. Shortly after McConnel arrived to meet with farmers over the water problems he learned that the county sheriff was having trouble keeping the peace among pea pickers and "that he and his deputies had not had much sleep for almost a week, going day and night." It quickly became clear to McConnel that he had walked into the middle of an ongoing conflict between workers and the produce companies that contracted them to pick peas. The General thought the dispute centered over wages.[63] Given the history of conflicts between workers and San Diego Fruit and Produce, one of the companies being struck, the strike is surprising only in the sense that it had not occurred sooner.[64]

Looking into the matter, McConnel learned that the companies were paying the pea pickers 70¢ per hundred pounds and an additional 15¢ per hundredweight if the picker stayed until the end of the season. Strike leaders objected to this for the reasons already discussed and demanded that management pay a flat $1 per hundredweight. When the companies refused about fifteen hundred workers went out on strike.[65] The sheriff told McConnel that about 90 percent of the workers were willing to work at the prevailing rate but that the remaining 10 percent "were keeping these pickers out of the field by threats of violence against themselves and their families."[66] The threat of violence even intimidated the sheriff, who claimed his deputies had been held the day before by "a gang of Mexicans," demanding that the deputies turn some prisoners loose who had earlier been jailed for "breach of the peace."[67] Asunción Pérez, a young boy from Idaho Falls, in Driggs with his family to pick peas, noted that trouble broke out when one of the company bosses, whom he remembered as "Mr. Howell" but it could have been Glen Hubbel, treated some of the Mexican workers badly and physically abused them. One worker retaliated, slashing him with a razor blade and sending him to the hospital. Pérez remembered that the company hired lots of armed men and they threatened "to massacre the Mexicans if they insurrected."[68]

Whatever the circumstances may have been, Gen. McConnel thought local authorities could handle it. On the morning of Aug. 14, however, he changed his mind. Upon emerging from a meeting with area water users he encountered an angry crowd of about 175 farmers "swearing that if they could not get order established by the civil authorities they would take the matter into their own hands and clean the Mexican camps themselves."[69] There seems to be little doubt that they would have attempted to do so. Just two summers before in the neighboring state of Washington, farmers had formed vigilante squads ("farmers' protective associations") in the Yakima Valley, armed themselves and loyal workers with pick handles and baseball bats, and confronted a group of strikers in the apple orchards. "A brief battle ensued, with bats and missiles flying. After a few minutes the farmers because of superior numbers and arms forced the workers to surrender. They were then surrounded and herded in mass to Yakima where 61 of them were booked in the county jail."[70] It certainly was not out of the question that something similar could happen in Driggs. Although Gen. McConnel could not make the decision to declare martial law, he was convinced that the local police could not handle the situation. The county's prosecuting attorney S.H. Atchley and other officials agreed and Atchley sent the governor a telegram urging him to intervene militarily.[71] The conflict had escalated from a dispute over wages between labor and the produce companies to one in which the farmers became directly involved with the prospect of economic ruin if they lost their pea crop. In their anger they lashed out at the strikers. Believing one of the Mexicans recently released from jail to be a strike leader they gave him thirty minutes to leave town, thought better of it, and prepared to do him serious bodily harm. Only his quickness enabled him to elude the mob and possibly saved his life.[72]

Idaho national guardsmen arrived in Driggs on the morning of Aug. 15 under the command of Colonel F.C. Hummel. In his Aug. 27 report Hummel stated that the strike had been "fomented by a few Americans and about 150 Mexican agitators.[73] He explained that after discussing the matter with a number of "prominent citizens… county officials and packing company officials it was plainly apparent that a large majority of the 1500 Mexicans engaged in harvesting the pea crop were being prevented from working by about 150 to 200 Mexican agitators and about 6 or 8 American agitators" dissatisfied with the wages. "It was also apparent," he continued, "that a large majority of the Mexicans were satisfied to work but were being prevented from working by threats of injury and death to the women and children." He reported that "certain Mexicans" visited them at night and "threatened them with death." They also visited the workers in the field and threatened them if they did not join the strike.[74] McConnel's account to the governor further tarnished the image of the strike leaders by claiming that they were "men who do not want to work themselves" and prevented the majority who did from doing so. Furthermore, he alleged that "there is pelnty [sic] of liquor circulating among the Mexican pickers, and also there is great evidence of Mariahuana [sic] being sold, which makes them very crazy after smoking it."[75]

Newspaper accounts seem to agree with the reports that Hummel and McConnel submitted, indicating that no one talked to the strikers or to the workers directly. No evidence indicates that anyone, public official, military officer, or journalist, tried to understand the workers' point of view or question the veracity of the company and official explanations of events. The picture that emerges is distorted and incomplete without the voice of the workers. And with the exception of Asunción Pérez's memories of an incident that occurred fifty-five years earlier the authors have yet to encounter a version of the story from the Mexicans' side. We do know that workers' representatives from outside the area and the Mexican consul in Salt Lake City attempted to obtain information and offered to send in people to negotiate a settlement.[76] However, Gov. Ross preferred to allow Hummel and McConnel to handle the affair. During the afternoon of Aug. 15 and the next morning Col. Hummel's troops entered three Mexican labor camps and arrested about 125 "Mexicans who were causing the trouble." Another "30 or more Mexicans were picked up on the streets of Driggs." These, together with "a few American agitators and some parasites and camp followers," were held under guard until paid the wages still owed them. Troopers then loaded them into trucks furnished by the packing companies or forced them into their own cars and trucks and escorted them to the county line where they told them not to return to Teton County.[77] The next day the remaining workers returned to the fields. The strike had come to an end.

It was clear at the time, and still is, that workers, regardless of their citizenship or ethnicity, had suffered violations of their civil rights (see Fig. 2.4). This was not unusual for American labor in other states during the Depression, and especially for migrant

Fig. 2.4. Mexican peapickers in Teton Valley, Idaho, 1930s
(photo courtesy of the Valley of the Tetons Public Library, Victor, Idaho).

agricultural labor. In Yakima, Wash., farmers' vigilante groups in the above-mentioned 1933 incident beat workers and packed them off to jail, and authorities built a stockade of heavy timbers strung with barbed wire at the top and a catwalk for patrolling purposes on the outside. Into this "bull pen" (reminiscent of those built in the 1890s by northern Idaho authorities to incarcerate striking miners and others caught in police or military dragnets)[78] the sixty-one farmworkers were herded to await trial. The *Yakima Morning Herald* reported that "several were lashed by the officials in the jail, then released and 'taken for rides' by vigilantes. One worker claimed that he was left beside the road with a swastika clipped in his hair and the red letters 'U.S.S.R.' painted on his welted back."[79] The bullies' cruelty was only matched by their ignorance. During that same year in California's San Joaquin Valley, local law authorities armed growers against striking cotton pickers who then fired into a crowd of men, women, and children assembled for a mass meeting, killing two and wounding another ten. One of those killed was president of the *comisión honorífica* investigating the strike for Mexican Consul Enrique Bravo.[80] One would hope that given this recent history of violence in other western states, Idaho's Gov. Ross dispatched the National Guard to Driggs to prevent its occurrence there, although no evidence exists that he was so motivated. If the governor was expecting applause for his actions he must have been disappointed when he came under fire from the Nampa and Boise Trades and Labor Councils. Affiliates of the American Federation of Labor, the Councils drew up a resolution condemning the governor's decision to impose martial law in Teton County. Published in the *Idaho Daily Statesman,* the resolution accused the governor of violating workers' constitutional and civil rights by sending troops to force them to end their strike for a just wage.[81] In its annual convention that same year, the Idaho State Federation of Labor adopted a resolution opposing the use of the Idaho National Guard in strikes.[82]

The pea pickers lost the strike at Driggs, but events leading up to the confrontation between labor and capital gives ample demonstration that these workers were not about to accept whatever company officials meted out to them without a struggle. Anything but passive victims, they protested what they considered to be unfair wage practices, requested help from the Mexican consulate, took their case to the courts, and finally, out of desperation, went on strike when the company and the farmers were most vulnerable as their ripe peas were about to burst their pods awaiting harvest. This would not be the last time that companies like San Diego Fruit and Produce, Yaqui Fruit, or Randolph Marketing and others would face worker opposition to shrinking wages, contractor abuses or miserable living conditions. Attempts to maximize profits at worker expense meant confrontations would continue in Idaho's fields and in those of neighboring Northwestern states throughout the 1930s, into the 1940s and beyond.

The role of the Mexican consulate in Salt Lake City as it sought to protect its citizens working in Idaho is an example of the limitations imposed by Mexico's inferior power position relative to that of the United States. Prior to 1929 American agriculture and industry pressured the U.S government to keep the border open. But when the economy weakened and opportunities dwindled for both U.S. citizens and immigrant labor, pressure mounted for Mexicans to return to Mexico. Repatriation, forced or otherwise, drove hundreds of thousands of Mexicans and even many Americans of Mexican heritage into Mexico. Owing to Mexico's precarious economic position repatriation overwhelmed the government and put severe strains on its already meager social infrastructure.[83] In Idaho, as elsewhere, Mexicans, even though legal residents recruited to the state when times were good, were now perceived as unwelcome and unwanted competition for what jobs were available. Consular officials in Salt Lake City knew that their citizens had a tough time finding work in Idaho, but acknowledged that the large produce companies were some of the few employers that would readily hire Mexicans.[84] Efforts to establish *comisiones honoríficas* as well as charitable organizations like the *Cruz Azul* (Blue Cross) were intended partially to provide protection and support for Mexican citizens living in Idaho. When workers called on the consulate to aid them in their disputes with San Diego Fruit and Produce Company, officials had to be careful to exercise the greatest diplomacy and to be as nonconfrontational as possible. The consulate's only power was moral. It could request information, investigate, and urge the companies and the state government to do the right thing, to treat the workers justly and humanely. Beyond that, it was powerless. This would change after Mexico and the United States signed the *bracero* agreement as a part a World War II alliance. As contract laborers, Mexican *braceros* had the power of their government behind them, backed up by international treaty to make sure that the agreements were kept. So when Mexican field workers in Twin Falls, Idaho, struck over payment of wages in an incident in 1945 farmers were forced by prior treaty agreements to honor workers' wage demands.[85] Again, in 1947, responding to allegations of discrimination and harassment of Mexicans in certain Idaho communities, the Mexican consul temporarily eliminated Idaho from the *bracero* program.[86] As long as the *bracero* agreement lasted between the United States and Mexico, Mexican *braceros* could look to their government and expect to receive at least minimal protection.

Finally, the foregoing account should demonstrate that Idaho's image of a state with a poor civil rights record is not a recent tag placed upon it by the presence of a few white supremacists that took up residence in the northern part of the state. Mexicans have faced discrimination, hostility, and injustice in Idaho throughout the twentieth century. Strides made toward correcting some of these abuses during the last twenty years do not mean that the past was a myth. Rather, the past was very real. Those who experienced abuses kept up the pressure to bring about changes so that the future would be better for their children and grandchildren. Farm labor advocates like Leo Morales and others, who worked so hard to eliminate agriculture's exemption from the minimum wage and to license farm labor contractors and force them to post bonds, know from personal experience that Idaho has become a better place for them only because they wouldn't have it any other way.

Endnotes

1. Leo Morales, "Farm Labor Bill Will Aid Idaho," *Idaho Statesman,* Jan. 31, 2002, Local 9. For the full text of the law see Idaho Code, Title 44, Chapter 16.
2. Gregory Hahn, "Kempthorne Signs Farmworker Bill," *Idaho Statesman,* Mar. 22, 2001, Main 1. For related *Statesman* articles see Jan. 9, 2001, Local 4; Mar. 13, 2001, Main 1; and Dec. 31, 2001, Local 4. The full text of the law is in Idaho Code, Title 44, Chapter 15. Leo Morales interviewed by Errol Jones, June 12, 2002, Boise, ID, tape in possession of Errol Jones.
3. Dale N. Duncan Jr., "The Struggle for Equal Coverage: The Battle for Workers Compensation in Idaho's Fields," in *The Hispanic Experience in Idaho,* ed. Errol D. Jones and Kathleen Rubinow Hodges (Boise, ID: Department of History, Boise State University, 1998), 136.
4. Ibid., 154.
5. Quoted in James D. Cockroft, *Outlaws in the Promised Land: Mexican Immigrant Workers and America's Future* (New York: Grove Press, 1986), 38.
6. A number of histories examine the early agricultural development of Idaho. For example, see articles by Hugh T. Lovin, "Free Enterprise and Large-Scale Reclamation on the Twin Falls-North Side Tract, 1907–1930," *Idaho Yesterdays* 29, no. 1 (1985): 2–14; "'Duty of Water' in Idaho: A 'New West' Irrigation Controversy," *Arizona and the West* 23, no. 1 (1981): 5–28; and "A 'New West' Reclamation Tragedy: The Twin Falls-Oakley Project in Idaho, 1908–1931," *Arizona and the West* 20, no. 1 (1978): 5–24; Merrill D. Beal and Merle W. Wells, *History of Idaho,* 3 vols. (New York: Lewis Historical Publishing Co., 1959); Merrill D. Beal, *A History of Southeastern Idaho* (Caldwell, ID: Caxton Printers, 1942); Carlos Schwantes, *In Mountain Shadows: A History of Idaho* (Lincoln: University of Nebraska Press, 1991); Leonard J. Arrington, *History of Idaho,* 2 vols. (Moscow, ID: University of Idaho Press, 1994); and Todd Shallat, ed., *Secrets of the Magic Valley and Hagerman's Remarkable Horse* (Boise, ID: Black Canyon Communications, 2002), especially Chapter Six.

7. Errol D. Jones and Kathleen R. Hodges, "Writing the History of Latinos in Idaho," in *Latinos in Idaho: Celebrando Cultura,* ed. Robert McCarl (Boise: Idaho Humanities Council, 2003).

8. D. Worth Clark, "Idaho Made the Desert Bloom," *National Geographic,* June 1944. For the history of *braceros* in Idaho and the Pacific Northwest see Erasmo Gamboa, *Mexican Labor and World War II: Braceros in the Pacific Northwest, 1942–1947,* 2nd ed. (Seattle: University of Washington Press, 2000).

9. In 1907, the first bulletin of the Idaho State Historical Society announced that one of the main duties of the Society would be "To procure from pioneers narratives of their exploits, perils and adventures." By looking at subsequent publications, one can form a pretty clear idea of which pioneers they meant. *Idaho State Historical Society Bulletin* 1, no 1 (Apr. 1, 1908).

10. Lawrence A. Cardoso, *Mexican Emigration to the United States, 1897–1931* (Tucson: University of Arizona Press, 1980), 38–54. Gunther Peck, *Reinventing Free Labor: Padrones and Immigrant Workers in the North American West, 1880–1930* (Cambridge: Cambridge University Press, 2000). Peck's analysis demonstrates the control that labor agents and recruiters gained, or sought to gain, over workers they recruited.

11. Arthur F. Corwin, ed. *Immigrants and—Immigrants: Perspectives on Mexican Labor Migration to the United States* (Westport, CT: Greenwood Press, 1978), 110, 116. The Mexican-born population in the United States in 1910, 1920, and 1930 was 221,915, 486,418, and 639,017, respectively.

12. Typed copy of letter from Mexican Consul General to Gov. Moses Alexander, Oct. 1, 1918. William J.A. McVety papers, MS 307 box 1, folder 3, Idaho State Historical Society, Library and Archives, Boise, ID. This small collection of the private papers of William J.A. McVety contains some official correspondence from the time he spent as Labor Commissioner under Gov. Alexander.

13. Local newspaper articles during the decade of the 1920s suggest that many more Mexicans were in the state than indicated by the census. For example, "Mexicans to Harvest Beet Crop," *Idaho Farmer,* Oct. 13, 1921, 10, noted that Amalgamated Sugar Company brought over five hundred Mexican field hands into the Twin Falls district alone and was looking for more. The census would have counted more seasonal workers in Idaho in some years than in others owing to the time of year when the data was collected. The 1910 census was taken in June, the 1920 census in January, and the 1930 census in April. Margo J. Anderson, *The American Census: A Social History* (New Haven: Yale University Press, 1988). The Kansas beet farmer was quoted in Peck, *Reinventing Free Labor,* 41.

14. McVety papers, folder 3.

15. Hugh Lovin, "Moses Alexander and the Idaho Lumber Strike of 1917: The Wartime Ordeal of a Progressive," *Pacific Northwest Quarterly* 66, no. 3 (1975): 119.
16. Untitled report, McVety to Gov. Alexander, Oct. 24, 1918, in McVety papers, folder 3.
17. McVety papers, folder 3.
18. For a discussions of labor contracting, see Peck, *Reinventing Free Labor*, and Devra Weber, *Dark Sweat, White Gold: California Farm Workers, Cotton, and the New Deal* (Berkeley: University of California Press, 1994).
19. McVety papers, folder 3.
20. Erasmo Gamboa, ed., *Voces Hispanas: Hispanic Voices of Idaho* (Boise: Idaho Commission on Hispanic Affairs and Idaho Humanities Council, 1992), 9.
21. McVety papers, folder 3.
22. Ibid.
23. *Twin Falls Daily News*, July 19, 1924, 8.
24. Ibid., July 20, 1924, 8.
25. Ibid., July 27, 1924, 5.
26. Erasmo Gamboa, "Mexican American Railroaders in an American City: Pocatello, Idaho," in *Latinos in Idaho: Celebrando Cultura*, ed. Robert McCarl (Boise: Idaho Humanities Council, 2003), 36.
27. Ibid.
28. Ibid.; quotation in Mary Katsilometes Scott, "The Greek Community in Pocatello, 1890–1941," *Idaho Yesterdays* 28, no. 3 (1984): 33.
29. Gamboa, "Mexican American Railroaders," 37.
30. C.M. Gaxiola to Subsecretary of Consular Department, Ministry of Foreign Relations, Sept. 25, 1929, Salt Lake City Consulate File IV-261-30, Archivo Histórico del Secretario de Relaciones Exteriores, Mexico City, hereafter AHSRE.
31. As a recruiter, Porter traveled to Mexico during the winter to recruit Mexican laborers for the company. Utah and Idaho Sugar Company had been bringing Mexican workers into the state even earlier than this, possibly from the time it began operating in Idaho after building its first mill in Lincoln in 1903. An active Mormon, Porter was born in the Mormon settlements established in northern Mexico during the Díaz dictatorship. This would explain his ability with the Spanish language and his knowledge of Mexico. "Edson Porter Dies in Montana," *Idaho Falls Post Register*, Apr. 1, 1956, 2; Miranda Stringham, compiler/editor. *Old Ammon (The First Fifty Years) 1885–1935* (Rexburg, ID: Ricks College Press, 1984), 213; Leonard Arrington, *Beet Sugar in the West: A History of the Utah-Idaho Sugar Company, 1891–1966* (Seattle: University of Washington Press, 1966), 21–24.
32. AHSRE, IV-261-30.

33. C. M. Gaxiola to Juan Reyes, Sept. 25, 1928, AHSRE, IV-261-30.
34. For an explanation and a history of refrigerated railroads see John H. White, *The Great Yellow Fleet: A History of American Railroad Refrigerator Cars* (San Marino, CA: Golden West Books, 1986). Pacific Fruit Express, a major operator and owner of refrigerator cars, built and maintained cars in its shops at Pocatello and Nampa, Idaho. Anthony W. Thompson, Robert J. Church, and Bruce H. Jones, *Pacific Fruit Express* (Wilton, CA: Central Valley Railroad Publications, 1992).
35. *Idaho Daily Statesman*, June 5, 1931, 5.
36. Editorial, *Idaho Daily Statesman*, June 27, 1937, 4.
37. Ibid.
38. "Pea Pickers Quit When Company Cuts Wages: Several Fights Follow," *Idaho Daily Statesman*, June 9, 1931. According to this report the incident took place on a farm on the Idaho side of the Snake River near Ontario, Oregon. The Payette County sheriff and three deputies "quelled" the disturbance.
39. Glen Barrett, "Idaho Coal: H.F. Samuals and the Teton Basin Mines, A Black Diamond History." Unpublished mss. Boise State University Library, 1973, 36.
40. F.C. Madsen writing in the *Teton Valley News*. Quoted in Barrett, 37.
41. AHSRE File No. IV-193-22.
42. Gilbert G. Gonzalez, *Mexican Consuls and Labor Organizing: Imperial Politics in the American Southwest* (Austin: University of Texas Press, 1999), 49. See as well the groundbreaking work by Francisco E. Balderrama on the significant role in the Mexican community played by the Mexican Consulate in Los Angeles during the depression of the 1930s, *In Defense of La Raza, the Los Angeles Mexican Consulate, and the Mexican Community, 1929–1936* (Tucson: University of Arizona Press, 1982).
43. Gonzalez, *Mexican Consuls*, 49–52.
44. AHSRE, various communications included in File No. IV-193-22.
45. *Henry Moreno & Zacarías García v. San Diego Fruit and Produce Company.* Teton County, District Court Records, AR 245, Box 20003904, Case #807, Idaho State Historical Society Library and Archives, Boise. Reference to this case can also be found in AHSRE, File No. IV-193-22.
46. Ibid.
47. Mexican Consul at Salt Lake City Enrique Ferreira to the Secretariat of Foreign Relations, Dec. 18, 1930, AHSRE, File No. IV-193-22 Reg. No. 3158, Exp, 242/(73–47). The letter from the company is not in this file. Ferreira is translating and paraphrasing from it in his letter to his superiors.

48. Mexican Vice Consul at Salt Lake City Elías Colunga to Secretariat of Foreign Relations, Feb. 4, 1931, AHSRE, File No. IV-193-22, Exp. 241.8 /(73-54). The description of Rodríguez and the power he exercised over the workers evokes some similarities to the Italian padrone Antonio Cordasco described by Gunther Peck in his study *Reinventing Free Labor*, 15–31. Devra Weber, *Dark Sweat, White Gold*, describes contractor/worker relationship patterns in California's cotton fields during the 1920s and 1930s. What little we have found in the records on Idaho indicate relationships similar to those she discovered. See especially 69–78. For a description of Mexican labor contractors operating in the U.S. in the 1980s and 1990s see Daniel Rothenberg, *With These Hands: The Hidden World of Migrant Farmworkers Today* (New York: Harcourt Brace & Co., 1998).
49. Raúl Domínguez to Secretariat of Foreign Relations, Aug. 31, 1931, AHSRE, File No. IV-193-22.
50. Ibid.
51. Mexican Ambassador to the United States José Manuel Puig Casauranc to Consul Raúl Domínquez, Sept. 14, 1931, AHSRE, File No. IV-193-22, Exp. 73-0/241/103.
52. Colunga's five-page report to Raúl Domínguez dated Sept. 1, 1931, can be read in AHSRE, File No. IV-193-22. Rita Pérez confirmed much of this fifty-five years later when she told an interviewer: "At Driggs there was a clearing in the forest where we were allowed to either pitch tents or build shelters out of bark." Rita Pérez interviewed by Rosa Quilantán, Idaho Falls, ID, Aug. 25, 1991, quoted in Gamboa, *Voces Hispanas*, 20–21. In California's San Joaquin Valley the deplorable conditions in the labor camps "were a constant source of sickness, accidents, strain and conflict." Weaver, 72–73.
53. Colunga's report. One of the major grievances was the exploitation suffered by pea pickers under the labor contract system. Worker belief that contractors were unfairly profiteering from their labor touched off a massive strike in the pea fields in Alameda and Santa Clara counties, California, during April 1933. Stuart Marshall Jamieson, *Labor Unionism in American Agriculture*, Bulletin No. 836 (Washington, D.C.: U.S. Department of Labor, 1945, Arno Press reprint, 1975), 88–89.
54. Colunga report.
55. Ibid.

56. Raúl G. Domínguez to Secretariat of Foreign Relations, Sept. 3, 1931, AHSRE, File No. IV-193-22. The quotation is from Farm Security Administration, "Migratory Labor Camp Program," Sept. 10, 1941, Correspondence Concerning Migratory Labor Camps, 1935–1943, AD-124 (Housing), National Archives, Record Group No. 96, 16. Domínguez had good reason to be concerned about worker health conditions. The photos Colunga took portray intolerable living conditions. On Sept. 10, seventy Mexican workers signed a letter to the company demanding that Hubbel and Carranza be dismissed. Hubbel, they said, drove the men too hard, was "disrespectful to everyone and is not liked." See letter and photos in AHSRE, File No. IV-193-22.

57. Raúl Domínguez to Enrique Ferreira, Mexican Consul in San Diego, Sept. 15, 1931. AHSRE, File No. IV-193-22.

58. W.L. Springstead to Amando C. Amador, Consul of Mexico, San Diego, Mar. 26, 1932. AHSRE, File No. IV-193-22. Emphasis ours.

59. Ibid. Contains letters from the Salt Lake City and San Diego consulates to Foreign Relations detailing the ongoing negotiations with the company.

60. Raúl Domínguez to Secretariat of Foreign Relations, July 30, 1932. AHSRE, File No. IV-193-22, Exp. 73/54/524.9/6.

61. Jamieson, 80; AHSRE, IV-193-22, Exp. 73-54/240 "32," for contract.

62. Jim Gentry, *In the Middle and on the Edge: The Twin Falls Region of Idaho* (Twin Falls: College of Southern Idaho, Twin Falls Centennial Commission, 2003), 269-70.

63. M.G. McDonnell to Gov. C. Ben Ross, Driggs, ID, Aug. 14, 1935. Gov. Ross Papers, Idaho State Historical Society Library and Archives, Boise, ID, AR2/15, Box 1.

64. In his biography of Gov. Ross, Michael P. Malone says, "The few episodes of labor unrest in Idaho during this period [the 1930s] reflected the absence of concerted workers' organizations in the state." Malone's brief paragraph on the strike in Teton County completely ignores the Mexican presence and the struggles that migrant labor faced with falling wages and terrible working conditions throughout the 1930s. *C. Ben Ross and the New Deal in Idaho* (Seattle: University of Washington Press, 1970), 97.

65. M.G. McConnel to Gov. C. Ben Ross, Boise, ID, Aug. 21, 1935. Gov. Ross Papers. See also "Teton County Labor Strike Causes Martial Law Order: Troops Enroute to Driggs," *Idaho Daily Statesman,* Boise, ID, Aug. 15, 1935, 1, and *Idaho Falls Post-Register* Idaho Falls, ID, Aug. 15, 1935, 1. So far in our examination of Salt Lake City Mexican consular files we have found no reference to this strike.

66. McConnel to Ross, Aug. 14, 1935, Gov. Ross Papers.

67. Ibid. A thorough examination of Teton County District Court cases, both criminal and probate, failed to produce records of any arrests made during this time, which might indicate that, if indeed workers were held prisoner, they were there without charges filed against them, a violation of their constitutional rights.
68. J. Asunción Pérez interviewed by Rosa Rodríguez. Idaho Falls, 1991. Idaho Oral History Center, Boise, ID, 38.
69. McConnel to Ross, Aug. 14, 1935. Gov. Ross Papers.
70. Jamieson, Appendix K, 438.
71. For S. H. Atchley's telegram see Gov. Ross Papers; "Teton County Labor Strike Causes Martial Law Order; Troops Enroute to Driggs," *Idaho Daily Statesman*, Aug. 15, 1935, 1.
72. McConnel to Ross, Aug. 14, 1935. Gov. Ross Papers.
73. F.C. Hummel Report on Martial Law Duty to the Adjutant General of Idaho. Boise, ID, Aug. 27, 1935. Gov. Ross Papers.
74. Ibid.
75. McConnel to Ross, Aug. 14, 1935. Gov. Ross Papers.
76. Charles W. Hope, Director Regional Labor Board, telegram to Gov. C. Ben Ross. Seattle, WA, Aug. 15, 1935; Hermenegilro Robles, Consul of Mexico, letter to Gov. C. Ben Ross, Salt Lake City, UT, Aug. 16, 1935. Both telegram and letter together with Ross's response are in Gov. Ross Papers.
77. Hummel's report to the Adjutant General, Aug. 27, 1935. Gov. Ross Papers.
78. J. Anthony Lukas, *Big Trouble: A Murder in a Small Western Town Sets Off a Struggle for the Soul of America* (New York: Simon & Schuster, 1997), 142,143, 146–54.
79. Quoted in Jamieson, Appendix K, 438.
80. An insightful account of the strike is given by Weaver, 79–111. See also Gonzalez, *Mexican Consuls,* 141–43; Abraham Hoffman, "The El Monte Berry Pickers' Strike, 1933: International Involvement in a Local Labor Dispute," *Journal of the West* 5, no. 7 (January 1973): 71–84. All three document the role of Mexican Consuls in their attempts to mediate agricultural strikes involving Mexican nationals in the early 1930s.
81. "Governor Ross Draws Attack of Labor Group," *Idaho Daily Statesman*, Boise, ID, Aug. 27, 1935. The newspaper published the resolution in its entirety. For Ross's written response to labor see C. Ben Ross letter to Nampa Trade and Labor Council, Boise, ID, Aug. 27, 1935. Gov. Ross Papers.
82. Idaho State Federation of Labor, "Resolution No. 14," *Proceedings of the Idaho State Federation of Labor Convention*, 1935, 33–34.

ERROL D. JONES & KATHLEEN R. HODGES

83. The body of literature on repatriation is substantial and growing. For example, see Cardoso, *Mexican Emigration*; Abraham Hoffman, *Unwanted Mexican Americans in the Great Depression: Repatriation Pressures* (Tucson: The University of Arizona Press, 1974); Francisco Balderrama and Raymond Rodríguez, *Decade of Betrayal: Mexican Repatriation in the 1930s* (Albuquerque: University of New Mexico Press, 1995); and for events in California, Camille Guerin-González, *Mexican Workers and the American Dream: Immigration, Repatriation, and California Farm Labor, 1900–1939* (New Brunswick: Rutgers University Press, 1994). For the impact of repatriation in Mexico and in the United States during the era of President Lázaro Cárdenas (1934–40), see Fernándo Saúl Alánis Enciso, "El proyecto de repatriación de Mexicanos de los Estados Unidos durante el cardenismo: la reaccion de la comunidad mexicana en San Antonio, Texas y en Los Angeles, California"; and John Dwyer, "The Repatriation Program of President Lázaro Cárdenas." Both papers were presented at the X Conference of Mexican and North American Historians at Fort Worth, TX, on Nov. 20, 1999.
84. Mexican Consular Report from Salt Lake City Consulate to the Mexican Secretariat of Foreign Relations for November 1932, in AHSRE. File No. IV-331-8.
85. Ben Mendoza, "Mexican Field Hands Strike for 80-cents Per Hour; Work Halts," *Times News* (Twin Falls), June 7, 1945, 1; "Wages Boosted to End Mexican Worker Layoff," *Twin Falls Times News*, June 8, 1945, 1.
86. Patricia Ourada, *Migrant Workers in Idaho* (Boise: Boise State University, 1980), 61.

Japanese and Mexican Labor in the Pacific Northwest, 1900–1945

Jerry Garcia

By the end of World War II approximately one million Mexicans,[1] Japanese, enemy aliens, and prisoners of war labored on the home front under assorted local, state, and federal agencies in an effort to resolve the wartime labor shortage in agriculture and other important industries.[2] The Emergency Farm Labor Program utilized numerous groups and organizations, including children, civilian prisoners, and victory groups, but the largest group of nonwhite workers consisted of Mexican nationals imported under a bilateral agreement between Mexico and the United States or in the form of Japanese labor recruited from the concentration camps administered by the War Relocation Authority (WRA) throughout the American West.[3]

Mexicans and Japanese were also used beyond the fields of agriculture; for example, these two groups were employed heavily in the railroad industry throughout the Pacific Northwest. Research on ethnic Mexicans and braceros in the Pacific Northwest is limited to a handful of studies completed almost single-handedly by historian Erasmo Gamboa, while the study of Japanese Americans in the region is more extensive.[4] No study, however, has examined these two groups in terms of the development of their racialization.[5] Thus, in this essay it is my intent to show that as World War II reached its end in 1945, the United States had developed a system designed to coerce, exploit, and subjugate a nonwhite labor force based on a long-standing tradition of racism. Beyond a historical analysis of Japanese and Mexican labor, this essay will examine the racialization of Asian (primarily Japanese) and Mexican workers and will explain how this process determined their treatment in the Pacific Northwest. It is hoped that a study of the characteristics of this process will enable a better understanding of the region's history during the first half of the twentieth century. Finally, although Japanese and Mexican workers were victims of abuse and exploitation, neither succumbed to their victimization, but rather each group employed a variety of strategies to contest such treatment. For example, throughout the war period Mexicans and Japanese often worked together in the Pacific Northwest. However, they were also often segregated from one another and rarely had contact beyond the work environment. Mexicans and Japanese Americans had much in common regarding their position in U.S. society. They also formed alliances in the early twentieth century to protest their treatment as laborers.[6] However, during World War II and with the arrival of Mexican nationals and the imprisonment of Japanese Americans it was rare to see these two groups socializing let alone forming alliances, protesting, or striking. Yet, this is exactly what happened in the Pacific Northwest in the summer of 1943 in one of the rare strikes organized by Japanese American internees and Mexican braceros.

Historical Antecedents: The Racialization of Asians and Mexicans

The treatment of Mexican nationals in the Pacific Northwest during World War II was shaped by two historical factors: first, the racialization of ethnic Mexicans residing in the United States, and second, the immigration policies directed toward Mexico in the first half of the twentieth century. It can be argued that the racialization of the Japanese began with the arrival of the Chinese to the United States in the mid-nineteenth century and the subsequent challenge to their "whiteness" by the California courts in the 1854 case, *People v. Hall* that ruled Chinese were not white. This ruling, based on the concept of whiteness during this era, began a roller coaster ride for Asians seeking U.S. citizenship.[7] When Japanese laborers began to arrive in large numbers at the end of the nineteenth century, they too faced "the same rigid racial and ethnic stratification of the labor market as did the Chinese, and their employment experience was similar."[8] By and large, the end of the nineteenth century witnessed the emergence of a European American dominated American West structured to provide the utmost advantage at economic, political, and social levels. When ethnic groups such as the Chinese or Japanese challenged the hegemony of whiteness along the Pacific Coast and Mountain regions, laws were created to ensure their subordination and to obstruct their path to economic independence.

As a result, Mexicans and Japanese struggled for decades under a process of racialization. This racial formation is defined by the concept of whiteness and the privileges accorded to those who can claim it, or as Robert Miles writes in *Racism*,

> Those instances where social relations between people have been structured by the signification of human biological characteristics in such a way as to define and construct differentiated social collectivities… The concept therefore refers to a process of categorization, a representational process of defining an Other (usually, but not exclusively), somatically.[9]

Furthermore, Tomás Almaguer argues that "it was the simultaneous interaction of both structural and ideological factors that ultimately shaped the trajectory of the historical experiences [of Mexicans]."[10] Thus, for Mexicans this racialization began long before first contact with European Americans, which is generally considered the 1820s. Various historians have examined this development, and most agree that by the time of first contact, various forms of literature circulated during the colonial and early national period that depicted Mexicans in a negative light had distorted the view of Mexicans.[11]

The actual catalyst for the widespread animosity toward Mexicans and their maltreatment, however, was the Texas-Mexican War of 1836, and the Mexican-American War that ended with the signing of the Treaty of Guadalupe Hidalgo in 1848. More importantly, by the dawn of the twentieth century, through a process of economic, political, and social transformation, many Mexicans in the United States lived under an apartheid system where segregation was rampant, rights as citizens were challenged, and their labor was exploited.[12]

U.S. governmental reports confirm the prevailing attitude toward ethnic Mexicans in the United States at the turn of the twentieth century. For example, in 1901 the Industrial Commission reported that "the Mexican peon laborer was little if any better than the Japanese coolie" and that "the competition of the Mexican was quite as disastrous to white labor as was that of the Chinese and Japanese."[13] Notably, in a 1908 government-sponsored report, Victor S. Clark wrote, "The Mexican is docile, patient, and usually orderly in camp, fairly intelligent under competent supervision, obedient and cheap. If he were active and ambitious, he would be intractable and would cost more. His strongest point is his willingness to work for a low wage."[14]

Although the presence of Mexicans in the Pacific Northwest can be documented as far back as the 1800s, permanent Mexican communities did not emerge until the early twentieth century.[15] The emergence of these communities in the northwest was the result of the development of Mexico's northern region and the American West at the turn of the twentieth century, both of which pushed hundreds of thousands of Mexicans northward. The full effects of the 1910 Mexican Revolution with regard to emigration also cannot be appreciated unless put into a similar human context. By the end of this violent period of upheaval in Mexico, approximately 10 percent (in excess of 1,000,000)[16] of Mexico's population (approximately 15,160,000 in 1910)[17] had fled to the United States. This movement resulted in a sizeable increase in the Mexican population along the U.S-Mexican border estimated to be over a half million in 1900,[18] and tripling in size by the 1920s.[19] The significance of these numbers is twofold. One, employment for people of Mexican origin in the American Southwest became competitive and increasingly scarce as the number of new arrivals swelled. Two, this competition triggered intra-group rivalry that developed into tension between the long-established Mexican American community and the recently arrived Mexicans.[20] Thus, Mexican immigration along the border region, competition, and scarcity of work created economic tension among Mexicans and Mexican Americans that resulted in the significant movement of this population to regions outside of the Southwest. Furthermore, the increased development of the Northwest, including the expansion of its industries, caused a northward movement. For example, the Pacific Northwest became the beneficiary of the Carey Act of 1894 and also the Newlands Act of 1902, both of which provided funding for the development of its agricultural zones.[21]

By the end of the 1920s, U.S. experimentation with imported foreign labor also had caused a substantial growth in the Mexican population beyond the Southwest. One example, the precursor to the *Emergency Farm Labor Program* of the 1940s, was the *Temporary Admissions Program* of 1917. This contract labor system attempted to alleviate labor shortages during World War I by providing a constant flow of workers from Mexico into various regions of the United States. That the 1917 agreement ever came to fruition is surprising, considering prevailing attitudes toward immigrants at the time. In fact, the United States had recently implemented prohibitions against the use of contract labor but suspended them as the country entered World War I.[22] Immigration restrictionists and xenophobes lobbied hard for the exclusion of Mexicans, but growers and industrialists who relied on cheap labor convinced the U.S. Congress to exempt Mexicans from provisions of the Immigration Act of 1917, and in particular, the $8 head tax and literacy test.[23]

As a result, approximately 80,000 Mexicans worked in agriculture, railroads, mines, and canneries in the United States during World War I.[24] In this era Alaska, Oregon, and Washington had thriving fishing and cannery industries that employed Asian and Mexican labor. For example, by 1917, over fifteen hundred Mexicans and Mexican Americans worked in Alaska canneries. By the end of World War I, however, those numbers dropped significantly due to some of the worst working conditions and practices ever seen in the canning industry. As noted, this first attempt to import labor was plagued by failures and problems, some of which assured that guarantees made to Mexican laborers would go unfulfilled.[25] Finally, nativist,[26] patriotic societies, the American labor movement, eugenicists, and congressmen who challenged the exemptions given to Mexicans convinced President Wilson to rescind the temporary labor program shortly after the war.[27]

By the early 1920s Mexican immigration accounted for roughly 2 percent of all immigration to the United States, and was considered minor in comparison to European immigration. As a result, legislation emerging during this period was primarily focused on restricting Eastern and Southern European immigration. As many scholars have indicated, the prevailing attitude was that most Mexican immigrants were simply sojourners, not likely to remain permanently, and certainly not interested in citizenship. Furthermore, Clare Sheridan indicates that "anti-immigration forces raised the specter of a permanent Mexican presence in the United States not as citizens, but as a peon class injurious to national character or Americanness."[28]

Additional concerns over Mexican immigration were raised after the the Johnson-Reed Act passed in 1924. This legislation established a quota system, which numerically restricted immigration on the basis of a national origins formula, but Western Hemisphere countries including Mexico were exempt from quota restrictions. The aim of the Act was to decrease the flow of Eastern, Southern, and Asian immigration, which it did, as well as to favor the continued stream of Western and Northern Europeans. Although lingering debate remained about the importation of Mexican laborers, in the end the powerful capitalist interests and Department of Agriculture won out and Mexican immigrants remained exempt from the national origins quota. Nevertheless, the public debate over Mexican immigration provides insight regarding the racial attitudes toward Mexicans. Interestingly, proponents *and* opponents of Mexican immigration each made their pitch with racial overtones. An underlying theme emanating from opponents of Mexican immigration throughout the early twentieth century was based on the racial threat posed by "undesirable" foreigners such as Mexicans. For example, the Congressional Record of 1928 reported the following from Congressman Box of Texas:

> The Mexican peon is a mixture of Mediterranean-blooded Spanish peasants with low-grade Indians who did not fight to extinction but submitted and multiplied as serfs. Into this was fused much Negro slave blood. This blend of low grade Spaniard, peonized Indian and Negro slave mixes with Negroes, mullatos and other mongrels and some sorry whites, already here. The prevention of such mongrelization and degradation it causes is one of the purposes of our laws which the admission of these people will tend to defeat.[29]

Similarly, proponents argued that the work Mexicans performed was labor that white Americans would not do because of the long hours, low wages, and poor working conditions. Moreover, proponents go on to say, the very nature of the Mexican is what makes them desirable for agricultural work and exempt from immigration legislation: "docility, patient, obedient, cheap, and culturally and psychologically suited to perform the arduous manual labor required in these industries."[30] Therefore, in the eyes of many, Mexican immigrants were ideal laborers who would come to the United States during peak harvest periods and return to Mexico once the work was done. The supposed transitory nature of the Mexican satisfied xenophobic and nativist feelings that Mexicans should not remain permanently, thus minimizing their threat to the dominance of the power structure of the Southwest and other regions of the United States.

The first two decades of the twentieth century also represent a period when the ethnic Mexican population in the United States continued to be racialized by various agencies, groups, and individuals, ensuring that Mexicans remained marginalized and at the lowest level of the economy, and thereby assuring a cheap and tractable workforce. Moreover, Mexican immigration, facilitated by the push of the Mexican Revolution, the pull of economic opportunities in the United States, and favorable immigration legislation, made it possible for thousands of ethnic Mexicans to move beyond the traditional southwest.

The Amalgamated, American, and the Utah and Idaho Sugar Companies were also partially responsible for the movement of Mexicans into the Northwest and Mountain regions of the country. These corporations created the sugar beet industry of the Northwest, a labor-intensive crop that required an army of workers for cultivation and harvest.[31] The end of the 1920s witnessed a discernible movement of Mexicans from the Southwest into the Rocky Mountain region and eventually into Montana, Idaho, Oregon, and eastern Washington.[32] By 1930, the U.S. Census recorded Mexicans permanently residing in the region as 1,278 in Idaho, 1,568 in Oregon, and 562 in Washington; but these numbers do not account for the Mexican migrant labor force that resided in the region only part of the year.[33]

Similar to the plight of the Mexican worker, Asian laborers (Chinese and Japanese) faced formidable obstacles in their transition to the United States. The initial phase of Asian immigration into the Pacific Northwest consisted of Chinese laborers who came to the United States in significant numbers during the last quarter of the nineteenth century. For example, attracted by the gold rush of the American West, Chinese could be found as early as 1852 in southwestern Oregon and 1856 in southern Idaho.[34] By the late 1860s, Chinese in Idaho were considered such a threat to white miners that the territory passed a "foreign" miners tax in an attempt to curtail the flow of Chinese into the territory. Nevertheless, "[the] measure ultimately did little to restrain Chinese migration to the Boise Basin."[35] The Chinese in Idaho are illustrative of the initial Asian movement into the Pacific Northwest, where according to census data, Chinese residing in Idaho numbered 4,274 by 1870. Between 1870 and 1880, over 123,000 Chinese immigrated to the United States with the 1880 census count indicating 87,828 Chinese Americans.[36] Nonetheless, the Chinese Exclusion Act of 1882, coupled with new mining techniques that required large amounts of capital and a rise in nativism that created economic impediments, resulted in diminishing returns for the Chinese that caused their numbers to dwindle considerably by 1890. By the turn of the century, many Chinese in the Pacific Northwest either had returned to China, or had moved into urban centers.[37]

The economic and political misfortunes of the Chinese, along with the restrictions placed on them, created the opportunity for Japanese immigration to the United States. The early phase of Japanese labor immigration to the Pacific Northwest began in the late nineteenth and early twentieth centuries, with contract laborers employed in agriculture, railroad, fishing, and lumber industries (see Fig. 3.1).[38] Permanent settlement for Japanese immigrants began in the early twentieth century, when many Japanese laborers became farmers throughout the Pacific Coast. According to the 1900 Census, California, Washington, and Oregon had a combined Japanese American population of 18,629,[39] 2,501 of which resided in Oregon, and 5,617 in Washington, respectively. A short decade later the combined Japanese populations of Oregon and Washington was well over 16,000.[40]

Due to its inland location, Idaho had a relatively small Japanese population at the turn of the twentieth century that would remain so up until World War II, even though documentation demonstrates Japanese movement into Idaho between the late 1890s and the early twentieth century. According to some sources, Japanese laborers first appeared in Idaho in substantial numbers (approximately 1,000 in 1892) to work for the railroad lines in and around

Fig. 3.1. *Japanese Loggers, Snoqualmie Lumber Co., Washington State circa 1925 (photo Courtesy of University of Washington Libraries, Special Collections, UW11555).*

Pocatello.[41] The Japanese in Idaho encountered the same resistance to their presence as their counterparts in other regions and were encouraged to depart; in fact, in the late nineteenth century, as Japanese began to move into various locales throughout Idaho, the native white citizens petitioned for their removal:

> The Japanese have within the past four months completely demoralized the laboring interest of southern Idaho. They have superseded the honest white section hands along the Union Pacific railway, from Huntington to Pocatello, and have run white workers from farms and orchards. They are filthier than the Chinese, and they work for lower wages. They are virtually the serfs of the men who are said to be fraudulently importing them, and they are controlled by "slave drivers."[42]

An undated document prepared by a representative of the Meiji Foreign Office of Japan around the late nineteenth century confirms that most of the Japanese laborers in Idaho were railroad workers numbering about four hundred. The report provides an overall description of the climate in Idaho for Japanese immigrants, suggesting that Japanese laborers suffered from a dual wage system and poor working conditions. Furthermore, the racial animosity toward the Japanese was exploited by a private contractor who used the workers' overtime wages to pay bribes and business expenses, and who forced them to purchase all their groceries from him since he was in the grocery business. Finally, the report states that the contractor deducted all expenses prior to paying wages using suspect accounting practices and thus creating the appearance of cheating the workers of their real wages.[43]

Individuals such as Henry Fuji came very early to the state of Idaho. En route from Seattle, Fuji and several brothers arrived in Nampa in 1907 to pursue farming. Upon arrival, however, they were employed in the sugar beet and railroad industries in Idaho and Montana where they earned $1.25 for a ten-hour day (see Fig. 3.2). Mr. Fuji indicated that he lived and worked mainly around Emmett, Idaho, with about fifteen other Japanese. He also recalled that many Japanese were recruited from such places as San Francisco and Hawaii, resulting in approximately eight hundred Japanese working in and around Nampa.[44]

Fig. 3.2 Japanese Beet Workers, Pacific Northwest circa 1920s
(photo Courtesy of University of Washington Libraries, Special Collections).

Eventually, Mr. Fuji started a truck garden business in Emmett. Although he indicated very little animosity emanating from the local population, he did state that around 1915 individuals coming from California campaigned for the enactment of "anti-Japanese land law" legislation.[45] As in other western states, the record shows that in 1923 Idaho, Montana, and Oregon each passed alien land laws that prohibited aliens ineligible for citizenship from purchasing land for agriculture and restricted leases to three to five year periods.[46] Mr. Fuji indicates that he had purchased land before the enactment, which he was not forced to give up, but that after the passage of the law he was allowed to lease additional land only for five years at a time, which allowed him to keep farming. In 1918, Mr. Fuji and his wife, Fumiko, moved to Nampa, where he began to farm approximately eighty acres. During World War II, the Fujis were allowed to remain in Idaho, keep farming, and travel throughout Idaho with a permit. Mr. Fuji does recall the many restrictions placed upon Japanese, such as not being able to walk in groups of three or more or further than twenty-five miles from their home[47] Mr. Fuji and his wife eventually became U.S. citizens in 1953, after the McCarran-Walter Act repealed the last vestiges of the "aliens ineligible" clause for naturalization.[48]

The treatment of the Japanese in the Northwest was similar to that of Mexicans with racial animosity remaining acute in various regions. For example, in 1905 a disturbance in northwestern Washington broke out between Japanese and white workers at the Alaska Packers Association Cannery. In the final analysis this disturbance was minor in nature; nonetheless, it provides insight into the precarious position of Japanese living in this region in the early twentieth century. The Whatcom County Sheriff report contains the following:

> I made a careful investigation of the trouble
> between the whites and the Japs at the Alaska
> Packers Association Cannery in Semiahoo, and find
> the whole trouble arose from the fight between
> young (Ira) Parks and the Japs. The Japs seem to be
> a low grade or low element.[49]

Besides using language that was typical of the day, the report seems to identify the "Japs" as the culprits who in the end deserved what they got, according to Sheriff Williams: "a good black eye." Because of exaggerated claims surrounding the incident, however, the State of Washington Adjutant General and the Imperial Japanese Consul in Seattle requested an investigation of the incident. Even though each of their reports downplayed the event as a simple brawl between workers, the cannery company bowed to pressure from the Sheriff's office and shipped all the "Japs" back to Portland.[50]

By the first and second decades of the twentieth century various state, regional, and federal laws were enacted in an attempt to prevent Japanese citizenship, land ownership, leasing, and miscegenation, much of which is well-documented history. A few illustrations from the Pacific Northwest provide a sense of continuity regarding the pattern of racialization. For example, Japanese living in the Pacific Northwest came under attack by such groups as the Asiatic Exclusion League of North America. As early as 1908 this organization wrote to then Washington State Gov. Albert E. Mead requesting his help in excluding undesirable "Orientals" in an effort to "save America for the American people and their posterity."[51] On June 9, 1921, Washington State legislators passed a bill stating that aliens "ineligible for citizenship" also became ineligible to purchase, lease, or inherit land.[52] In 1922, the Cable Act slightly changed the consequences for those American women who married "aliens ineligible for citizenship," that is, Japanese, Chinese, and other "Asians."[53] As various barriers and restrictions emerged regarding the naturalization of Asians,

97

some Japanese challenged the concept of whiteness as a precondition for citizenship.

Takuji Yamashita, from Tacoma, Wash., represented one of the more interesting challenges to the concept of whiteness and U.S. citizenship. In 1892 Yamashita emigrated from Japan to Tacoma, where he worked and graduated from high school. Then he applied to and was accepted to the University of Washington Law School. In 1902, Takuji Yamashita received his naturalization certificate conferring U.S. citizenship and passed the state bar exam. Admission to the state bar, however, was limited to U.S. citizens. Although he had a certificate of naturalization, it was called into question because of his Japanese ancestry. Based on the 1790 naturalization law stating that "only free white persons" could be naturalized, amended after the Civil War to include individuals of African ancestry, Yamashita was denied. A court challenge ensued regarding Yamashita's citizenship status and his certificate of naturalization was voided which in effect barred him from practicing law. Eventually the Supreme Court heard his case in 1922, and ruled in favor of the State of Washington, affirming that Japanese were not eligible for naturalization under federal law because they were not considered white.[54]

The first decades of the twentieth century provided many challenges to Japanese and Mexicans regarding citizenship and whiteness. As the 1920s came to an end, the first signs of an economic collapse appeared within the United States and with it, a search for a scapegoat.

One of the great tragedies of the 1930s besides the economic fallout from the Great Depression was the mass deportation from the United States of over one million ethnic Mexicans—an estimated half of whom were U.S. citizens of Mexican ancestry.[55] It is difficult to ignore the similarities between the 1930s deportations of Mexicans and the 1940s round-ups of Japanese. In each case a vulnerable ethnic group was targeted for activities that constituted a brazen violation of the constitutional rights of American citizens. These deportations represent an important link in the chain of racialization of the ethnic Mexican population of the United States during the 1930s. Although very little has been written regarding the removal of Mexicans from the Pacific Northwest, one source indicates that officials interested in lowering incarceration costs agreed to commute the jail sentences of Mexican prisoners if they consented to deportation. As a result, ninety Mexican prisoners at McNeil Federal Penitentiary in the state of Washington were shipped back to Mexico in 1932.[56]

In conclusion, these historical antecedents provide background regarding the arrival of Mexicans and Japanese into the Pacific Northwest and the treatment they received from the predominately white population of the region. Although not passively accepted by either group in the first two decades of the twentieth century, this treatment indicated what lay ahead in 1940s. Furthermore, the movement of Mexicans and Japanese into the northwest, including such places as Alaska and Montana, provides the historical framework for the racialization of both groups in the Pacific Northwest. Finally, the agricultural development of the Yakima Valley in Washington, the Willamette Valley in Oregon, and the southern region of Idaho such as the Boise Valley created the momentum for the migratory patterns of Mexicans out of the Southwest and Rocky Mountain region during the early twentieth century. Some of the oldest Japanese and Mexican communities in the Pacific Northwest are located in these fertile valleys, as indicated by the 1940 census that recorded 14,565 Japanese residents and 2,400 individuals of Hispanic origin residing in Washington.[57] During that same year Oregon reported a Japanese population of 4,071, and 1,280 Hispanics in the Willamette Valley and Hood River,[58] while Idaho counted approximately 1,200 Japanese, residing mostly in its southern region, and 2,720 people of Hispanic origin.[59]

JERRY GARCIA

Japanese Internees and Mexican Braceros

Despite repeated attempts in the early twentieth century to prevent Japanese Americans from becoming integrally tied to the agriculture economy of the Pacific Northwest, it is evident that this is what transpired over the first four decades of the twentieth century.[60] An important development for Japanese self-sufficiency and their integration into the agricultural industry was the shift from wage labor to tenancy, or the leasing of farmland by the first decade of the twentieth century.[61] Indeed, by the beginning of the 1940s, Japanese Americans were such an important component of the agriculture economy as growers and laborers that their removal from along the Pacific Coast created a temporary decline in farm production. Furthermore, many sources indicate their removal was responsible for the importation of thousands of Mexicans by the fall of 1942 in California and the following year into the Pacific Northwest. According to the Department of Agriculture, by the fall of 1942, 1,329,000 people had left work on the farms to enter the Army and into other vocations.[62] For example, C.C. Teague, president of the Agriculture Council of California testified, "The agriculture labor problem is greatly aggravated in California and Oregon by the removal these people [Japanese] who had worked in specialty crops."[63] The removal of the Japanese was not simply a matter of labor. Testimony from other agricultural interests point to additional consequences not anticipated with the Japanese roundups. For example, a lack of expertise in farm management emerged with the Japanese incarcerations as explained by John Cooter, representative of the War Manpower Commission,

> ...Another thing that very seriously affected the situation here was the removal of the Japanese. They were skilled in their trade, and probably 20,000 to 30,000 of those skilled agricultural workers were removed when the Japanese were removed... When they were taken away, a part of

the land which they used was taken over by other farmers in the community, and on those farms that had experienced management, but in many other cases absolutely inexperienced help was put in charge of the farms. Now, we didn't have good supervision on those farms, and also had inexperienced help to do the job and it took more people all the way around.[64]

It then became apparent that the removal of the Japanese from along the coastlines of California, Oregon, and Washington had multiple effects. First, their removal created a drop in crop production, even though more acreage was put into production a year after their evacuation, which lends to the belief that crops on the former Japanese farms were inefficiently planted and harvested the year following the removal. Secondly, the Japanese roundups created a drop in the overall number of laborers along the Pacific Coast. Third, even if testimony regarding the effects of the Japanese removal from agriculture was exaggerated, it nevertheless created the impetus for the recruitment and importation of Mexican labor that was used in Idaho, Oregon, and Washington. Thus, by the early phases of the war, the strategy of the War Manpower Commission was to openly target these two groups for the sugar beet and other industries:

> Employment of Japanese from war relocation camps along with the use of Mexican labor under an agreement with the government are contemplated in a program to harvest the country's sugar beet crop next spring and summer. Speaking before representatives of the war manpower commission and the sugar beet industry who are meeting here [Kansas City] F.W. Hunter, chief of the agriculture division of the WMC disclosed plans for the large scale use of Mexicans and Japanese.[65]

To address the growing concern over the lack of agricultural laborers, growers and the U.S. government embarked on this two-pronged approach. First, they attempted to enlist the help of the very people they incarcerated, the Japanese Americans. Second, the recruitment of foreign labor, principally Mexican, became a top priority in 1942. The Japanese concentration camps dotting the western landscape became de facto labor camps in which Japanese labor was procured for agricultural fields of the American West, including the Pacific Northwest. The U.S. government was aware that approximately 45 percent of the Japanese interned had either operated their own farms or were hired hands in agriculture prior to the war.[66]

Furthermore, besides the racial animosity the Japanese faced, they also encountered hatred due to their economic success, which provided additional incentive for individuals and organization to declare Japanese Americans as untrustworthy, dangerous, and in event of a war, un-American. For example, in *By Order of the President* Greg Robinson reports journalist Ernest O. Hauser's statement that:

> ...Japanese farmers, having a virtual monopoly
> on vegetable production in California, will send
> their peas, potatoes, and squash full of arsenic to
> the markets, throwing the population into panic.[67]

Robinson further declares that greed and economic self-interest played a large role in the anti-Japanese movement and eventual evacuation of Japanese Americans into concentration camps. Organizations such as the Western Growers Protective Association, the Grower-Shipper's Vegetable Association, and the White American Nurserymen of Los Angeles used wartime emergency as a means to remove the Japanese, or as the Growers-Shipper's manager told the *Saturday Evening Post*, "We're charged with wanting to get rid of the Japs for selfish reasons. We might as well be honest. We do. It's a question of whether the white man lives on the Pacific Coast or the brown man."[68] In the end, the economic self-interest and racism on part of the European American community combined with the culpability of U.S. government caused the roundup and incarceration of ethnic Japanese into concentration camps beginning in early 1942. What followed were the importation of Mexican nationals and the exploitation of Japanese labor residing in the concentration camps.

With the removal of over 120,000 Japanese from California, Oregon, and Washington, agricultural and governmental officials soon realized that, by their own hand, they had sabotaged the war effort by removing a vital component of the agricultural economy, the Japanese. An incarcerated Japanese American, George S. Ishiyama, while at Heart Mountain, Wyoming, served as the camp director for Information and echoed this very sentiment to Paul McNutt, Chairman of the War Manpower Commission:

> I do not know if you are aware of the tremendous manpower that lies dormant within these projects. This terrible waste of human energy, to my way of thinking, especially in time of war, is as much an act of sabotage as any direct act to "throw a monkey wrench" into the mechanization set up for the effective prosecution of this war. It is indeed a deplorable situation when industry and agriculture are so sorely in need of efficient labor that more constructive use is not being made of this vast source of human energy.[69]

Some of the first Japanese released from the concentration camps for agricultural labor began working right after their incarceration. In late May 1942, a first group of fifteen left their imprisonment to thin sugar beets in the southeastern corner of Oregon. The Farm Security Administration housed them at a labor camp located in Nyssa, Oregon. By June, "about a hundred Japanese" from Portland and other assembly centers were working there.[70] Nevertheless, initially, some of the Japanese in the concentration camps refused to sign up for agricultural work. By and large, this refusal stemmed from the inability of the authorities and growers to guarantee their safety. For example, the following is a partial transcript of a recorded telephone conversation that took place between employees of the Bureau of Employment Security in October 1942 attempting to ascertain why Japanese have not been secured for work in Montana:

Mr. Warders:	Have the 500 Japanese that you spoke to me about the other day that you thought might be secured, have they been able to get them yet?
Mr. Lamport:	No, we have no word that we got any of them.
Mr. Warders:	The Japs have not arrived?
Mr. Lamport:	No.
Mr. Warders:	Is there any reason for that?
Mr. Lamport:	The only reason is their timidity about leaving the camp.
Mr. Warders:	Japs are timid about leaving camp?
Mr. Brennan:	This is Brennan speaking.
Mr. Warders:	Yes, Brennan.
Mr. Brennan:	Their idea is that they won't be courteously treated, that they are not safe when they leave the camp. That's the older ones. The ones we got out are the younger more venturesome type.[71]

By the end of 1942 some ten thousand Japanese journeyed from the camps to perform agricultural work.[72] Like Mexicans, Japanese living and performing agricultural work in the various communities throughout the Pacific Northwest encountered animosity. For the Pacific Northwest, the most prevalent form of hostility was manifested with racial slurs, stone throwing, and intimidation. An exception would be the shots fired at the home of a Japanese family living in Nampa, Idaho, shortly after Pearl Harbor was attacked.[73] Ironically, when Idaho was facing its labor

woes in 1942 many of the growers first turned to the use of
Japanese workers. Idaho's vehemently anti-Japanese Gov. Chase
Clark led the opposition to Japanese Americans in the state, and
opposed their use as laborers.[74] Idaho's anti-Japanese sentiment
seemed to emanate from the governor's mansion, since Gov. Clark
went on record many times espousing his views on the Japanese,
particularly with regard to the War Relocation Authority's plan to
establish the Minidoka concentration camp in south central Idaho
or with regard to other Japanese attempting to voluntarily resettle
in Idaho from the coastal states. For example, to inquiries made
about possible land purchase by some Japanese Gov. Clark
retorted,

> I am not ready to sell the State of Idaho to the
> Japanese for a few dollars while our American boys
> are dying to prevent Japs from taking the State of
> Idaho and our entire nation by force of arms... I
> also want to suggest to you the possibilities in that
> the ones born here are more dangerous than the
> ones born in Japan... those born here are taught
> that Japan is heaven and their emperor the
> Almighty.[75]

In the end, the wartime labor shortage in Idaho convinced
Gov. Clark to seek the use of Japanese laborers. The other
Northwest states followed a similar pattern and by the end of 1942
Japanese internees were heavily engaged in agricultural activities
throughout the region. Shortly after the removal of the Japanese
from the coast, the importation of Mexican nationals began.

In 1943, Mexican braceros began arriving to the Northwest.
During the next four years Idaho, Washington, and Oregon
utilized a combined 46,954 Mexican laborers.[76] After domestic
workers, Mexicans represented the largest form of labor in the
region. According to reports, the Emergency Farm Labor Program
contracted 7,000 braceros to work in Washington, Oregon, and

Idaho during the first year (see Fig. 3.3).[77] As the Northwest need for labor peaked during harvest periods, many rural areas in Eastern Oregon, Washington, and Southern Idaho suffered acute shortages due to a low population density and a lack of experienced farm laborers.

Fig. 3.3. Mexican Braceros in Oregon, 1943
(photo Courtesy, Oregon State University, Special Collections).

It should also be noted that although Mexicans were used extensively in agriculture, various railroad companies throughout the Northwest employed thousands of Mexicans as maintenance workers. With the exception of Barbara Driscoll's study on Mexican Railroad workers, this aspect of the bracero program remains underdeveloped.[78] Initially, the use of Mexicans in the railroad industry was not part of the agreement signed by the United States and Mexico; however, the railroad industry was able to convince both governments that it suffered from an acute shortage of maintenance workers and thus was able to import Mexicans for use on various lines.[79] More importantly, its administration was entirely separate from the farm labor program and many of the logistics for its operation fell under the Railroad Retirement Board (RRB). The majority of railroad braceros worked in Washington, Oregon, California, Nevada, and southern Arizona.[80] One other area that scholars have neglected regarding the bracero program is the high number of Mexican deaths occurring during the war years. Although most studies on the bracero program mention these fatalities, they fail to provide a complete analysis and no study makes any connection to the notion of racialization as a possible culprit for the apparent neglect, maltreatment, and disregard for the lives of Mexican workers.

Due to the high number of Mexicans imported to the United States, it is reasonable to assume that some accidental deaths would occur considering the occupational hazard of working in agriculture, and in particular, the railroad industry. However, a large number of Mexican deaths in civilian occupations and in a noncombat environment should not have been expected. The evidence indicates that many of the Mexican deaths that occurred on and off the job could have been prevented, and that negligence on part of the employer and medical personnel and a sense of disregard for the lives of Mexicans was prevalent in many areas in which they worked. Finally, many of the death certificates examined are suspiciously questionable in regard to cause of death.

As a whole, the number of deaths of braceros in the United States is not precise, but Driscoll's study provides an indicator in that eighty-nine braceros died while under the employment of just one line, the Southern Pacific Railroad, during the duration of the program.[81] This does not include bracero deaths in the agricultural sector. Approximately thirty-five railroad lines employed Mexicans during the war period and almost all recorded Mexican deaths. For example, the Southern Pacific, Northwestern Pacific Railroad, and the San Diego and Arizona Eastern Railway recorded fifty-five Mexican deaths for the period 1943–1945.[82] Deaths of braceros occurred in many locations and under various circumstances. As an illustration, the following is a common pattern of deaths that can be found throughout the bracero program at the national and regional levels.

For the period from June 22 to July 27, 1943 (approximately one month) the Southern Pacific Railroad recorded the death of three Mexican nationals. According to the death certificates all died from "heat prostration."[83] No evidence indicates that the railroad company took any precautionary measures after the first death in June. Subsequently, documents show that two additional individuals lost their lives from working under similar extreme conditions. These three deaths were of a great concern to the Mexican government, which lodged a formal complaint with the U.S. government accusing the railroad of negligence and not providing adequate or timely medical attention to the injured. The Mexican Consul, in his letter to the State Manpower Director, had testimony indicating that the crew foreman refused to provide a doctor's order for at least two Mexicans who had become gravely ill, one by the name of Salvador Vasquez Huante who eventually died.[84] Although the Southern Pacific Railroad responded to the Mexican inquiry, its own investigation absolved any of its employees of negligence.

During 1943–1945, one source puts the number of Mexican nationals killed working for the railroad companies in Pacific Northwest at fourteen.[85] Mexican braceros in the Pacific Northwest were also killed in the agricultural industry. Gamboa's study states that eighteen braceros died in agriculture during 1945 from a variety of causes and that those deaths prompted the U.S. Public Health Service to organize a conference to look into the matter.[86] As a further illustration, during March–April 1945 three Mexicans were killed in Washington and Oregon. On Mar. 13, 1945, Ignacio Garnica Espinosa, a Mexican bracero and a member of a section gang repairing a broken line in Portland, Oregon, was struck by an automobile and died from his injuries. On Mar. 14, 1945, Mexican bracero Carlos Mendoza Morales died after being struck by a train while working for the Northern Pacific Railway in Winlock, Wash. On Apr. 23, 1945, Felix Sotelo-Murillo, a Mexican bracero imported from Queretaro, Mexico, to work for the Northern Pacific Railway Company in Tacoma was instantly killed after being struck in the head by a train in the vicinity of Puyallup, Wash. Although these deaths occurred in separate regions of the Northwest, they nonetheless share some commonalities with a national pattern in that most of these deaths appear to have been preventable had proper training been implemented or simple precautionary measures taken. The pattern of deaths became so pervasive even before 1945 that a Mexican Consul asked for an investigation regarding the deaths and that compensation be provided by the railroad companies.

Through a series of letters to the War Manpower Commission in 1944, San Francisco's Mexican Consul Alfredo Elias Calles attempted to ascertain the number of braceros killed while in railroad employment, a list of their names, and benefits or compensation to be paid. The work contracts signed by braceros, whether in agriculture or railroad employment, made no provisions to pay death benefits, funeral expenses, or for the transportation of the deceased back to Mexico. Technically, the Railroad Retirement Board (RRB) was under no obligation to make such payments, but as a gesture of goodwill and according to a "Gentlemen's Agreement" referred to in Section 17 of the War Manpower Commission (WMC) Field Instructions No. 187 agreed to pay funeral expenses of $130 and $150 to be given to the beneficiary. The Mexican Consul argued that such payments were inadequate, a mere pittance that did not fully compensate for the loss of the worker.[87]

In sum, for every year that the bracero program existed large numbers of Mexican deaths were recorded. Mexican officials and the braceros themselves complained, went on strikes, wrote collective letters of protest, attempted civil action, and in some cases demanded that they be returned to Mexico. No evidence has been found showing that an employer of braceros was ever held responsible for one Mexican death. In the end, the life of a bracero amounted to $150 plus funeral expenses and only a handful of the deceased were ever returned to Mexico. Most remain buried in local cemeteries where they died in the United States. Resistance to bad working conditions, unfair wages, poor diet, and abusive employers are plentiful in regard to the braceros and Japanese internees in the Pacific Northwest. Although collective action by these two groups was rare during the war period, the Pacific Northwest recorded one of these singular events.

Collective Resistance: The Japanese-Mexican Strike of 1943

Dayton, Wash., is a small rural community located in the southeastern region of the state. During the 1940s the town was well known for producing and canning crops such as asparagus, peas, and beans for the war effort. Due to the intensive labor required for these crops, Japanese Americans, Mexicans, and German prisoners of war all worked simultaneously in this community. The treatment and attitude toward the Japanese and Mexican workers serves as a striking example of the impact of ethnicity on the dominant culture.

Dayton remained sparsely populated on the eve of WWII and experienced some of the worst labor shortages in the state. Furthermore, this region grew a high concentration of peas that required hundreds of laborers to harvest and preserve. Very early in 1943 it was determined that Mexicans would be used to cut asparagus. But since an adequate supply of such workers could not be found, various farm labor entities decided to gauge community reaction to using Japanese internees as an alternative. In February 1943, the front-page headline of the *Chronicle-Dispatch* suggested "Maybe Get Jap Labor for County Harvest Operation."[88] In April 1943 it became evident the region needed additional laborers for the summer harvest of the pea crop. Under the guidance of the War Relocation Authority (WRA) a community meeting was held to check sentiments about importing Japanese labor. This meeting provides interesting insight into the prevailing attitudes toward Japanese Americans and Mexicans. According to Clarence Johnson, who probably voiced the sentiment of the meeting and the county when he summed up the whole matter, "I don't like the

Japanese, but we are destitute for labor to harvest the crops, and I think we should bring them in. Winning on the food front is every bit as important as on the battlefront. And I think the people will treat them fairly." Community members asked the WRA to compare the Japanese to Mexican labor. The response indicated that, generally speaking, the Japanese are better educated and resented [Japanese] classification in the same category as Mexicans. Also, according to the report, many of them speak better English than European Americans and have good sanitary habits.[89]

This short passage is a telling sign of the times and the contradictions faced by Japanese and Mexican laborers in the Pacific Northwest. On the one hand the Japanese are described as a better ethnic group than the Mexican and one that conforms to the European American mores of the time, yet they faced severe prejudice based on their ethnicity. The report further states that "they are educated," unlike the supposed ignorant masses that hail from Mexico. The Japanese take on further characteristics of whiteness when they too, supposedly, resent the Mexicans, and according to the official, speak better English than whites… ascending to a greater whiteness by their mastery of the English language.[90] Lastly, explicit in the town hall dialogue is the notion that a good citizen is determined by cultural conformity to the habits of the dominant culture. In another article, War Food Administration officials described the Mexicans in Dayton as "sober, industrious, and altogether inoffensive." In the end, during the summer of 1943 Dayton officials requested and received over two hundred Japanese laborers who worked alongside Mexican braceros (see Fig. 3.4).[91]

In the summer of 1943 a group of Mexican braceros and Japanese internees went on strike at the Blue Mountain Cannery facility located in Dayton. What prompted this unusual form of unity in this small rural community? According to available records, either on July 20 or 21, a white female came forward stating that she had been assaulted and described her assailant as

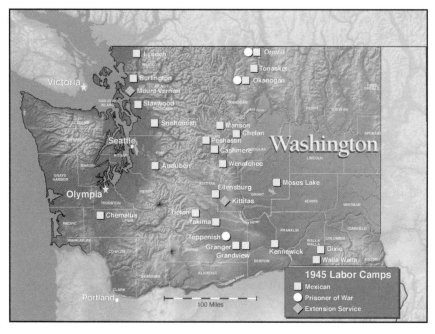

Fig. 3.4. Map of Mexican and Prisoners of War labor Camps in Washington State, 1945 (photo courtesy of Washington State Extension Service).

"looking Mexican."[92] Prior to any investigation and immediately after the alleged victim came forward, authorities from the prosecutor's and sheriff's office imposed a mandatory "restriction order" on both the Mexican and Japanese camps. Since no investigation transpired and neither the Japanese nor Mexican laborers were questioned, they collectively decided to strike during the heart of pea harvest to protest their unfair treatment.

Mid-July represented the height of the pea-canning season with literally hundreds of thousands of bushels for the war effort in jeopardy. The decisions by a variety of individuals regarding this case are significant because they revolved not around the safety of the alleged victim, or great concern about violating the bracero treaty or that somehow the Japanese had been lumped in with the Mexicans, but harvesting and canning the peas for the war effort. During a meeting between farm labor agents, city authorities, and Blue Mountain Company officials the alleged assault seemed to be glossed over. Most concerns revolved around restarting production. Farm labor supervisor Walter E. Zuger stated:

> I questioned several of my personal acquaintances around town in an effort to learn the story behind the issuance of the "restriction order" and what the general opinion was concerning the difficulty. The amazing thing was that no one was particularly upset over the assault case, apparently doubting that it happened or feeling that it was solicited. They all wanted to know when the Mexicans and Japanese were going back to work.[93]

Furthermore, the United States Employment Service received inquiries from the San Francisco War Food Administration, Gov. Langlie of Washington, War Food Administration in Seattle, and an unidentified colonel from Tacoma, Wash., all telling him that they wanted those peas canned even if they had to send in the army, and also offered to send him twenty-four "Jeeps" loaded with soldiers.[94] Another newspaper of the region, the *Walla Walla Union-Bulletin* reported that 170 Mexicans and 230 Japanese stopped working. The newspapers avoided the topic of the assault and simply stated that the Mexicans and Japanese were protesting the restrictive order. According to the *Walla Walla Union-Bulletin* the restriction order read as follows:

> Males of Japanese and or Mexican extraction or parentage are restricted to that area of Main Street of Dayton, lying between Front Street and the easterly end of Main Street. The aforesaid males of Japanese and or Mexican extraction are expressly forbidden to enter at any time any portion of the residential district of said city under penalty of law.[95]

On July 22 a meeting was held at Blue Mountain Cannery attended by three United States Employment Service (USES) employees, including the area supervisor; a member of the WRA; two Cannery officials; and two Mexican individuals serving as interpreters. At this meeting it was learned that all of the Japanese and about seventy of the Mexicans wanted to return to their place of origin. Later that same day the three USES representatives, the WRA member, and Walter E. Zuger, Assistant State Farm Labor Supervisor met with the Columbia County Sheriff, the Mayor of Dayton, the prosecuting attorney, and a city councilman. According to Walter Zuger's report the city councilman indicated that the City Council refused to approve the "restriction order" and therefore it was not in effect. The prosecuting attorney protested, stating that "the restriction was not unreasonable and that public opinion made it necessary that something be done."[96] By the end of the meeting the sheriff's office and prosecuting attorney signed a statement to the USES that in effect nullified and voided their illegal "restriction order."

Within forty-eight hours this strike had been resolved. On the night of July 22 officials met with the Japanese and Mexican workers. After negotiating approximately two hours it was determined that at least seventy Mexicans still wanted to be returned or shipped somewhere else and the Japanese still wanted to be returned to the camp. However, by the next morning only a handful of Mexicans refused to return to work and most of the Japanese remained.[97] Furthermore, according to reports, it had been determined by the farm labor authorities that the Mexican nationals had not even arrived in Dayton until after the alleged criminal attack had taken place. None of the published accounts indicates why the Japanese were restricted along with the Mexicans. However, amid the negative treatment and attitudes toward the Japanese internees it took very little for that animosity to rise to the surface, a pattern of discrimination then found throughout the Northwest.

Zuger followed up on this investigation and found a tremendous amount of hostility between Dayton citizens and cannery officials that stemmed from people's perception that various government agencies allowed the cannery "to have its way." However, although Zuger was told that year-round cannery workers and the local European American workforce agitated against the cannery's methods of bringing in Japanese and foreign workers without consulting the community or taking into consideration the social implications,[98] public meetings held and reported on by local newspapers easily rebut this contention. Zuger's report also suggests a possible motive on the part of the local cannery workers to sabotage and fabricate an alleged assault in order to rid themselves of the Japanese and Mexicans. No hard evidence was ever found regarding this, but Zuger's report considered it a possibility in not so many words. What became of the alleged assault and the victim remains a mystery. After July 21, none of the handful of reports on this incident or newspaper accounts ever mentioned it or her again. By the end of summer the pea harvest produced a bumper crop, and the ensuing war years saw Mexicans, and Japanese and German prisoners of war, continuing as sought-after labor to help harvest the crops in the Dayton region.

Conclusion

The treatment of Japanese and Mexicans during the first half of the twentieth century in the Pacific Northwest had been predicated on a long history of European American traditions. These traditions held that individuals of European stock, or those that could cling to the notion of "whiteness," were the favorite sons and daughters of the United States. By definition, the 1790 Naturalization Act stated that "only free white persons" could be naturalized and this caveat would remain in place well into the twentieth century. This contested terrain over whiteness created racial hierarchies within the United States and began the process of racialization for such ethnic groups as Japanese and Mexicans. Although these two groups share some parallel experiences, they also have some differences regarding their movement and incorporation within the United States. Nevertheless, by the early twentieth century both groups had become the "other" within the racial hierarchy of the United States and fought to maintain their viability.

As the Japanese and Mexicans made their way to such places as Idaho, Oregon, and Washington, their treatment was not based on their interaction with European Americans of that region, but on previous contacts made by other Asian groups or unfounded perceptions based on secondary contact. The treatment the Japanese faced in the Northwest was based on the legacy and racialization of the Chinese who came before them. For Mexicans, the only contact European Americans residing in the Northwest had with them prior to first contact in the early twentieth century was through literature, popular culture, or newspaper accounts that depicted Mexicans in an unfavorable light.

Throughout the first four decades of the twentieth century Japanese and Mexican laborers in the Northwest oftentimes worked side by side for similar prevailing wages, and both groups have been described as hard working and industrious even though they faced much animosity. Although some locals in the region came to accept them during World War II, beyond the field or cannery Japanese and Mexicans interacted little. Furthermore, in the mindset of the European American population Mexicans and Japanese represented two divergent groups. Mexicans, although seen as inferior, were allies of the United States during the war period. Although the Mexican braceros were imported via an international treaty guaranteeing certain conditions and rights, albeit violated repeatedly, this group appears to have been more readily accepted than the Japanese Americans who were divested of their property and possessions, rounded up, sent to assembly centers and then concentration camps to be farmed out as laborers denied their freedom and liberty. To the European American community the Japanese presence represented the enemy. It did not matter that the majority were Japanese Americans and loyal citizens of the United States. A large portion of the European American community associated Japanese Americans with the Empire of Japan. To illustrate, a long time European American resident of Emmett, Idaho, was interviewed decades after the war and in response to being asked about her knowledge of Japanese internment stated,

> Yes, I knew that they [Japanese] were and I felt that it was for their own protection because of the very incident that happened there. As far as I have ever heard, they received good treatment. They were not brutally beaten or any of that type of treatment that our people received in their prison camps.[99]

The general populace, the U.S. government, and military authorities were unable and unwilling to distinguish between Japanese nationals and those that attacked the United States and Japanese Americans. The concentration camps created for the Japanese also represents what many scholars consider as simply a link in a chain of racism that stretches back to first contact between Asians and whites on American soil. Throughout the Pacific Northwest Japanese and Mexicans faced a form of racism and discrimination that transcended ethnicity and race with one that included nationalism. However, as this paper has shown, Mexicans and Japanese found ways to protest and resist their unfair treatment in the Pacific Northwest.

In the final analysis, despite the ambiguous treatment of the 47,000 Mexican braceros and over 20,000 Japanese workers sent to the Pacific Northwest, they were vital in securing economic victory for the United States. In a show of remorse in the late twentieth century, the U.S. government paid reparations for the illegal roundups, loss of property, and confinement in concentration camps of Japanese and Japanese Americans. However, how do you compensate individuals who lost their livelihood, possessions, land, and property? More importantly, how do you return those lost years of imprisonment and the indignity suffered by loyal American citizens? For Mexican nationals, the bracero program continued unabated until 1964 with over four million workers entering the country during that period.[100] However, importation of braceros to the Pacific Northwest ended in the early 1950s when the cost became prohibitive. Those braceros who entered the Northwest created the foundation for the development of Mexican communities in regions such as the Columbia Basin, Yakima Valley, Mt. Vernon, the Willamette Valley and eastern Oregon, the Snake River Valley and other areas of southern Idaho (see Fig. 3.5).

Fig. 3.5. Mexican Braceros sorting Unions, Moses Lake, Wash., 1956 (photo Courtesy, Driggs Family Collection).

Endnotes

1. In this essay, when I speak of Mexican Americans I am referring to American citizens of Mexican descent, regardless of their length of residence in the United States. I use the term Mexican immigrants when referring to citizens of Mexico residing in the United States. Although all of these groups historically have recognized important distinctions between and among themselves, all have been subject to varying degrees of prejudice and discrimination in the United States, regardless of their formal citizenship status. Thus, when referring to the combined population of all persons of Mexican ancestry or descent living in the United States, I employ the term ethnic Mexicans. These definitions can be found in David G. Gutiérrez. "Significant to Whom?: Mexican Americans and the History of the American West," *Western Historical Quarterly* 24, no. 4 (November 1993): 520n1.

2. Louis Fiset, "Thinning, Topping, and Loading: Japanese Americans and Beet Sugar in World War II," *Pacific Northwest Quarterly* 90, no. 3 (Summer 1999): 123. For an estimate on the number of braceros and prisoners of war used as farm laborers see Wayne D. Rasmussen, *A History of the Emergency Farm Labor Supply Program, 1943–47.* Agriculture Monograph No. 13. U.S. Department of Agriculture, Bureau of Agriculture Economics, September 1951.

3. Other foreign laborers included Jamaicans and individuals from Barbados. Barbadians, Jamaican, and German POWs were smaller in number in comparison to Mexican and Japanese workers. Although there was a clear distinction between Mexican nationals and Mexican Americans, in the public perspective they were the same.

4. Unless quoting a U.S. government document, official or other individual, I will be using the terms imprisonment or concentration camps throughout this essay to describe the confinement of Japanese during World War II. For a further discussion on this see Raymond Y. Okamura, "The American Concentration Camps: A Cover-Up through Euphemistic Terminology," *The Journal of Ethnic Studies* 10, no. 3 (Fall 1982): 95–108.

5. For a detailed analysis on braceros and the incarceration of Japanese during World War II see, for example, Roger Daniels, *Concentration Camps USA: Japanese Americans and World War II* (New York: 1971); Roger Daniels, *Prisoners Without Trial: Japanese Americans in World War II* (New York: Hill and Wang, 1993); Jeffrey F. Burton, et al. *Confinement and Ethnicity: An Overview of World War II Japanese American Relocation Sites* (Seattle: University of Washington Press, 1999); Alice Yang Murray, *What Did the Internment of Japanese Americans Mean?* (New York: Bedford/St. Martin's

Press, 2000); Tetsuden Kashima, *Judgment without Trial: Japanese American Imprisonment during World War II* (Seattle: University of Washington Press, 2003); Wayne D. Rasmussen, *A History of the Emergency Farm Labor Supply Program, 1943–1947* (Washington, D.C.: U.S. Department of Agriculture, 1951); Ernesto Galarza, Merchants of Labor: *The Mexican Bracero Story: An Account of the Managed Migration of Mexican Farm Workers in California 1942–1960* (Santa Barbara: McNally & Lofton, 1964); Richard B. Craig, *The Bracero Program: Interest Groups and Foreign Policy* (Austin: University of Texas Press, 1971); Erasmo Gamboa, *Mexican Labor & World War II: Braceros in the Pacific Northwest, 1942–1947* (Austin: University of Texas Press, 1990); Kitty Calavita, *INSIDE THE STATE: The Bracero Program, Immigration and the I.N.S.* (New York: Routledge, 1992).

6. For example, the Japanese-Mexican Labor Association was formed in 1903 in Oxnard, California, to protest unfair labor practices of the Western Agricultural Contracting Company such as paying the workers in script and withholding payment until the end of their contract. Although the Association was only partially successful, this illustrates the historical alliances made by these two groups.

7. Tomás Almaguer, *Racial Fault Lines: The Historical Origins of White Supremacy in California* (Berkeley: University of California Press, 1994), 162. Hereafter cited as Almaguer, *Racial Fault Lines*.

8. Ibid., 184.

9. Robert Miles, *Racism* (London: Routledge Press, 1989) as cited by Chor Swang Ngin and Rodolfo D. Torres, "Racialized Metropolis: Theorizing Asian American and Latino Identities and Ethnicities in Southern California," 373, in *Asian and Latino Immigrants in a Restructuring Economy: A Metamorphosis of Southern California*, ed. Marta López-Garza and David R. Ruiz. (Stanford University Press, 2001).

10. Almaguer, *Racial Fault Lines*, 3.

11. For an excellent discussion on the origins of anti-Mexican sentiment in the United States and the treatment of Mexicans before and after 1848 see the following studies: Martha Menchaca, *Recovering History Constructing Race: The Indian, Black, and White Roots of Mexican Americans* (Austin: University of Texas Press, 2001); *Racial Fault Lines*; Arnold De León, *They Called Them Greasers: Anglo Attitudes toward Mexicans in Texas, 1821–1900* (Austin: University of Texas Press, 1983); Reginald Horseman, *Race and Manifest Destiny: The Origins of American Racial Anglo-Saxonism.* (Cambridge: Harvard University Press, 1981).

12. For an excellent discussion on the transformation see Alamaguer, *Racial Fault Lines* and Menchaca, *Recovering History Constructing Race.*

13. Report of the Industrial Commission on Immigration, 15, no. 759 (1901): n22 as quoted in Gilberto Cardenas, "United States Immigration Policy

toward Mexico: An Historical Perspective," *Chicano Law Review* 2 (Summer 1975): 70. Hereafter cited as Gilberto Cardenas.

14. U.S. Department of Labor, Mexican Labor in the United States, Bulletin No. 78 (1908): 466–522.

15. For a detailed analysis of the early arrival of Mexicans in the Pacific Northwest see Erasmo Gamboa, "Mexican Mule Packers and Oregon's Second Regiment Mounted Volunteers, 1855–1856," *Oregon Historical Quarterly* 92 (Spring 1991); and "The Mexican Mule Pack System of Transportation in the Pacific Northwest and British Columbia," *Journal of the West* 29 (January 1990).

16. Lawrence A. Cardoso, *Mexican Emigration to the United States, 1897–1931* (Tucson: The University of Arizona Press, 1980), 38.

17. Héctor Aguilar Camín and Lorenzo Meyer, *In the Shadow of the Mexican Revolution: Contemporary Mexican History, 1910–1989* (Austin: University of Texas Press, 1993), 71.

18. Oscar J. Martinez, *Mexican-Origin People in the United States: A Topical History* (Tucson: University of Arizona Press, 2001), 7–8

19. Ibid., 14.

20. David G. Gutiérrez, *Walls and Mirrors: Mexican Americans, Mexican Immigrants, and the Politics of Ethnicity* (Berkeley: The University of California Press, 1995), 40. (Hereafter Gutiérrez , *Walls and Mirrors.*) Gutiérrez provides an excellent analysis of this rivalry and its consequences.

21. Carlos A. Schwantes, *The Pacific Northwest: An Interpretive History* (Lincoln: The University of Nebraska Press, 1989), 203–204. Hereafter cited as Schwantes, *The Pacific Northwest.*

22. Manuel García y Griego, "The Importation of Mexican Contract Laborers to the United States, 1942–1964," in *Between Two Worlds: Mexican Immigrants in the United States*, David G. Gutiérrez (Wilmington: Scholarly Resources, Inc., 1996). Hereafter cited as Manuel Garcia y Griego.

23. Rodolfo Acuña, Occupied America: A History of Chicanos, 4th ed. (New York: Longman Press, 2000), 174–75. Hereafter cited as Acuña, *Occupied America.*

24. Oscar J. Martínez, *Mexican-Origin People in the United States: A Topical History* (Tucson: University of Arizona Press, 2001), 28.

25. Juan Ramon García, *Operation Wetback: the Mass Deportation of Mexican Undocumented Workers in 1954.* (Westport, CT.: Greenwood Press, 1980), 21.

26. This definition of nativism refers to an ultranationalist group, not to be confused with its anthropological definition. As Rodolfo Acuña defined in *Occupied America*, "'Nativism' in this text refers to ultranationalist group of Euroamericans who considered themselves the true Americans, excluding even the Indian..."

27. Neil Foley, *The White Scourge: Mexicans, Blacks, and Poor Whites in Texas Cotton Culture* (Berkeley: University of California Press, 1997), 45.

28. For a more detailed analysis see Clare Sheridan. "Contested Citizenship: National Identity and the Mexican Immigration Debates of the 1920s," *Journal of American Ethnic History* 21, no. 3 (Spring 2002): 3–35.

29. Gilberto Cardenas, Congressional Record. 2817–18 (1928), 69–70n2169.

30. Gutiérrez. *Walls and Mirrors*, 46.

31. Erasmo Gamboa, *Mexican Labor and World War II: Braceros in the Pacific Northwest, 1942–1947* (Austin: University of Texas, 1990; Seattle: University of Washington Press, 2000), 8.

32. See Erasmo Gamboa's work on braceros in the Pacific Northwest for a further analysis of this movement.

33. Paul S. Taylor. *Mexican Labor in the United States: Migration Statistics, Vol. 4* (Berkeley: University of California Press, 1933). The 1930 census used for the first time the word *Mexican* to enumerate persons born in Mexico or having parents born in Mexico. In prior censuses, the nearest categories to this were provided by the classification "foreign born whites whose country of birth was Mexico." However, the 1930 Census represents the only time such a category was used. In 1930 only 65, 968 persons of Mexican birth or parentage were returned as white, and 1,422,533 as Mexican.

34. Liping Zhu, *A Chinaman's Chance: The Chinese on the Rocky Mountain Mining Frontier* (Niwot: University Press of Colorado, 1997), 26–27. Hereafter cited as Zhu, *A Chinaman's Chance.*

35. Ibid., 47.

36. Roger Daniels, *Prisoners without Trial: Japanese Americans in World War II* (New York: Hill and Lang, 1993), 4. Hereafter cited as Daniels, *Prisoners without Trial.*

37. Zhu, *A Chinaman's Chance*, 189–90. According to the author, some of the economic barriers created by the Idaho state legislature were an 1891 law prohibiting aliens from obtaining mining claims, tunnel rights, mill sites, quartz mills, water rights, and other mining related properties, as well as the law passed in 1897 making it illegal to employ any alien who had not become a naturalized citizen, thus barring almost all Chinese.

38. Yuji Ichioka, *The Issei: The World of the First Generation Japanese Immigrants, 1885–1924* (New York: The Free Press), 57–59.

39. Daniels, *Prisoners without Trial*, 8.

40. Chris Friday, *Organizing Asian American Labor: the Pacific Coast canned-salmon industry, 1870-1942.* (Philadelphia: Temple University Press, 1994), 93.

41. Robert C. Sims, *Japanese American Contributions to Idaho's Economic Development.* A Publication of the Center for Research, Grants, and Contracts, Boise State University, May 10, 1978, 3. Hereafter cited as Sims, *Japanese American Contributions to Idaho's Economic Development.*

42. *Idaho Daily Statesman*, July 26, 1892, 8, as cited by Robert C. Sims, *Japanese American Contributions to Idaho's Economic Development*, 4.

43. Ronald L. James, ed., "Meiji Foreign Office Report on Idaho," *Asian American Comparative Collection Newsletter*, Supplement 19, no. 1 (March 2002), 5. This very interesting document originally in Japanese was translated into English. Although brief, it provides detailed information on the working and living conditions for the Japanese in Idaho. Included in the narrative are wage rates for Japanese in comparison to white workers and the overall observations made by the Meiji Foreign Office representative.

44. Henry H. Fuji interviewed by Mrs. Robert Alexander and Mrs. Cecil Hungerford. Boise: Idaho Oral History Center, Idaho Historical Society, Aug. 23, 1971. Hereafter cited as Henry H. Fuji.

45. Ibid.

46. Raymond Leslie Buell, "Some Legal Aspects of the Japanese Question," in *Japanese Immigrants and American Law: The Alien Land Laws and Other Issues*, ed. Charles McClain (New York: Garland Publishing,Inc., 1994), 3–23.

47. Henry H. Fuji.

48. Ibid.

49. Letter to Hon. A.E. Mead, Governor of the State of Washington from Andrew Williams, Sheriff, Whatcom County, Wash., Aug. 12, 1905. Japanese Exclusion, Box 2E-2-16, Papers of Gov. Mead, Washington State Historical Archives.

50. Ibid.

51. Letter to W.E. Mead, Governor of Washington from D.S. Wright, Asiatic Exclusion League of N.A. (North America) and Statistician of International Organization and Secretary of Local Branch, Mar. 30, 1908. Japanese Exclusion, Box 2E-2-16, Papers of Gov. Mead, Washington State Historical Archives.

52. Gabriel J. Chin. "Twenty Years on Trial: Takuji Yamashita's Struggle for Citizenship," In *Race on Trial: Law and Justice in American History*, ed. Annette Gordon-Reed (Oxford: Cambridge, University Press, 2002), 103–17. Hereafter cited as *Race on Trial*.

53. Clare Sheridan, "Contested Citizenship: National Identity and the Mexican Immigration Debates of the 1920s," *Journal of American Ethnic History* 21, no. 2 (Spring 2000): 4.

54. *Race on Trial*. This article will provide the complete background on Yamashita as well as a detailed analysis of the court case. Yamashita was eventually interned at the Minidoka concentration camp during World War II and died in Japan in 1957. The State of Washington Supreme Court admitted Takuji Yamashita to the state bar in 2001.

55. Francisco E. Balderamma and Raymond Rodríguez, *Decade of Betrayal: Mexican Repatriation in the 1930s* (Albuquerque: University of New Mexico Press, 1995), 122.
56. Ibid., 51.
57. U.S. Bureau of Census, "Characteristics of the Population," *United States Census of Population: 1940*, vol. 2, part 7.
58. U.S. Census Office, Sixteenth Census of the United States, 1940 as cited in Appendix A in *The Hood River Issei: An Oral History of Japanese Settlers in Oregon's Hood River Valley*, Linda Tamura (Urbana and Chicago: University of Illinois Press, 1993), 283.
59. Sims, *Japanese American Contributions to Idaho's Economic Development.*
60. Some of these attempts include the 1907 Gentlemen's Agreement between the United States and Japan to prevent Japanese laborers from entering the United States. The emergence of the so-called "yellow-peril" and the enactment in 1913 of the California Alien Land Law created a sense of hysteria within white communities throughout the Pacific Coast. Although not directly mentioning the Japanese the law referred to those aliens ineligible for citizenship, which included all Asians who would be prevented from owning land. Lastly, states such as California and Oregon enacted miscegenation laws that furthered attempted to stamp the notion of "whiteness" in the region.
61. William S. Hallagan, "Labor Contracting in Turn-of-the Century California Agriculture," *Journal of Economic History* 40, no. 4 (December 1980): 757–76.
62. Investigation of Western Farm Labor Conditions. Hearings before the Special Committee to Investigate Farm Labor Conditions in the West. United States Senate, Seventy-fifth Congress, Second Session on S. Res. 299, A Resolution to Investigate Agricultural Labor Shortages in the Western States in Connection with the Prosecution of the War. In Four Parts, PART I, Sacramento, California, Nov. 23, 24, and 25, 1942. United States Government Printing Office: 1943, 21. Hereafter cited as Investigation of Western Farm Labor Conditions.
63. *Investigation of Western Farm Labor Conditions*, 24.
64. Ibid., 186–87.
65. *The Minidoka Irrigator*, Mar. 13, 1943.
66. Luis Fiset, "Thinning, Topping, and Loading: Japanese Americans and Beet Sugar in World War II," *Pacific Northwest Quarterly* 90, no. 3 (Summer 1999): 124.
67. Greg Robinson, *By Order of the President: FDR and the Internment of Japanese Americans* (Cambridge: Harvard University Press, 2001), 89.
68. Ibid., 90.

69. Letter from George S. Ishiyama to Paul S. McNutt, Chair, War Manpower Commission, Washington, D.C., Feb. 3, 1943. Records in the National Archives & Records Administration, Rocky Mountain Region Archival Operations. RG211, War Manpower Commission, central correspondence files, Region XI, Series 269, Box 106, Wyoming, ES 533.19, February 1942 to Sept. 30, 1943.

70. Roger Daniels, *Prisoners without Trial: Japanese Americans in World War II* (New York: Hill and Wang, 1993), 74. Hereafter cited as Daniels, *Prisoners without Trial.*

71. Bureau of Employment Security, Office of the Director, Record of Long Distance Telephone Conversation from A.W. Warders, Washington, D.C. to Mr. O.C. Lamport and Mr. James Brennan, Helena, Montana, Oct. 7, 1942, 11:20 a.m. Records in the National Archives & Records Administration, Washington, D.C. RG211, War Manpower Commission, central correspondence files, entry 115, box 49.

72. Daniels, *Prisoners without Trial*, 74–75.

73. Kelly L. Strough, "The Japanese American Farm Labor Experience in the Treasure Valley during World War II: Racism, Economic Necessity, and the Failure of American Leadership," Master's Thesis, Boise State University, 1989, 27.

74. Gamboa, *Braceros in the Pacific Northwest*, 28.

75. Robert C. Sims, "'A Fearless, Patriotic, Clean-Cut Stand': Idaho's Governor Clark and the Japanese-American Relocation in World War II," *Pacific Northwest Quarterly* (April 1979): 76; see also *The Japanese Farm Labor Experience*, 48.

76. Washington State Extension Service Emergency Farm Labor Specialist Report, Annual Narrative Report Farm Labor Program for Washington 6 (1945): 1–3. See also Plan of Work, 1946 Extension Farm Labor Program Washington 7 (1946): 1; Oregon State University Extension Service. *Fighters on the Farm Front: A Story of the 1943–1946 Oregon Emergency Farm Labor Program.* Extension Circular 492 January 1947. (Corvallis: Oregon State University, 1947); and Erasmo Gamboa, *Mexican Labor and World War II: Braceros in the Pacific Northwest, 1942–1947* (Seattle: University of Washington Press, 1990), 58.

77. Specialist County Visitation Report, Walter E. Zuger, Conference State Farm Labor Supervisors, Portland, Aug. 18, 1943, 1.

78. Barbara Driscoll. *The Tracks North: The Railroad Bracero Program of World War II* (Austin: Center for Mexican American Studies, University of Texas, 1999). Hereafter cited as Driscoll, *The Tracks North.*

79. Manuel Garcia y Griego, *Mexican Contract Labor, 1942–1964*, 50–51.

80. Ibid., 51.

81. Driscoll, *The Tracks North*, 117.

82. Letter from Southern Pacific Company, E.E. Mayo, Chief Engineer to J. Macklin, Regional Director Railroad Retirement Board, Mar. 21, 1945. SUBJECT: Mexican Nationals – Deaths Reported. National Archives and Records Administration Pacific Region (San Francisco), Record Group 211, Series War Manpower Commission XII, Box 2966, Mexican Track Workers' Deaths Jan–Jun 1945.

83. Letter from Herbert Connor, Manager, Federal Security Agency, Yuma Office to Henry K. Arneson, State Manpower Director, Arizona, Aug. 19, 1943. National Archives and Record Administration Pacific Region (San Francisco), Record Group 211 War Manpower Commission, Region XII, Series Regional Central Files, 1942–1945, Entry 269, Box 2964, Folder 6-2-2 Mexican Deaths LM&U 1943. The three Mexicans killed were Salvador Vasquez Huante, Salvador S. Ramirez, and Antonio Osario Amaro.

84. Letter from Morelos Gonzales, Acting Consul, Mexico, to Mr. Henry K. Arneson, State Manpower Director, War Manpower Commission, Arizona, July 30, 1943. National Archives and Record Administration Pacific Region (San Francisco), Record Group 211 War Manpower Commission, Region XII, Series Regional Central Files, 1942–1945, Entry 269, Box 2964, Folder 6-2-2 Mexican Deaths LM&U 1943.

85. Partial list of Mexican Deaths. National Archives and Record Administration, Record Group 211 War Manpower Commission, Region XII, office files, War Manpower Representative in Mexico, 1943–1946 (D), entry 196, Box 3.

86. Gamboa, *Braceros in the Pacific Northwest,* 117.

87. Memorandum to Regional Manpower Director, Region XII from A.W. Motley, Acting Director Bureau of Placement, Subject: Deaths of Mexicans Nationals – Letter from Mexican Consul, Mar. 10, 1944; Memorandum to Lawrence A. Appley from W.K. Hopkins, Regional Director, WMC, Region XII, Subject: Death of Mexican Nationals – Letter from Mexican Consul, Feb. 2, 1944. National Archives and Records Administration Pacific Region (San Francisco), Record Group 211 War Manpower Commission, Region XII, Central Files, 1942–1945, Box 2965, Folder 6-2-2 Mexican Track Workers Deaths January–June 1944.

88. "Maybe Get Jap Labor for County Harvest Operation," *The Chronicle-Dispatch,* Feb. 11, 1943, 1.

89. "Importation of Japanese for Harvest Is Discussed," *The Chronicle-Dispatch,* Apr. 1, 1943, 1.

90. Ibid.

91. Co-operative Extension Work in Agriculture and Home Economics, State College of Washington and the U.S. Department of Agriculture Co-operating, Specialist Record of County Visit, Columbia County, Walter E. Zuger, Assistant State Farm Labor Supervisor, July 21–22, 1943. Hereafter Co-operative Extension Work.

92. Ibid.
93. Ibid.
94. Ibid.
95. "Cannery Shut Down By Work Halt." *Walla Walla Union Bulletin*, July 22, 1943.
96. Co-operative Extension Work.
97. Ibid.
98. Ibid.
99. Audrey Haakonstad, interviewed by Teresa R. Funke. Boise: Idaho Oral History Center, Idaho State Historical Society, Oct. 9, 1991. The incident Mrs. Haakonstad refers to in the quote regards a confrontation that occurred in Emmett, Idaho, during the war years. According to Haakonstad, a longtime Japanese American resident went into a bank in Emmett and was confronted by a female who said, "Why don't you go home where you belong," and spit in his face.
100. Garcia y Griego, *Mexican Contract Laborers*, 1942–1964, 49.

Race, Labor, and Getting Out the Harvest: The Bracero Program in World War II Hood River, Oregon

Johanna Ogden

Migrant populations are created in large and complex forces in their home country and on their new shores. This is no less the case for the arrival of thousands of Mexicans to the Pacific Northwest during World War II. Under the auspices of an emergency agricultural labor act executed between the U.S. and Mexican governments in August 1942 titled Public Law 45 (commonly known as the Bracero Program), over two hundred thousand Mexican laborers were transported to the United States during World War II, with roughly five thousand traveling annually to Oregon beginning in 1943. Several hundred of these men lived and worked in Hood River.

The agreement executed between the two governments was to guarantee the following: Mexicans were to be only short-term laborers with a written contract (in Spanish and English); they were to be paid prevailing U.S. wages for their work; they had the right to organize; they would not be used to supplant U.S. laborers or be pressed into military service; and the U.S. government would provide round-trip transportation to and from Mexico and ensure adequate living arrangements. These conditions remained largely intact for the duration of the war.[1] However straightforward the terms of the U.S.-Mexico contract, it was intertwined with the inequalities of national status between the two countries, and powerful wartime politics and changes in U.S. society.

The Bracero Program occurred within and contributed to a larger transformation of the Pacific Northwest. The region underwent significant quantitative and qualitative demographic changes as workers of many nationalities streamed in to fill the tens of thousands of wartime industry and agricultural jobs.

Simultaneous to the infusion of multinational laborers into the
Northwest labor pool was the reprehensible internment of the
Japanese. The arrival of thousands of Mexican Bracero laborers
occurred in the midst of this social maelstrom.

While providing an overall analysis of the Northwest Bracero
Program in *Mexican Labor and World War II: Braceros in the Pacific
Northest, 1942–1947*, Erasmo Gamboa also notes, "Although the
bracero program was national in scope; local, federal, and state
officials tailored the federal farm labor system to meet regional
labor market demands."[2] As a result, analyzing the experience of
particular locales, varying as they do by crops, settings,
development, and interaction with the braceros, may add to a
collective understanding of this historical moment. Not only crop
and market forces affected and influenced regional and local
approaches to the Bracero Program, but also an area's attitude
about political and social issues. One issue in particular that
shaped how the Mexican workforce was used and accepted was
the area's attitude toward and reliance on Japanese farmers and
laborers. As Gamboa explains, "[t]he quietude in these small
communities, broken by the anxiety and emotionalism surrounding
the world crisis, often translated into increased racial intolerance.
The hardest blows were dealt to Japanese American residents in
the Northwest... it is important to note that the relocation of the
Japanese American communities, especially from key agricultural
places... only served to exacerbate an already strained labor
supply."[3] Despite much longstanding distrust of their presence,
Hood River's Japanese residents were critical players in the area's
fruit production prior to World War II. However, unlike other
areas of the Northwest where prejudices against the Japanese also
ran deep, Hood River never consented to accept interned Japanese
on work release despite an acute labor shortage. Consequently,
Hood River's reception of the bracero laborers was conditioned by
great necessity *and* a great generalized intolerance that underscores
the truth of Gamboa's observation that "the passage of the Alien
Registration Act of 1940 encouraged the hostility directed against

the Japanese Americans to spread later to other groups, including Mexican nationals and Mexican Americans."[4] Thus, while the *contractual* terms of the Bracero Program established the Mexican laborers as temporary and seasonal, the virulent anti-Japanese, anti-immigrant atmosphere in Hood River—the focus of this research—significantly shaped the town's *expectation* that these Mexicans should not stay either as permanent or as landowning members of the community. The demands of Hood River's wartime agriculture production was inextricably linked to that community's history and notions regarding race, immigration, and entitlement, and entwined the fate of its Japanese residents and newly arrived Mexican braceros.

World War II and Northwest Labor Needs

If the "labor shortage was the most serious obstacle encountered by farmers" in the Northwest prior to World War II, as argued by Erasmo Gamboa, this critical shortage was exacerbated many times over with the outbreak of the war. The Second World War brought important and lasting changes to the Pacific Northwest. Although no region of the United States escaped the impact of the war, few if any experienced a more rapid or intense transformation than the Pacific Northwest. Wartime social and economic pressures scarcely left a corner untouched. In what would prove to be a classic understatement, the *Portland Oregonian* observed on April 6, 1941: "Few persons realize the magnitude of the national defense efforts in the Pacific Northwest."[5]

Whatever one thinks of Pearl Harbor and the resulting U.S. entry into the war, there is no arguing that it brought dramatic, far-reaching, and almost immediate changes into U.S. society. The Pacific Northwest was no exception. Seattle Boeing grew from five thousand to fifty thousand jobs seemingly overnight. The Kaiser shipyards in Portland grew their own city of Vanport, and worked around the clock. People from around the country poured into the

Northwest to meet the massive needs of these war industries. Simultaneously huge national agricultural quotas were set to meet U.S. and Allied troop provisions, and Northwest farmers geared up to meet this challenge.

Northwest agriculture particularly suffered from a shortage of laborers during these times as men throughout society were recruited and enlisted into the armed forces. Compounding agriculture's historic shortages, wartime industries paid substantially better wages than agriculture and thus siphoned workers. Many of the remaining domestic migrant workers who would otherwise have been available for the fields understandably chose to cast their lot with Boeing, Kaiser, and the like. Schoolchildren and especially women assisted, but were unable to meet the heavy agricultural demands on their own. As this was the situation throughout the country, the federal government began looking for laborers outside the United States and in 1942 entered into active negotiations with Mexico for the importation of Mexican citizens that resulted in the Bracero Program. While workers were recruited from other countries (the Bahamas, Jamaica, and Newfoundland), Mexico was by far the single largest provider of laborers.

Taken as a whole, the wartime laborers who rushed in to fill the Pacific Northwest's industrial and agricultural jobs provided not just a major quantitative change to the region's demographics, but also introduced significant qualitative changes. This influx of tens of thousands of laboring men and women included thousands of southern blacks (attracted especially into the manufacturing industries), and Mexican nationals (recruited into the agriculture and railroad sector). World War II also included the persecution and internment of the Japanese, fueled especially by the hysteria and jingoism following the bombing of Pearl Harbor. Overall, race and racial politics would prove to be important features and components of change, much of it foisted upon the region by the "magnitude of the defense efforts" in the Pacific Northwest. Hood River was a microcosm of these dynamics.

RACE, LABOR AND GETTING OUT THE HARVEST

Hood River: Early History

Hood River, a sidebar of the Oregon Trail, did not see white settlement until the 1850s and 1860s, with more growth in the 1880s arising from the railroad linking the Columbia River Gorge to Portland. Most early settlers relied on cattle for their livelihood, though experiments in fruit growing began early. Clearing the land for orchards and accumulating the horticultural knowledge of suitable varieties had to wait for surplus time and funds. By the 1890s, a farmer growers union had been established based primarily on the initial success of strawberries in the area. The population grew slowly but steadily. The building of the Cascade locks on the Columbia River provided reliable market transport to The Dalles and Portland (respectively up and down river from Hood River), but large-scale irrigation capability remained key for further development of fruit production. This too was solved near the turn of the century, with land values nearly tripling in the wake of the construction of "the ditch" (as the new irrigation system was called). By the early 1900s Hood River's chief product was apples, for which it became widely known, and the valley began to burgeon with orchards, growers' marketing organizations (the most enduring of which was the Hood River Apple Growers Association, now Diamond Fruit Growers), warehouses, and the like. The town itself grew, gaining more permanent buildings, services.[6] Hood River had become a town with its life's blood rooted in agriculture.

While the majority of Hood River settlers were of European descent, Japanese immigrants also arrived in the valley relatively early on.[7] "The Chinese Exclusion Act of 1882 had curtailed the West Coast supply of Chinese laborers,"[8] and "[b]y 1897, when the Alaska gold rush drained the Northwest of laborers, the transcontinental railroads began to solicit Japanese workers as an inexpensive labor force."[9] Issei[10] men first arrived in Hood River in 1902, employed to lay a spur line from Hood River to outlying Parkdale.[11] Lumber companies also began to employ Japanese laborers. Finally, the farming opportunities and beautiful setting attracted Japanese laborers. The Issei gained experience and capital, increasingly moved from laborers to renting and leasing farms, and many became landowners.

Throughout the years, the Japanese were subjected to racial discrimination and hostility whatever their role. Their housing was most often segregated, and their economic successes were often blamed for downturns in white/European employment. The initial expectation of most Japanese, which perhaps conditioned their adaptability to hard and inhospitable conditions in the Northwest, was to maximize savings and return to Japan. But by 1905, one-third of Issei in Oregon were landowning farmers, and 1908 saw the first recorded deed to a Japanese landowner in Hood River County.[12] The 1923 Oregon Alien Land Law Act, introduced into the Oregon Legislature by a Hood River politician, prevented those ineligible for citizenship to own land, forcing Issei to either entrust their holdings to Caucasian contacts or to hold land in the name of their (citizen) children. This law is indicative of the tenuous claims to community-member status that the Japanese held as nonwhite landowners in the eyes of the dominant white community. It would also seem to indicate that the later appeals to prevent Mexican laborers from settling permanently in the Hood River valley during World War II were rooted in deeply held perceptions of white superiority and entitlement.

While small in absolute numbers in Hood River, the Japanese community had made itself felt in this agriculturally centered town. Three-fourths of those Japanese scattered through the valley were involved in farming, becoming a force in vegetable, strawberry, asparagus, and pear production. The head of the Apple Growers Association stated that in 1942 Japanese growers held 16 percent of the orchards in Hood River,[13] yet comprised only between 6 percent and 10 percent of the town's population. Japanese were both members and served on the board of directors of the Apple Growers Association, an organization with increasing importance to the town.

RACE, LABOR AND GETTING OUT THE HARVEST

Japanese successes in Hood River combined with an anti-Japanese hysteria along the entire West Coast increased mistrust. Despite marginal lands and low wages, these immigrants had not only stayed and succeeded, but also had become economic mainstays in the community. While some white community members accepted and welcomed the Japanese presence in Hood River, others did not, periodically resulting in ugly racist persecution. The period following the bombing of Pearl Harbor provided one of those moments.

Hood River and World War II: Harvest Demands

With most young men drafted or enlisting and laborers seeking employment in the war industries, World War II brought a desperate and unenviable labor shortage for growers nationally as well as in Hood River. Beginning in 1942, the labor shortage in Hood River threatened people's livelihoods and put years of hard work and investment at stake by crippling the ability to harvest and maintain the orchards. Compounding this were both patriotic and market pressures imposed by production quotas for the Allied food needs. The *Hood River News* (HRN) provides an excellent view into a small, singularly focused community desperate to solve a problem their collective well-being relied upon. The fact that for several years running the status of agricultural labor continued to be front page and prominent news is indicative of both the economic base of the town and of the critical nature of the problem.

As the weeks and pages from January to December of 1942 unfold, the frantic scramble to get out the crop is almost palpable in the press. The labor shortage, apparently without exaggeration, was termed the "most serious orchard labor shortage ever known in the history of the Hood River Valley."[14] Given the overall importance of agriculture, it was a statewide concern with governmental attention.[15] Everything and everyone was tried.[16] A national model, Oregon women were formed into a "Women's

135

Land Army" and were a backbone of reserve labor with as much as 50 percent of Hood River women assisting in the orchards. Schools altered their vacation and daily schedules so that children could be of assistance.[17] Social clubs were engaged. Trains came from Portland with "weekend recruits."[18] At the height of the pear season, the *HRN* states, "Town Deserted; Business Folk Pick Pears"[19] as businesses closed and owners and employees alike took to the orchards to assist. Conscientious objectors, philosophical and/or religious opponents to World War II held in a nearby work camp, were mobilized out of confinement. Notably, however, Hood River was the only area in the Northwest to refuse the labor of interned Japanese to get out their crop.

By a hair's breath, the trees were pruned, the fruit was thinned, and the 1942 harvest was successful. But when the USDA raised agricultural production goals for the war even higher for 1943, Hood River farmers—and farmers all across the country—were intent on solving the acute shortage of agricultural laborers.

1943 proved to be considerably different with the infusion of Mexican nationals via the federal Bracero Program. An article from the 1943 *HRN* regarding the local apple harvest is indicative that while still stretched, the feeling of panic had subsided. Titled, "Apple Harvest Makes Progress in Valley,"[20] the article states, "In a few days it is expected the apple harvest will be in full swing... If good weather prevails, it is probable that the entire apple crop will be finally gathered in and under considerably less heroic conditions than those which prevailed in Hood River valley one year ago."[21] While braceros only provided approximately 10 percent of the agricultural labor force statewide during the war years, the fact that they were men, and a skillful and flexible force, made them a critical component.

Braceros in Hood River: A Reliable and Controlled Workforce

To give some sense of the scale of the Bracero Program nationally, 75,000 workers were requested by agricultural interests in 1943, with 52,131 actually arriving.[22] Of that total, Oregon utilized 5,000 men, with roughly 600 assigned to Hood River. Certainly in Oregon, Mexican nationals solved the labor shortage dilemma more than their numbers indicate (see Fig. 4.1).

Fig. 4.1. Mexican Braceros in Hood River, Ore., circa 1943 (photo courtesy of Oregon State University Special Collections).

In addition to the general labor shortage of the Northwest region, Gamboa notes an important particular as applied to Hood River, that being that the "intense oscillation between peak demand and lull, and the often arduous nature of the work itself, exacerbated an already critical [labor shortage] problem."[23] This translates into small year-round labor needs, but large and very time-sensitive requirements at harvest. Braceros, at the beck and call of farmers, provided the large, capable, short-term infusion farmers needed.

JOHANNA OGDEN

In the 1944 Annual Hood River Extension Report, Agent Sadie Bennett provides important statistics regarding the number of "placements" of bracero workers. "Placements" are not equivalent to persons. A laborer may be placed in varying farming jobs throughout the season. Thus, "placements" refers to jobs filled, and is larger than the total number of workers utilized. According to Agent Bennett, the total number of Mexican laborers was approximately 600. The *total* number of seasonal placements (for harvesting, pruning, picking, and the like) was 6,872 (with Mexicans filling 5,481 of those positions, or nine times the actual number of Mexican laborers in town)[24] contrasted with 196 year-round positions (with Mexicans filling 151 positions).[25] The fall pear harvest alone required 2,003 placements, 1,766 of which were filled by Mexican nationals. The numbers are similar for the cherry and apple harvests. Thus the Extension Agent summarizes the importance of this labor infusion as follows:

> [I]t is the observation of this office that the many excellent reports of good work, especially among the ranch crews, overbalanced all bad points in the program. We could not have harvested our fruit without this Mexican help. Of the total placements made from the Labor office, 80% were Mexican Nationals, and 20% other help.[26]

Additionally, Mexican agricultural laborers provided a critically flexible and reliable resource. In a *Hood River News* article, J.R. Beck, head of the OSC Extension Service stated,

> The approximately 5,000 Mexicans working in Oregon at the farm labor peak will represent only about ten per cent of the total number of seasonal workers... They will play a vital part in the harvest, however, by taking up the slack in hop and prune pickers, by maintaining a labor balance so an

> adequate supply of bean pickers will be available,
> and by taking over when thousands of youngsters
> return to school in September... and also is work
> not well adapted to smaller youngsters, the
> Mexicans will fill an important gap...[27]

By comparison, it is instructive to review Hood River press accounts regarding the problems with the traditional American, non-bracero migrant laborers during the war years. The following coverage is indicative of the situation:

> While it was obvious that a number of orchard
> workers were coming into the valley, following the
> closing of the hop and other harvests... growers
> admitted that one of the most serious problems they
> now have to contend with is that of keeping pickers
> after they have started on the job, for many —and
> especially when the picking is not entirely to their
> liking—decide to try another orchard and, if they
> fail to find the kind they are seeking, they leave the
> area.[28]

Thus, traditional migrant, U.S.-born laborers could not be counted on to stay through a harvest if it was difficult (light crop, high growing fruit) and easier, faster money could be made in a harvest elsewhere. Wartime gas rationing also increased the unreliability of their migratory work patterns. An *Oregonian* editorial put it as follows, "Some [farmers] declare their preference for the Mexicans over the jalopy brigade of white migrants that followed the crops in pre-war days. The main consideration there, however, appears to be that the southerners, who are on loan from the Mexican government to ours, stay put, whereas the native transients are here today and gone tomorrow."[29] By contrast to the so-called "jalopy brigade," the control over Mexican braceros must have felt like a godsend to growers. Braceros were not free to follow the best work and pay. From the point of recruitment in Mexico, to transport and assignment to individual farms in the States (and barring the very few labor disputes), farmers (and their agent, the U.S. government) literally commanded Mexican nationals. Not only could they be counted on as a controlled labor force, but they could also be moved at will based on farmers' needs.

In Hood River the Bracero Program was administered under a single contract with the Traffic Association, a subcommittee of the Apple Growers Association, the sole representative contractor for the many individual orchards. The Extension Service then managed all labor requests through the Apple Growers Association. The business argument for this arrangement was the greater flexibility in meeting the shifting labor needs of the growers and the ability for cost accounting to be based on actual use. The Apple Growers Association levied a fee for all growers to cover the cost of housing and transport costs from Mexico. However, a curious "Mexicans as community property" language is also spawned in the pages of the *Hood River News*. Part of this rhetoric also contains the development of an assumption of those to be "inside" the delineated community and those who are "outside," that is, Mexicans.

First, the *HRN* was used as an organizing tool in the "allocation"[30] of Mexicans to local growers, with the Apple Growers Association or local Extension Agent questioning terms of employment, transportation issues, and coordination questions with other growers and/or governmental agencies.[31] While the newspaper was also used to report on and mobilize women, schoolchildren, and the broader Hood River community to assist growers, one salient difference stands out. As the vast majority of Mexicans in Hood River were solely Spanish speaking (and the *HRN* was and is an English press), this was a discussion *without but about* these laborers. In other words, Mexicans were not privy, and thus external, to this community discussion about their lives.

Other events raise the question of the defined community. In an article entitled, "Urges Safety for Farm Workers,"[32] the *HRN* reports, "Elimination of accidents in connection with farm motor vehicle transportation will be the goal of the safety program in Oregon in connection with observance of National Farm Safety Week…" The article goes on to describe the understandable concern for the thousands of youth transported to and from farms to assist in the labor emergency with no guidelines for safety in this transport. The article ends, "Last year there were no serious traffic accidents involving young people going to and from farms in Oregon and… said the observance of safety precautions would enable the state to repeat this record this year."[33] However, two weeks prior to this article, a serious farm vehicle accident occurred in Hood River involving Mexican braceros. Such accidents were one of the serious perils facing the bracero workers, yet no mention was made of any of this by either the *Hood River News* or governmental officials sponsoring this "National Farm Safety Week." This could be argued as nothing more than an error of omission. But oversights can also be windows into unexpressed convictions, such as who falls within the bounds of community concern.

Further, in the few down times between orchard tasks, the *Hood River News* was utilized as a sort of labor hall for Mexicans. Articles such as the following appear: "Jobs Urgently Needed for Mexican Labor,[34] "Jobs Needed for Mexicans,"[35] "Mexicans To Help Local Home Owners."[36] The Apple Growers Association changed the bracero work rules to allow the Mexican laborers to work for private homeowners digging basements or doing construction, to lay roads for the county or work in the lumber industry. The economic aspect of this is rather succinctly expressed in an article titled, "Traffic Group Ups Assessment: Unemployed Mexicans Is Serious Problem."[37] The "serious problem" is defined as the unproductive cost of unemployment, and a tariff was levied on all growers to defray the expense. The article goes on to note, "Meanwhile, the Traffic Association… is urging all local government bodies and individuals in the valley and town to furnish work for Mexicans to the end that all be employed at least 75 per cent of their working time and thus keep the board bills incurred down to a minimum."[38] In all of this, Mexicans are, in public-speak, the external resource/commodity to be used by the community of growers and the town dependent upon them. The Hood River community as a whole had an economic interest in ensuring a successful fruit harvest that required the infusion of these Mexican laborers throughout the season despite any periodic lulls in their workload. The community, seemingly at the growers' urging, opted to maintain a ready supply of orchard laborers even if it required financial support from them as a whole. Making these men—or others of their countrymen—permanent, self-reliant members of the community, however, was *not* an option. Not surprisingly then, one of the many articles urging the community to do their part to help employ the Mexican laborers also provides the assurance that, "Under the contract entered into by our own government, Mexicans who are to work in Hood River valley will be shipped back to Mexico immediately after harvesting of the fruit crops."[39]

Beyond Hood River, the many articles appearing in the *Oregonian* during the war years discussing new race relations and their ongoing meaning for the state based on Oregon's changed demographics *never* included Mexicans, despite over 10,000 Mexican laborers having traversed Oregon by 1945 (see Fig. 4.2).[40] Mexicans were not considered as within the existing or continuing definition of community.

Race in Wartime Hood River: Attitudes toward the Japanese and Braceros

The lack of community inclusion of Mexican braceros by the extant community of Hood River could be viewed simply as the result of the dictates of agricultural economics and a basic public acceptance of the federal contractual guarantee that these laborers

Fig. 4.2. Mexican Braceros weighing Hops in Oregon, circa 1944 (photo courtesy of Oregon State University Special Collections).

would be only temporary additions to the region. But in reality, the treatment of and attitude toward the Mexican bracero laborers was also deeply shaped by and rooted in Hood River's history and attitudes toward race, citizenship, and landownership. This took concentrated expression in the political and social interplay between the wartime Japanese internment and the arrival of bracero laborers.

At the start of World War II, Hood River's Japanese population was estimated at 6 to 10 percent.[41] Much like Mexican braceros, however, the Japanese in Hood River had influence well beyond their numbers as successful orchardists and through other types of businesses. With the outbreak of World War II Japanese community members were evacuated and interned as a virulent anti-Japanese and anti-foreigner sentiment dominated Hood River. This was fueled by wartime politics but linked to the longer history of racism and exclusion dating to before Oregon's 1923 passage of the Alien Land Law initiated in Hood River.

On June 21, 1943, the City Council of Hood River unanimously passed an anti-Japanese and anti-immigrant resolution introduced by the Hood River Post of the American Legion. Its salient points included the following: that Japanese are undesirable and unassimilable as U.S. citizens; that all persons of Japanese ancestry should be deported; that the U.S. Constitution should be amended to limit citizenship to those persons born to citizens; and that a call to revoke existing citizenship for all Japanese then in the United States should be issued.

Months prior to the City Council's adopting the resolution, the *Hood River News* prominently covered the reactionary discussion over how to solve what was termed the "Japanese problem." The local Grange organizations came out in favor of the American Legion resolution and aided the public debate. Announcing the Grange's backing of the Legion resolution, the *Hood River News* reports, "[The American Legion speaker] gave an excellent speech on the Japanese situation, in which he contrasted the selfish cruelty of Shintoism on the one hand with the broadening, tolerant Christianity of the United Nations on the other. The Negro problem, with its tendency to develop crowded locations, the breeding of lawlessness and the apparent impossibility of solving this problem, he declared, helped the Legion to adopt a resolution to the effect that the Japanese be not permitted to concentrate here or elsewhere in the United States."[42] Not only, then, is this resolution anti-Japanese, but also broadly anti-immigrant and racist in its genesis.

A front-page article days prior to the City Council adoption of the resolution titled "Grange View on Japanese Problem" warrants quoting at length. In classic reactionary populism, State Grange Master Tompkins summarizes the Asiatic Exclusion Act as pro-labor (U.S.), and notes with pride the Grange's efforts in its passage. It goes on:

> The several west coast states have laws
> forbidding the lease or ownership of land by
> Asiatics. In 1922, Oregon passed a law which forbid
> leasing or owning of land by those "who were not
> eligible to citizenship under federal law." Many ways
> were found to defeat these laws, particularly by the
> Japanese, who were determined to gain ownership
> of land by one pretext or another. After moving
> into our [sic] richest farm lands, they soon became
> employers and the sons and grandsons of our
> pioneers, who sought to maintain high standards of
> living, could not compete with the Japanese and
> were forced out of business and into hiring
> themselves to the Japanese landlords.
> At the beginning of this war the Japanese
> owned or controlled vast acreages of the richest
> farm lands in the western states. The Japanese are
> now purchasing many tracts of the best agricultural
> lands in our midst. Such procedure by the Japanese
> is a direct challenge to us and steps must be taken
> at the opportune time to see that it is stopped.[43]

Of particular note is this article's proposition that the Japanese own the "best agricultural lands" and that is a "direct challenge to us," seemingly meaning to whites. The explicit assumption is that the valley and the right to land ownership belongs to that same "us." It is perhaps superfluous to add that this same campaign lobbied against the Japanese residents returning to Hood River after their internment had been ended. "...[O]nly 40.3 percent (186 out of 462) of the prewar Hood River Japanese did return to the valley. This contrasted with like figures of 68.9 percent in the state... "[44] Pearl Harbor become a flash point triggering Japanese evacuation, internment, appropriation of orchards, and an influential white community verdict that no new (nonwhite) immigrant would again be a permanent resident *or* landowner.

The first Mexican bracero workers arrived in Hood River close on the heels of the evacuation and internment of the Japanese, and in the midst of the continuing anti-Japanese, anti-immigrant political atmosphere. It would be virtually impossible for this venomous mood not to spill onto this new immigrant group. The most significant means are not necessarily expressed in daily racist encounters or remarks. More telling is the often explicit expectation that these people were not considered members of the community nor anticipated to become so. Specifically, a broad community assumption expected that Mexicans would remain temporary, landless laborers, returnable to sender.

A *Hood River News* article titled, "Many Mexicans Are Leaving for Homeland: Only Three of Six Hundred Remain Here"[45] begins with several laudatory paragraphs regarding the Mexican laborers' efforts and skills at pruning, thinning, and harvesting, having made the decisive difference in a successful harvest. It then continues, "The fact that practically all of the Mexicans have returned to Old Mexico, at least until next spring, has put an end to rumors that the danger of numbers of them becoming permanent residents had any foundation… "[46] Lest one think this is just the parochialism of a small-town press, the "big-city" *Portland Oregonian* reassures and succinctly summarizes Hood River's attitude toward its (former) Japanese residents and the town's subsequent fears regarding Mexicans. The editorial states,

> This writer encountered a curious reaction among Hood River growers at the height of the pear crop. The Mexicans are good workers, they affirmed. And trouble in the camps? Not a single criminal charge against a Mexican worker had reached the Hood River county district attorney's office. Strikes or wage difficulties? None. Do you want them back next year? Well, maybe. Maybe not. Anyway, if Mexicans are needed next year, the same workers shouldn't be sent.

Hood River county, it will be remembered, had a considerable population of Japanese and Japanese-Americans. Many of the latter owned land and employed the numerous members of their families and friends' families at wages far below the cost of white labor. White growers and white workers felt that the Japanese created unfair labor conditions which were reflected in the fruit markets and in living conditions generally. Hood River county hopes that the Japanese will not return to their lands when the war ends.

Orchardists and workers feel no antipathy toward the workers from our friendly neighbor, Mexico, but they are frank to say that they do not wish these workers to return and become landowners.[47]

Societies are such that one seemingly simple, if large, contract for laborers such as the Bracero Program becomes intertwined with other societal dynamics and history at play, producing unanticipated results. Here, the temporary work contract for Mexican laborers converged with a valley beset with misplaced patriotism and outright racism toward its Japanese residents, creating the explicitly anti-immigrant and whites-only landowning atmosphere toward Mexicans so succinctly summarized by *The Oregonian* above.

Thus, a powerful confluence of race/cultural/political exigencies on the one hand and agricultural economics on the other converged to shape Mexicans' first major entry into Hood River. The life cycle and agronomics of the orchards required large, flexible, and dependable infusions of labor made desperately short by the larger labor issues of World War II. The history of and resentment toward Japanese settlement in Hood River flowered post Pearl Harbor into a virulently racist, anti-immigrant atmosphere. Otherwise put, on a multitude of levels, Hood River desperately needed Mexican laborers who didn't stay, and those needs were multifaceted in their genesis.

The Bracero Program as a Win/Win Situation

In 1943, the Governor of Oregon, thanking the repatriating Mexican laborers, stated, "…we hope… that you have found it as profitable to you as it has been to us…,"[48] implying the Bracero Program to be a win/win situation for all concerned. A (rather bad) poem appeared on the front page of the *Hood River News* with a similar theme:

Welcome men, from Mexico
To weather so unreasonable,
To have three warm days in a row
Just doesn't seem quite feasible.
We appreciate your able help,
Right gladly do I say so;
And perhaps you will reciprocate
And appreciate our peso![49]

There is little question that the thousands of Mexican laborers who took part returned to Mexico with larger sums of money than likely would have been garnered had they stayed in their home country. But this is an incomplete equation from which to evaluate the win/win claim.

An inherent inequality of nations lies behind the invention of the Bracero Program. That one country's resource is their people to be exported and used for another country's economic gain represents a fundamental disparity of power and means. While U.S. agricultural incomes rose and their enterprises expanded during the war years, Mexico experienced significant agricultural dislocation due, in part, to the exodus of over two hundred thousand laborers, many of them farmers, to the United States.[50]

In Hood River, the economic power of orchardists grew during World War II and positioned them for further expansion post-war.

While much ink in the *Hood River News* during the war years was given to growers' loud complaints over price and wage ceilings, a more subtle story exposed rising agricultural profits and land speculation. For example, Roy Webster, head of the Oregon, Washington, and California Pear Bureau purchased a large orchard in Hood River in 1944, noting a "lifelong dream" and positive orchard financial prospects.[51] As the war progressed, articles in the *HRN* highlighted increased profits, along with the potential of large and profitable European markets for the post-war years.[52]

Available and favorable farm loans also merit frequent mention during the war years, along with a number of articles documenting the capital development of the orchardists in the form of the expansion and/or building of cold storage packing facilities.[53] In short, many growers prospered during World War II, and were poised for significant expansion following it. The increased need for and reliance on landless laborers that developed during the war has continued as an increasingly significant dynamic between the United States and Mexico up to and including the present time. Finally, post–World War II Mexico saw the extension of U.S. agribusiness into Mexico on a large scale, in turn contributing to the further undermining of indigenous farms and the creation of an increasing number of landless peasants migrating in search of work.

The relatively small sums carried home by these men to Mexico seems an absurd equivalent to the agricultural dislocations and overall inequalities the Bracero Program contributed to and presaged, not the "win/win" claimed. The Bracero Program per se was not the sole cause of these inequalities. But it is both contributory and reflective of the pattern of domination of U.S. agricultural interests over Mexico and its people, and the creation of a permanent, migratory Mexican underclass in the United States.

Conclusion

World War II is a time replete with tales of heroism and sacrifice in American culture, and is often viewed as an ideal of national unity and patriotism. As is frequently the case for national myths, that is a partial picture and dependent on the teller. In this instance, Mexicans were imported to solve an acute labor shortage. Were it not for these "foreigners," farming quotas would not have been met. Yet Mexican laborers do not occupy a war hero status in the Pacific Northwest. Most residents know nothing of the Mexican presence or role during these years. Instead, what has endured since the war is a two-tier workforce, with Mexicans (and now Latinos more broadly) an enduring, and often disdained, landless underclass in the Pacific Northwest.

The arrival of bracero workers in Hood River arose from wartime production necessities, but was entwined with volatile issues of national status, race, and class. This mix transformed a seasonal work contract into a social and political belief that these Mexicans were not to become permanent, landowning members of the community. The invitation was to work, but it straightforwardly was not an open-ended invitation to stay and share in the fruits of one's labor. Despite the PR spin of the times equating "bracero" with helping hand/arm, it is ironic the program is named for a body part, a piece, of a human laborer. This, unfortunately, continues to be relevant for our times.

Endnotes

1. For a more complete discussion of these contract terms see Erasmo Gamboa, *Mexican Labor and World War II: Braceros in the Pacific Northwest, 1942–1947* (Austin: University of Texas Press 1990), 40–41.
2. Gamboa, xiii.
3. Ibid., 26.
4. Ibid.
5. Carlos Arnaldo Schwantes, *The Pacific Northwest* (Lincoln and London: University of Nebraska Press, 1996), 408.

6. Drawn from *History of Hood River County 1852–1982*, published by the Hood River County Historical Society, 1982.
7. Beyond where explicitly cited, this section draws heavily from Linda Tamura, *The Hood River Issei* (Urbana and Chicago: University of Chicago Press, 1993).
8. Ibid., 63.
9. Ibid.
10. Issei are first-generation Japanese immigrants to the United States. Nisei are their children born in the United States.
11. Tamura, 70.
12. Ibid., 82.
13. "Japanese in H.R. Valley," *Hood River News* (hereafter *HRN*), Mar. 13, 1942, 1.
14. "Town Deserted; Business Folk Pick Pears," *HRN*, Sept. 18, 1942, 2.
15. "[Governor] Sprague Takes Hand in Labor Situation: Plight of Farmers Is Growing Serious," *HRN*, May 8, 1942, 2.
16. "All Available Labor Must Be Utilized: Prospects of Transient Help Not Improving," *HRN*, July 24, 1942, 10.
17. "High Schools Open 6 Weeks Late: Leaders Adopt Plan to Help Fruitgrowers," *HRN*, Feb. 20, 1942, 9.
18. "Portland Will Send 1000 To Pick Apples: Special 20 Car Train To Be Here Sunday," *HRN*, Oct. 23, 1942, 1.
19. "Town Deserted; Business Folk Pick Pears," *HRN*, Sept. 18, 1942, 2.
20. "Apple Harvest Makes Progress," *HRN*, Oct. 1, 1943, 1.
21. "50,000 Needed For Harvesting," *HRN*, Aug. 18, 1944, 2 (quoting J.R. Beck, head of the OSC Extension Service).
22. Wayne D. Rasmussen, *A History of the Emergency Farm Labor Supply Program, 1943–1947* (Agriculture Monograph No. 13, U.S. Department of Agriculture, Bureau of Agricultural Economics, September 1951), 215.
23. Gamboa, 3.
24. Sadie Bennett, Farm Labor Assistant, "1944 Annual Farm Labor, Hood River County" (Hood River County Extension Service, 1944), Table 2.
25. Ibid., Table 3.
26. Ibid., 9.
27. "50,000 Needed For Harvesting," *HRN*, Aug. 18, 1944, 2.
28. "Shortage of Orchard Labor Still Acute," *HRN*, Oct. 2, 1942, 1, 8.
29. "Our Mexicans Are Homesick," *The Oregonian*, Sept. 29, 1943, 10.
30. "200 Mexicans Are Coming to Valley," *HRN*, June 4, 1943, 1.
31. See, for example, "200 Mexicans Are Coming to Valley," *HRN*, June 4, 1943, 1; "Mexicans May Be Sub-Contracted," *HRN* July 23, 1943, 9; and "Harvest Labor Scales Set," *HRN* Sept. 17, 1943, 5.
32. *HRN*, July 28, 1944, 4.

33. Ibid.
34. *HRN*, Aug. 6, 1943, p. 1.
35. *HRN*, July 28, 1944, 1.
36. Ibid., 12.
37. *HRN*, Aug. 14, 1944, 1.
38. Ibid.
39. "200 Mexicans Are Coming to Valley," *HRN*, June 4, 1943, 1.
40. For example, see "Racial Issues Found Urgent," *The Oregonian*, Jan. 29, 1945, 3.
41. "Valley Loses 10 Per Cent of Its Population," *HRN*, May 22, 1942, 4; and Tamura, 74.
42. "Grange Backs Legion's Stand," *HRN*, Feb. 19, 1943, 1.
43. *HRN*, June 18, 1943, 1, 2, 8.
44. Tamura, 226.
45. *HRN*, Nov. 12, 1943, 1.
46. Ibid., 5.
47. "Our Mexicans Are Homesick," *The Oregonian*, editorial, 10.
48. "Mexicans Are To Be Thanked," *HRN*, Oct. 8, 1943, 7.
49. "Viva Mexico!" *HRN*, June 18, 1943, 1.
50. "Migration of Mexicans Is Now at End," *HRN*, Sept. 24, 1943, 1.
51. "Webster Talks on Future of Valley Fruit," *HRN*, Mar. 24, 1944, 1, 2; see also "Farm Land Boom Is Still a Threat," *HRN*, Mar. 17, 1944, 5.
52. For example, see "Farm Income For '42 Breaks All Records," *HRN*, Aug. 13, 1943, 4; and "Urges Planning For Post-War Fruit Export," *HRN*, May 4, 1944, 1.
53. For example, see "Farmers Are Now Repaying Loans," *HRN*, Sept. 10, 1943, 10; "Farm Bureau To Expand in County," *HRN*, Mar. 17, 1944, 1; and "WPB Says O.K. to Parkdale Cold Storage," *HRN*, Apr. 7, 1944, 1.

Mexican American and Dust Bowl Farmworkers in the Yakima Valley: A History of the Crewport Farm Labor Camp, 1940–1970

Mario Compean

Farmworkers have long been central to the agricultural economy of the Pacific Northwest. This is especially true of the Yakima Valley in Washington State that became one of the leading regions in agricultural production in the Nation by the 1930s.[1] Farm laborers of various ethnic groups, especially migrants, have made a substantial contribution toward meeting the labor demands in the region in the decades since 1900s. The Crewport Farm Labor Camp in the Yakima Valley mirrors this history of migrant workers of varying ethnicity doing their part, making significant contributions to meet the labor needs of agricultural production in the region.

Historical Overview: Migrants to the Pacific Northwest

The families who came to Crewport in the early 1940s initially assumed that the Camp was to be only a temporary place of residence. However, many of these families became permanent residents at the Camp, and a permanent resident community of Dust Bowl and Mexican American families developed during the 1940s.and 1950s. The story of why the destinies of these Mexican American and Dust Bowl families converged at the Crewport Farm Labor Camp is rooted in a movement of people in search of work and a better life under the impulse of the forces of agricultural expansion, social catastrophe, and war.

The movement of people to the farm economy of the Pacific Northwest began at the turn of the twentieth century.[2] It was a population movement set in motion by the expansion of agricultural production that came with the advance of irrigation.

In the decades prior to 1930 the pace of this movement was slow. In the 1930s, however, sugar beet production grew substantially as the Utah and Idaho Sugar Company carried on an aggressive expansion drive. Increased sugar beet production brought with it a parallel increase in the demand for farm labor that attracted many migratory workers to the region. Another social force that spurred the movement of migrant agricultural laborers to the Pacific Northwest was the droughts that brought the farm economy of the Plains states to a halt in the 1930s. The collapse of the agricultural economy in the drought states[3] displaced many farmers, and as their lands ceased to be productive, many were forced to migrate to the western states and the states of Idaho, Washington, and Oregon in order to escape the crisis and start their lives anew.[4] World War II was a third social force that brought farm laborers to the Pacific Northwest. The accelerated growth of the defense industries created a high demand for labor. Military service and migration of rural labor in search of high-paying jobs in the wartime industrial centers located primarily in cities such as Portland and Seattle drained the labor supply in the agricultural areas. In the Yakima Valley, for example, a crisis in the supply of farm labor developed in 1941 and again in 1942.[5] Yakima Valley farmers turned to imported Mexican contracted labor and to Mexican American migrant workers from the Southwest to resolve the crisis in labor supply. Expansion of sugar beet production, the ecological catastrophe in the Plains states, and the demands of the wartime economy accelerated the movement of migrants to the region during the 1930s and 1940s.

Several studies have documented the entry of migrant farm laborers into the Pacific Northwest since 1930. Richard Wakefield and Paul H. Landis, and Carl F. Reuss and Lloyd H. Fisher have examined the migration patterns of Dust Bowl migrants into several regions of Washington State, including the Yakima Valley, with a focus on their adjustment problems as new settlers in the State.[6] Carl F. Reuss, Paul H. Landis, and Richard Wakefield

examined the experiences and living conditions of these
farmworkers in the Hop industry in the Yakima Valley.[7] The study
of the history and migration patterns of Mexican and Mexican
American[8] farm laborers in the Pacific Northwest has only begun
to emerge recently and is a field with much promise to interested
historians. Erasmo Gamboa's seminal studies of Chicano and
Mexican farmworkers in the Yakima Valley examine the
experiences of these peoples in the context of the expanding
agricultural industry of the region.[9] However, Gamboa' work
primarily focuses on the World War II era braceros. More recently,
community studies have begun to document the entry and
settlement of Mexican and Mexican American agricultural
workers in the Columbia River Basin in Eastern Washington.
Gilberto Garcia examined the experience of these workers in
Othello, Wash., over a period of four decades, with a focus on the
emergence of a sense of community as many of the migrants
settled permanently in Adams County.[10] Jerry Garcia has authored
a similar study of Chicanos and Mexicanos in the town of Quincy
covering a period of forty-five years that examines the movement
of ethnic Mexicans beyond the Yakima Valley.[11] Jerry Garcia has
also done a pioneering study that began the important task of
documenting the experiences of Chicanas in Washington State.[12]
All of these studies have made an enormous contribution to the
literature on the history of migrant farmworkers in Washington
State and the development of Mexican communities in the Pacific
Northwest. These studies, however, examine neither the dynamics
of social relations among the farm laborers in the context of labor
camps nor the relations between farm laborers of different ethnic
backgrounds. This essay makes an important contribution to this
body of work by focusing on the social life and relations between
Dust Bowl and Mexican American migrant laborers in the context
of a labor camp, and by shedding light on the experiences of
women farmworkers in the Yakima Valley.

MARIO COMPEAN

A Home for Migrant Workers

The Crewport Farm Labor Camp was home to several hundred migrant farm labor families for almost three decades. During the first decade of its life the Camp made the transition from a migrant population to a community comprised of permanent residents from the drought states and Mexican American families from the Southwest. By the early 1950s, however, the Camp residents were mostly Mexican Americans from the Southwest. The story of these people, as told by those who lived there and by others who knew and associated with them, is the story of working-class families engaged in a constant struggle for survival. It is the story of parents and their children, of poverty-bound families who wanted the best life they could have. It is the story of ordinary people who worked hard and made many sacrifices to achieve their life goals. This essay is a first step in reconstructing the history of Crewport based on the recollections of the narrators interviewed for this project who generously shared their life stories with the interviewers.[13]

Crewport existed officially as a migrant farm labor camp from May 1941 to December 1968.[14] It originated in the severe drought and strong winds that hit the Plains states during the 1930s, whipping up dust storms from 1933 until the end of the decade. When the storms subsided, the farmlands and the agricultural economy of the affected states were devastated as production dried up. The loss of income and inability to pay taxes and retire debt forced many families to migrate to the western and Pacific states to start their lives anew. The states affected by drought and the storms are known in history as the Dust Bowl, and the farm families that fled them came to be called Dust Bowl migrants or drought refugees.[15]

The Crewport Farm Labor Camp opened its doors for the first time in May 1941. The Farm Security Administration (FSA) built the camp to house displaced farmers and other uprooted Dust Bowl refugees. Most of these "drought refugees" hailed from the southern Plains states while those from the northern plains settled mostly in Western Washington. The Camp was first called the "Granger Farm Workers Camp" because of its proximity to the City of Granger, Wash. Initially dust bowl families were the only ones housed at the camp. Soon thereafter Mexican American migrant farmworkers from the Southwest, mostly from Texas, also called Crewport their home. They were recruited to the Yakima Valley in the early 1940s in response to the farm labor shortage caused by World War II. They joined the dust bowl families at Crewport and formed a community of permanent resident farmworkers of mixed ethnicity. Camp population continued to change through the 1950s. Eventually most of the drought refugees relocated elsewhere in the Yakima Valley or in other regions of the State. By the late 1950s Mexican American families comprised most of the Crewport population. Many of the Mexican Americans settled in nearby Granger after authorities announced the Camp's closing late in 1968 (see Fig. 5.1).

*Fig. 5.1. A view of the Crewport Labor Camp, circa 1943
(photo courtesy of William and Helen Cochran).*

A Community of Farmworkers

One interesting dimension in the history of Crewport is that the camp developed as a community of permanent resident farmworkers. The camp served as a temporary home for migrants following the seasonal flow of farm work but it also evolved as a home for farmworkers who resided there the year round. This development of Crewport as a community of permanent resident farmworkers is partially explained by the original purpose of the camps when the FSA built them with the goal of resettling displaced dust bowl farmers. The FSA staffed and managed the camps.[16] Most dust bowl migrants who arrived at Crewport in the 1940s understood that the camp was to be their residence until they could reestablish themselves in farming. To help them achieve this goal FSA staff provided a myriad of services and encouraged residents to engage in and organize activities that reinforced notions of responsibility, self-help, and self-sufficiency. This can best be seen by looking briefly at the services and activities for residents at Crewport.

Camp residents published a weekly newsletter, the *Leader*, for about two years starting with the first issue in October 1941, scarcely four months after the Camp opened for the first time in May of that year.[17] This first issue of the newsletter, as did subsequent issues, reported on services available to the residents and activities organized or sponsored jointly by residents and staff for the benefit of the residents. A myriad of programs and services were available to Crewport residents. These included a nursery and school for young children, a hot lunch program for children under age seventeen, a library and a clinic, a cooperative grocery store, a community hall for activities, and a job placement service. Several clubs and committees that attempted to meet the varied needs of the residents were also organized. These included the Recreation Committee, the Women's Club, the Sewing Club, a Craft and a Cooking Club, and an "Indian Club." In addition, a Camp Council served as an auxiliary to the Camp manager and staff in the management and governance of the Camp.

Crewport residents, under the tutelage of the Camp staff, also engaged in many activities that served to instill and reinforce a notion of shared status and identity, a community bound by common interests. For example, people were reminded to keep the Camp clean and benefit all residents by properly disposing of waste. But it was the grocery cooperative store that was apparently the Camp staff's preferred vehicle for the resocialization of the residents. Camp staff continually emphasized the benefits of the concept "cooperation." This ideology stressed harmonious relations and mutual support between the residents. Howard Wilson, the Camp manager, continually invoked the ideology of cooperation as exemplified by his statement in the first issue of the *Leader*, as a means ideally suited to further the cause of economic advancement for the Camp residents and others. His "Manager's Letter" included a concise, explicit statement of the ideology of cooperation, "It is high time that farmworkers learned that alone they are helpless. The farmers are learning it. All Granger's and Farmer's Union members are going in for ALL-OUT cooperation. We who live from the soil, whether it is as farmers or farm laborers, are finally beginning to realize that, as individuals, we are too small, too insignificant to compete with efficiently organized industrial farms and processing plants. We are beginning to realize that there is no basic difference between the farm laborer and the farmers." A clear indication that political socialization of the residents was a key goal of Camp staff was the statement by Camp Manager Howard Wilson, "There's no need for bloody revolution to change this condition. There's no need for any sort of revolution. There is need only that farmers and the farm laborers assert the rights they now have as citizens of this great country, that they ORGANIZE AND COOPERATE, so that they may do business in the same efficient manner that the big industrial farmers and processors do. THEY CAN'T DO IT AS INDIVIDUALS BUT THEY CAN DO IT BY COOPERATION." Together the programs, services, and activities with the ideology of cooperation served to reinforce notions of a shared identity and community among Crewport farmworkers.[18]

Mexican Americans were recruited to the Yakima Valley soon after the Crewport Camp opened in 1941 to meet the labor demands created by U. S. involvement in World War II.[19] Some of these families "settled out" of the migrant stream and also made Crewport their permanent residence, creating an ethnic mix of white dust bowl and Mexican American migrants who lived side by side and interacted with each other. At least one Mexican American family lived at the Camp in 1941. According to the first issue of the *Leader*, the Camp's newsletter, has a person by the name of Lupe Martinez among the more than seventy names appearing on the Grocery Cooperative membership list.[20] Apparently there was an increase of Mexican Americans among the residents at Crewport by the following year because the Sept. 4, 1942, edition of the *Leader* saw the need to publish a Spanish version of Camp Manager Howard Wilson's "Manager's Letter" translated by a Mexican American women named Elvira Flores. Wilson emphasized the themes of cleanliness and hygiene, and informed Mexican Americans that rules governed the residents' conduct and daily activities at the Camp. He exhorted the residents to do their part in helping to keep the "community" (the Camp) clean and orderly. Interestingly, Wilson emphasized that all Camp residents had equal rights regardless of "color" or nationality, and that racial bias and prejudice were not acceptable because that was "what Hitler was trying to do." He further encouraged Mexican American residents to report to him if they encountered prejudicial treatment from other residents, and to participate in Camp activities and programs. He invited them to visit his office anytime they had questions regarding Camp life and services.

Mexican American farmworkers at Crewport engaged in other activities that complemented the efforts of Wilson and other Camp staff to promote a sense of community and a shared identity among the residents. Mexican Americans promoted a shared ethnic identity by practicing cultural customs and traditions that they brought with them from the Southwest. The daughters of Celedonia Robles, for example, recalled that when one of their siblings decided to get married the prospective groom's parents paid a formal visit to their mother to ask for her hand in marriage, as was the custom in Mexican culture.[21] Mexican Americans also interacted with the dust bowl migrants in activities that promoted friendly relations between the two groups. Celedonia Robles frequently visited with neighbors who were always willing to lend her a helping hand in making ends meet to support her nine children. Both Mexican Americans and white residents also interacted with one another in sports activities. Leroy Blankenship and Pete Dodd recalled that each group had a baseball team that played against each other even though the Mexican Americans knew little English.[22] These activities apparently promoted relations between Mexican American and dust bowl residents at the Camp that were free of racial or ethnic conflict and promoted the sense that Crewport was one community of farmworkers regardless of ethnicity (see Fig. 5.2).

The residential ethnic mix at Crewport is of significant import to historians interested in the study of race relations. The story told by the Crewport narrators reveals that relations between white and Mexican American residents were quite friendly and harmonious. That racial conflict among residents in Crewport was not present stands in stark contrast to the experience of

Fig. 5.2. Mary Esparza, Joan Sweezea's best friend, circa 1951; the Esparza and Sweezea families resided at Crewport in the latter 1940s and 1950s (photo courtesy of Clete Sweezea).

Mexican American and Mexican farmworkers in the Southwest. This is especially so when we recall that Crewport emerged at the end of the "tragic decade" for the thousands of Mexicans repatriated to Mexico during the era the Great Depression, when government policy and racial hostility converged to stamp U. S. history with a black social stain analogous to the internment of Japanese Americans during World War II. Instead of hostility toward one another, white and Mexican American migrants coexisted at Crewport in a friendly environment and created substantial social bonds with one another. White narrators recalled their perceptions back then of their Mexican American neighbors in very positive terms.[23] Mexican American residents, they said, were a friendly people who seemed to enjoy life despite their poverty. In turn Mexican American narrators spoke of friendship bonds they established with the white migrants,[24] and of help they received from them. Narrator Celedonia "Sally" Robles moved to Crewport from the Rio Grande Valley in Texas with her nine young children because her husband died and her mother already lived there. Robles spoke fondly and appreciatively of whites, both Crewport residents and members of the larger community, who helped her to make ends meet as sole support of her nine children.[25] Frank Gonzales also has fond memories of social life at the Crewport Camp. Apparently race and ethnicity did not erect rigid social boundaries between the residents. He related that his father maintained friendly relations with some of their white neighbors at Crewport, "We use to live right next to Helen and Bill Cochran. They were on one side of us, and there used to be another man who lived on the other side, Mr. Gray. That's what I remember, Mr. Gray. We use to know the mail lady before Helen; her name was Ms. Autry... Dad likes going there [annual Crewport Reunion] cause he knows Pete Dodd. He likes talking to Pete Dodd, Orvella and Rose..."[26]

How is this absence of ethnic conflict among Crewport residents explained? A possible answer emerges when we pose the question: how did the host community relate to the Crewport residents, both white and Mexican American? According to the narrators the host community did not think highly of Crewport residents. Narrators recalled incidents of racial and class discrimination that had a powerful impact on their lives. Narrator Leroy Blankenship related that his middle school music teacher "kicked" him off the school band because he could not read music even though he was an accomplished musician. He played the piano and several other instruments. Pete Dodd also recalled that his brother was stopped by the police because his car had Oklahoma license plates. The officer dragged him out of the car and cursed at him as he took him to jail. This and other incidents at school suggested to Dodd and Blankenship that Crewport residents were suspect because they were poor. Dodd recalled the prejudice Crewport residents encountered:

"It was 'Crewport Trash' that was us you know. And if you'd go to town, I mean if you went to town, you went to town very carefully and... Went to the movies, carefully walked in, sat down and sat there, got up [and] you left." Dodd reinforced his point further, "Uh-huh! A lot of prejudice you know. And... if you was [sic] in school and something was stolen, we always stole it you know..." Blankenship agreed with Dodd, "Well, it's amazing!... being called "Crewport trash" was very depressing to me as a child, because in my little old ten, twelve-year-old mind... I wondered; I'm no different from anybody else. Why would they point the finger at me... and call me that?"[27] Mexican American narrator Tomas Escobar was a teenager when his family resided at Crewport.[28] He recalled that while holding class one of his high school teachers made several disparaging "racist" comments about Mexicans. In reaction, Escobar got up from his desk, scuffled with the teacher, and "threw him out the window." Police arrested Escobar and charged him with criminal assault but the charge was dropped after several students, Mexican American and white, testified that the teacher had made "racist" comments several times prior to the incident with Escobar.

The social portrait that emerges from the narrators' life stories is that Crewport residents were seen as social outcasts. Host community members who had routine contact with Crewport residents confirmed the narrators' perception of racial and class discrimination. D. A. "Mickey" Leonardo and wife Martha were schoolteachers who owned and operated a photo studio and a farm. In these capacities they interacted routinely with camp residents. Crewport children were in their classes, and some of their parents were their business customers. As farmers the Leonardos also routinely hired Crewport residents to work their farm. Their son, Douglas Leonardo, remarked that some members in the host community did not appreciate the Crewport laborers' contribution to the local economy. "As farmers started becoming more self-sufficient in the area, they started looking down their noses at people at Crewport. I mean if you lived in Crewport and you wanted to go out with this farmer's daughter, he wouldn't want that to happen at all. Attitudes changed quite a bit, and it wasn't really nice to see around here." He noted that the labor of Crewport farmworkers made the Yakima Valley economy viable: "Crewport in a lot of ways made this valley economically viable during the late forties and fifties for as long as it was there. The valley was really pretty poor, really poor, until it started becoming self-sufficient, before some of the bigger farms started becoming self-sufficient. But they laid it on the back of Crewport. Crewport allowed these farms to grow around here... in the Yakima Valley."[29]

These narratives suggest that Crewport residents were aware, if only at the most superficial level, that the host community saw them as social outcasts. This awareness possibly helped forge a common identity, a nascent class consciousness perhaps, among the white and Mexican American Crewport residents. Narrator Leroy Blankenship suggested this when he commented "Well, I really like what Pete said a while ago... Crewport was just one big family... there was no status... big I's and little U's. We all stood on one platform, and on the same level together..."[30] (see Fig. 5.3).

Las Mujeres de Crewport

Another very interesting dimension of the Crewport Labor Camp history is the role of women residents. The "traditional" women's role we see in the history of patriarchy was apparently very much a part of the Crewport women's experience. Crewport women took care of the house; they cooked, did the laundry, and raised kids. Leroy Blankenship recalled fondly that his mother used to spread a tablecloth on the ground in the fields at lunch time on which to place the meal she had prepared for her children and husband.

Fig. 5.3. *Ira Sweezea picking fruit, circa 1947 (photo courtesy Clete Sweezea).*

Mexican American narrators Julia Saenz and Celedonia "Sally" Robles also experienced this "women's role" firsthand. In her narrative Saenz recalls that she cooked, did the laundry, and kept house for her brothers, father, and her invalid mother.[31] Sally Robles, a widow with nine children, was the sole provider for her family and also performed all the tasks of "women's" work.[32]

Seen through the feminist lens of women's historians a second social tier emerges in the experience of Crewport women. This is clearly visible in the narratives of Celedonia Robles, Julia Saenz, and Leroy Blankenship. Leroy Blankenship's narrative reveals that his mother worked the "double day." His mother performed all the tasks expected of women and she also worked in the fields.[33] This experience comes to full life in the Saenz and Robles narratives.

As stated previously, Robles was a young widow with nine children when she relocated to Crewport from Texas, so as head of her household she had to manage the dual role of raising her children and working to support them.[34] Julia Saenz is the epitome of the woman trapped in patriarchy. In her narrative she revealed that, as the oldest daughter in her family, she had to assume household responsibilities when her mother was paralyzed by a stroke. She had to do all the house chores and provide for her brothers and father in addition to working a full day in the fields with them six days a week. On Sundays Saenz had to do the laundry and prepare for the new work week. Consequently she had no social life as her brothers did; and did not marry until middle age. "Well like I told you, I never had friends that we'd sit and talk or whatever. No, everyday to work with my father and my brothers, get home and take care of my mother and do at home what ever had to be done and that was it. The only day we didn't work was Sunday; and that was to wash clothes for all week and get ready for Monday. And that was it"[35] (see Fig. 5.4). Other evidence appears to confirm that traditional culture pervaded the lives Mexican American families at Crewport. Angela Grajeda expressed concerned about the results of her work as a farmworker advocate in the Yakima Valley: "We did a survey, I think it was through Ellensburg [Central Washington University], in which we visited the families door to door in Sunnyside, Toppenish, Wapato, and Crewport and talked to both the husband and wife. We asked them what expectations they had for their daughters and sons. They responded that they hoped their daughters settled in a professional career like teacher aide and marry

Fig. 5.4. *Julia Saenz at her home in Zillah, Wash., April 2000 (photo courtesy Crewport History Project).*

166

a good man, and also hoped for the best for the son, a master mechanic [perhaps]." This suggested to Grajeda that the best expectations that parents had for their daughters was that they marry "a good man." The portrait that emerges from these narratives is that Chicanas like Saenz, Robles, and Grajeda were strong women who made the best of their lives despite the social boundaries imposed on them that emanated from traditional Mexican cultural values.[36]

A Community No More

The Crewport Farm Labor Camp entered a period of physical deterioration in the mid-1950s that culminated with the closing of the camp by 1970. Narrators note that some of the itinerant farm laborers that came from Texas during that time had large trucks. These migrants began taking beds and other furnishings from cabins with them when they left, chasing the seasonal flow of the crop harvest in the Pacific Northwest. Apparently others also intentionally damaged some of the cabins. By the mid-1960s the condition of the cabins and the apartments (barracks) had gone from bad to worse, just as the farmworker unionization movement was gaining momentum and calling attention to the plight of farmworkers. Farmworker advocates in the Yakima Valley focused their efforts on substandard housing, working conditions, and healthcare issues in the region, pressuring local and state authorities to address the problem. Angela Grajeda recalled conditions at Crewport when she became a farmworker advocate at age seventeen in the mid-1960s: "...but in those days the camp was pretty run down; the streets were bad and [the place looked] very abandoned. The places needed a lot of work, but some of the people still lived there in their own homes. They paid their rent and tried to better themselves."[37] As a result the Wash. State Health Board issued a revised strict housing code that required costly upgrades. Consequently Yakima County, which assumed ownership and operation of the Crewport camp in latter half of the

1940s, ordered its closure because of the high cost of upgrades. This decision played right into the designs of organized farmer alliances that had continually criticized the FSA operation of the farm labor camps because they considered them to breeding grounds for "Communist" labor organizers.

Ironically, the efforts of farmworker advocates in the Yakima Valley had the unintended consequence of helping organized farmer groups achieve their long-sought goal in the case of the Crewport camp closure.[38] The closing of the camp signaled its end as a community of dust bowl and Mexican American farmworkers in addition to ending the era of government operated labor camps in Wash. State. A new community, however, has emerged since then. It is a vibrant community of Mexican Americans and Mexican immigrants, mostly the latter, who have purchased and renovated the old cabins and homes and now call Crewport home. Some of the Mexican Americans are families who resided there when it was a labor camp (see Fig. 5.5).

Fig. 5.5. Josefa and Domingo Sanchez at their home at Crewport, August 2000 (photo courtesy Crewport History Project).

Endnotes

1. Erasmo Gamboa, "A History of the Chicano People and the Development of Agriculture in the Yakima Valley, Wash.," M.A. Thesis, University of Wash., 1973.
2. This historical overview of the movement of farm laborers to the Pacific Northwest and to the Yakima Valley draws on Gamboa's work and on recent oral histories in other regions of Wash. State. See Gilberto Garcia, "Mexicanos in Othello, Wash.: The Excluded Chapter in the History of Adams County," unpublished manuscript in author's collection; and Jerry Garcia, "The History of a Chicano/Mexicano Community in the Pacific Northwest: Quincy Washington 1948–1993," M.A. Thesis, Eastern Washington University, 1993. Also useful were several of the studies done by the Agricultural Experiment Station at the State College of Washington (now Washington State University) in the latter 1930s and early 1940s; for example, see Carl F. Reuss and Lloyd H. Fisher, *The Adjustment of New Settlers In Yakima Valley, Washington* (Pullman: State College of Washington Agricultural Experiment Station Bulletin No. 397, Rural Sociology Series in Population No. 6, Feb.1941).
3. The Federal Relief Administration designated fifteen states in this category: Colorado, the Dakotas, Montana, Minnesota, Missouri, Nebraska, Kansas, Texas, New Mexico, Wyoming, Oklahoma, Iowa, Arkansas, and Wisconsin, but only certain counties in the latter two states. Richard Wakefield and Paul H. Landis, *The Drought Farmer Adjusts to the West* (Pullman: State College of Washington Agricultural Experiment Station Bulletin No. 378, Rural Sociology Series in Population No. 4, July 1939), 6.
4. For an account of the impact of the dust storms see Donald Worster, *Dust Bowl: the Southern Plains in the 1930s.* New York: Oxford University Press 1979.
5. Erasmo Gamboa, "Mexican Migration into Washington State A History, 1940–1950," *Pacific Northwest Quarterly* 72, no. 3 (July 1981): 122–23.
6. Wakefield and Landis, *The Drought Farmer Adjusts to the West*; and Reuss and Fisher, *The Adjustment of New Settlers In Yakima Valley*.
7. Carl F. Reuss, Paul H. Landis, and Richard Wakefield, *Migratory Farm labor and the Hop Industry on the Pacific Coast with Special Application to Problems of the Yakima Valley*, Washington (Pullman: State College of Washington Agricultural Experiment Station Bulletin No. 363, Rural Sociology Series in Farm Labor No. 3, August 1938).
8. In this essay I use Mexican and Mexicanos to refer to Mexican immigrants and contract workers (braceros) and Mexican American, Chicanos, and Chicanas to refer to people of Mexican descent from the Southwest.

9. Erasmo Gamboa, *Mexican Labor and World War II: Braceros in the Pacific Northwest, 1942–1947* (Austin: University of Texas Press, 1990); Gamboa, M.A. Thesis; and Gamboa, "Mexican Migration into Washington State: A History, 1940–1950."

10. Gilberto Garcia, "Organizational Activity and Political Empowerment: Chicano Politics in the Pacific Northwest," in *The Chicano Experience in the Pacific Northwest*, 2nd ed.,ed. Carlos Maldonado and Gilberto Garcia (Dubuque, IA: Kendall/Hunt Publishing Company, 2001); "Mexican Communities in the State of Washington: A Case Study of Othello, Washington," in *The Illusion of Borders: The National Presence of Mexicanos in the Pacific Northwest*, ed. Gilberto Garcia and Jerry Garcia (Dubuque, IA: Kendall/Hunt Publishing Company, 2002).

11. Jerry Garcia, "Mexican Migration, Labor, and Community Formation: A Case Study of Quincy, Washington, 1943–1980," in *The Illusion of Borders: The National Presence of Mexicanos in the United States*, ed. Gilberto Garcia and Jerry Garcia (Dubuque, IA: Kendall/Hunt Publishing Company, 2002); Garcia, M.A. Thesis.

12. Jerry Garcia, "A Chicana in Northern Aztlan: An Oral History of Dora Sanchez Trevino," *Frontiers* 19, no. 2 (1998).

13. The interviews were conducted in 2000 and 2001 by the faculty, staff and students of the Crewport History Project, a joint project of the Chicana/o Studies Program and the Partnership for Rural Improvement at Yakima Valley Community College. Interview tape recordings are deposited at The Central Washington University Library. The Crewport History Project received funding support from several sources including the Center for Columbia River History with a grant from the U.S. Department of Education and the Kellogg Foundation Food System Professional Education Program at Washington State University. Dr. Laurie Mercier, Associate Professor of History, Washington State University, also provided valuable input to the Project. The author served as Research Coordinator for the Crewport History Project.

14. The official announcement was issued in late 1968 but the process of phasing out the residents was completed in the early 1970s.

15. For a discussion of the reasons that dust bowl migrants came to Washington state see Richard Wakefield and Paul H. Landis, *The Drought Farmer Adjusts to the West* (Pullman: State College of Washington Agricultural Experiment Station Bulletin No. 378, Rural Sociology Series in Population No. 4, in cooperation with the Division of Social Research of the Works Progress Administration, July 1939), 22–29.

16. See Joe J. King, "Sheltering Migratory Agricultural Laborers in the Pacific Northwest," *Sociology and Social Research* 26, no. 3 (January/February 1942).

17. The first issue of the newsletter, Vol. 1 No.1, Oct. 25, 1941, was published without a name and announced a contest for readers to name it. Vol. 1, No. 2, Nov. 2, 1941, carried the name *The Granger Leader* on its mast; subsequent issues shortened the name to *Leader*. The Crewport History Project secured photocopies of several issues of the newsletter from microfilm archival copies at the University of California at Berkeley covering the period October 1941 to September 1942.

18. The newsletter also actively promoted the ideology of cooperation by prominently inserting slogans in strategic places in each issue. See Vol. No. 1, Oct. 25, 1941.

19. Gamboa reports that Mexican Americans were recruited to the Yakima Valley in the 1940s because farmers saw them as a more cost-effective resource than Mexican contract workers, See Gamboa, "Mexican Migration into Washington State: A History, 1940–1950," 127.

20. The *Leader*, Vol. 2, No. 13, Sept. 4, 1942. It is not clear if this person was a woman or a man since the name Lupe is short for Guadalupe which is a common first name for both male and female Mexicans and Mexican Americans.

21. This practice of the use of cultural traditions and customs by Mexican Americans to promote a sense of community and ethnic identity in the Pacific Northwest is well known in the literature. See the Mexican Americans at the Columbia River Basin Ethnic History Archive at http://www.vancouver.wsu.edu/crbeha/browse.htm and the works by Jerry Garcia in note 2 and Gamboa in note 3 above. For the Robles account cited here see Celedonia "Sally" Robles, Interview, Crewport History Project, April 15, 2000.

22. Leroy Blankenship, Pete Dodd, and Rose Parker, Interview, by Dan Groves and Susan Bolton, Crewport History Project, Granger, WA, Feb. 25, 2000.

23. D.A. Mickey Leonardo, Martha Leonardo, and Douglas Leonardo, Interview, by Dan Groves, Pedro Cordova, Wade Decoteau, and Edgar Rosas, Granger, WA, May 30, 2000.

24. Frank Gonzales, Interview, by Dan Groves and Wade Decoteau, Crewport History Project, Ellensburg, WA, May 17, 2000.

25. Celedonia "Sally" Robles, Interview, by Mario Compean, Susan Bolton, Tomas Escobar and Angela Ornelas, Crewport History Project, Granger, WA, April 15, 2000.

26. Frank Gonzales, Interview, by Dan Groves and Wade Decoteau, Crewport History Project, Ellensburg, WA, May 17, 2000.

27. Leroy Blankenship, Pete Dodd, and Rose Parker, Interview, by Dan Groves and Susan Bolton, Crewport History Project, Granger, WA, Feb. 25, 2000.

28. Tomas Escobar, personal communication to the author, Yakima, WA, June 20, 2004.

29. D.A. Mickey Leonardo, Martha Leonardo, and Douglas Leonardo, Interview, by Dan Groves, Pedro Cordova, Wade Decoteau, and Edgar Rosas, Granger, WA, May 30, 2000.
30. Leroy Blankenship, Pete Dodd, and Rose Parker, Interview, by Dan Groves and Susan Bolton, Crewport History Project, Granger, WA Feb. 25, 2000.
31. Julia Saenz, , Interview, by Mario Compean, Susan Bolton, Tomas Escobar and Angela Ornelas, Crewport History Project, Zillah, WA, April 14, 2000.
32. Celedonia "Sally" Robles, Interview, by Mario Compean, Susan Bolton, Tomas Escobar and Angela Ornelas, Crewport History Project, Granger, WA, April 15, 2000.
33. Leroy Blankenship, Pete Dodd, and Rose Parker, Interview, by Dan Groves and Susan Bolton, Crewport History Project, Granger, WA Feb. 25, 2000.
34. Celedonia "Sally" Robles, Robles, Interview, by Mario Compean, Susan Bolton, Tomas Escobar and Angela Ornelas, Crewport History Project, Granger, WA, April 15, 2000.
35. Julia Saenz, Interview, by Mario Compean, Susan Bolton, Tomas Escobar and Angela Ornelas, Crewport History Project, Zillah, WA, April 14, 2000.
36. Angela Grajeda, Interview, by Dan Groves, Noemi Chapala, and Edgar Rosas, Crewport History Project, Sunnyside, WA, April 14, 2000. Grajeda at age 17 was already going against traditional Mexican cultural values. She was a student at Yakima Valley Community College engaged as activist in the incipient farmworker Movement in the Yakima Valley. Grajeda and her family did not reside at Crewport; rather she visited the Camp regularly in her work as a farmworker advocate.
37. Ibid.
38. In October of 1942, scarcely a year after Crewport was opened, the Camp newsletter, *The Leader*, reported that the National Farm Bureau had "launched an all-out war on the FSA" and that the bureau "had opened fire with all its guns in an effort to wipe the FSA" and with it presumably also eliminate the FSA farm labor camps. See *The Leader* Vol. 1, No. 15, 1942.

El Sarape Mural of Toppenish:
Unfolding the Yakima Valley's Bracero Legacy

Margaret A. Villanueva

Cuando me enfadé de 'El Traque' me volvió a invitar aquel
A la pizca del tomate y a desahijar betabel.

Allí gané indulgencias caminando de rodillas,
Haciéndoles reverencias tres o cuatro y cinco millas.

¡¡Ah, que trabajo tan mal pagado
por andar arrodillado!

—Bracero Corrido Song, in Herrera-Sobek, 1979

The immigration of Mexican workers and families into the United States since 1848 has been memorialized in heroic ballads (*corridos*) such as the one about the *betabeleros* who worked in beet fields across the West recorded by María Herrera-Sobek, above,[1] as well as on film, stage, canvas, and in fiction and nonfiction literature. Perhaps most strikingly, the immigration narrative comes to life in the Chicano/a murals painted on public walls across the American Southwest and border regions.[2] However, the emergence of murals commemorating the journey and settlement of Mexicans into the Northwest and Midwest has been given little attention in Chicana/o and Latino/a Studies due to a lack of attention to the dynamics of community-building beyond the Southwestern region.[3]

Immigration from Mexico and Texas into the Pacific Northwest began with the extension of national railroads into the region in the late 1800s, as Mexicans were gradually drawn into employment in salmon canneries, railroad construction, sugar beet and potato fields, and fruit orchards.[4] On public walls Northwestern artists are beginning to tell the story of this little-

173

known regional history of work, settlement, community-building, and labor-organizing.

The purpose of this chapter is to provide an analysis of an important local mural completed in a small town in the Yakima Valley in 2001. It explores connections between the realization of the *El Sarape* mural in Toppenish, Wash., the social and demographic context of the story it tells, and how the mural fits into the tradition of Chicano/a public art that emerged from the social movements of the 1960s and 70s.

Following the release of 2000 Census, the demographic growth of the Latino populations in the Northwest and Midwest suddenly attracted the attention of major newspapers and the national media, even though Latinos had long known that their national presence was a well-kept secret. Rapidly growing Mexican communities remained "hidden in plain sight," as artist Daniel DeSiga observes.[5] However, in the closing years of the twentieth century and the opening of the twenty-first, Latino communities in these two regions were organizing around mural projects that would add their stories to the walls of towns such as Toppenish and Sterling, Illinois.

The small towns of Toppenish and Sterling both had official "Mural Societies" in charge of initiating and approving citywide mural projects about local history, but the previous fifty-nine murals of Toppenish, and nine murals of Sterling gave no attention to the settlement and work of Mexicans who had been residents since the early twentieth century. Although official "Mural Societies" did not initially promote the painting of Latino/ Mexicano murals in either town, community pressure and the participation of local Latino and Latinas eventually led to a coordinated effort to have the large and colorful *El Serape* and *Adelante* murals painted on the public walls of Toppenish and Sterling, respectively.

In regard to the social context for Southwestern Latino murals, anthropologist Carlos Vélez-Ibáñez has noted that "of all the explosive expressions of U.S. Mexican struggles in the nineteenth and twentieth centuries, the mural movement is the most profoundly cultural in its organizational mutuality and *confianza*, its group mobilization and action, and the participation of diverse elements of the U.S. Mexican and other communities."[6] This struggle has quietly moved from the Southwest into other regions where Mexicanos and other Latinos are now "claiming a space on the walls."

When artist Daniel DeSiga[7] completed the 100' x 15' mural *El Sarape*, in August 2001, the Mexican community celebrated with a barbeque, block dance, and live music sponsored by the Farm Workers' Clinic (see Fig. 6.1). For some time, members of the Mexican community of Toppenish had been urging the local Mural Society to recognize their presence through a historical mural.[8] After the Mural Society moved the historical timeline for murals forward into the 1920s through the 1950s, *El Sarape* became the sixtieth Toppenish mural, and the first to depict the arrival of bracero workers from Mexico between 1942–1947.

Fig. 6.1. Section of El Sarape mural depicting Braceros in Toppenish, Wash. (photo courtesy of Daniel DeSiga).

Dr. Erasmo Gamboa, historian of the Bracero Program in the Pacific Northwest, explained the purpose of the mural and its historical roots in a dedication on July 23, 2001:

> This mural pays tribute to the generation of young Mexican Laborers known as Braceros that began to arrive in Toppenish in October of 1942. At the time, the fury of World War II consumed the energies of this nation and Mexico came to our aid. We asked these men to leave their homes in Mexico and journey to the Yakima Valley to help harvest the food necessary to feed the country and to defeat our adversaries in Europe and Asia. By the end of the war, thousands of Braceros had made an important contribution by "saving the crops" in Toppenish and surrounding Yakima communities. This artistic work honors the wartime Braceros and conveys the recognition they justly deserve. It is dedicated with the hope of fostering a new era of harmony among all the residents of Toppenish and between Mexico and the United States.[9]

Whether or not harmony is being achieved, people of Mexican descent now constitute the overwhelming majority population in Toppenish; and the growing numbers of Latino/a businesses, organizations, officials, and politicians in the town attest to a continual community-building process that began before World War II and promises to transform many such rural communities in the coming decades. The bracero mural points to a significant historical marker in the growth of the Latino community: the arrival of thousands of Mexican workers to the Northwest during a time of crisis.[10] However, it is unlikely that the *El Sarape* mural would have been painted if arrival in Toppenish through the Bracero Program was a singular event rather than part of an ongoing history of immigration, migration, and settlement.

Mexicans had come to the Northwest before the 1940s, and their presence grew in the closing decades of the century.

For Chicano, Mexican, and other Latino communities in the United States, creating public murals has been an integral part of community-building processes: moving beyond the marginal spaces of labor camps, *colonias* and *barrios,* establishing social networks and economic niches, appropriating social space, and forging alliances toward collective goals.[11] As historian Vicki Ruiz notes in her work on Mexican women's grassroots activism, "Claiming public space can involve fragile alliances and enduring symbols, rooted in material realities and ethereal visions."[12]

After 1947, Central Washington's agricultural workforce remained largely Mexican and Mexican American, with the continued movement and settlement of people from Texas, the Southwest, and Mexico. This ongoing process of migration and immigration, historian David Gutiérrez suggests, has "transform(ed) the cultural landscape, social life and practices, and use of public space" in many regions of the country because dating from the first large influx of Mexicans into the United States after 1900, one of the central animating themes of the Mexican diaspora has been the constant augmentation and cultural reinvigoration of existing Mexican American communities in the border states by Mexican immigrants, or the creation of new ethnic enclaves in far-flung pockets of settlement such as Washington's Yakima Valley in the Northwest or the *colonias* established in Midwestern industrial cities such as Chicago, Gary, and Detroit.[13]

Beyond their demographic presence, Mexicans and other Latinos find various channels to claim a place on the map and to create sense of belonging. Staking a claim for "identity, space, and rights," Latino newcomers and settled residents work toward building community.

Anthropologist Renato Rosaldo and his colleagues have been fine-tuning research and theory on the relationship between Latino culture and communities since 1987, and he recently coined the key term "cultural citizenship" to summarize the process whereby,

> groups form, define themselves, define their membership, claim rights, and develop a vision of the type of society that they want to live in. It includes how excluded groups interpret their histories, define themselves, forge their own symbols and political rhetoric, and claim rights. It includes how groups retain past cultural forms while creating completely new ones…Thus, cultural citizenship for Latinos involves the creation of a distinct Latino sensibility, a social and political discourse, and a Latino aesthetic, all of which flow out of the unique reality of being Latino in the United States and the desire to express that uniqueness.[14]

The Chicano/Latino mural movement has been a vibrant part of such efforts to claim social and political space and to develop cultural identities, Vélez-Ibáñez explains, because "murals served as a notice—a type of documentation of cultural persistence and continuance," for these public art works are a "singular means of expression through the communal participation of different voices."[15] Coming out of the social environment of a farm working family in Washington State, and the cultural environment of the Chicano arts movement of the greater Southwest and Northwest, the painter of El Sarape, Daniel DeSiga, has created a mural that provides a historical sense of belonging that can help move community-building efforts forward.[16]

In analyzing how Chicano/Latino mural art differs from its Latin American predecessors, Vélez-Ibáñez observes a number of characteristics shared by the El Sarape mural:

- Being located in space vacated due to historical elimination...or *filling "blank spaces" unfilled by others* (my emphasis)
- Incorporating various cultural populations into the mural statement, and changing as new populations become demographically or politically important
- Changing themes and symbols as larger social and economic issues emerge

El Sarape fills the space on a wall that is not in the center of the town, had not been selected for the prior sixty murals, and incorporates both Latinos and Anglos. Reading the mural from left to right, the farmworkers' tents recall early photographs of tent housing for the Yakama Indians when they were a major farm labor force in the 1800s (as depicted in Hops Museum photographs and earlier downtown murals). *El Sarape* also incorporates themes and symbols that go beyond the World War II Bracero Program period, such as the change from the use of a short to the less onerous long hoe for farmworkers achieved by United Farm Workers (UFW) organizing in Eastern Washington (see Fig. 6.2).

Vélez-Ibáñez goes on to emphasize the significance of "sponsorship" of a mural project, that is, how publicly or privately sponsored works "are less likely to be participatory, 'owned,' or communal in their relationship to the surrounding community."[17] Daniel DeSiga was faced with these limitations in designing a *bracero* mural: how to satisfy both official sponsors and a community that had faced a history of exclusion?

The artist shared early designs not only with local Latino community members and former braceros, but also with undergraduate college students from the Yakima Valley who attended the University of Washington.[18] Photographs and oral histories gleaned from some of the original braceros or their family members assisted DeSiga in maintaining local images and memories on the mural's facade. Final decisions on *El Sarape* and

*Fig. 6.2. Painting of "El Veterano" using a short-handled hoe
(photo courtesy of Daniel DeSiga).*

all Toppenish murals rest with the Mural Society that holds the
final word on the themes and details of the town's public murals.
Nevertheless, this mural has fulfilled the stipulation of Vélez-
Ibáñez that "sponsorship in and of itself is not necessarily the most
definitive factor."[19]

I agree with Erasmo Gamboa in the mural's dedication
(above), and the editors of *Latino Northwest* magazine, who placed
El Sarape on their Spring-Summer 2001 cover, that the mural
reflects community history and acknowledges Mexicans'
contribution to the town and the region. But I also argue that
through its sweeping scope and intimate detail, the mural surpasses
its officially approved origins and historic meaning, that in Vélez-
Ibáñez's terms, *El Sarape*'s sheer mural aesthetics and presentations
are "so generative within [the] community that the work 'captures'
the community itself and goes beyond it because of its
representation. This capturing is a reciprocal process, with the
community and mural reflecting each other, paradoxically, in
contrast to the actual or social environment."[20]

180

EL SARAPE MURAL OF TOPPENISH

The mural *El Sarape* is composed of vignettes painted within geometric bands that form a traditional Mexican blanket in the famous *Saltillo* style, which originated in northwestern Mexico and traveled into the American Southwest in the nineteenth century. Fringes and vertical black/red stripes comprise the ten-foot "blanket edges" on each side of the mural, while a dozen colorful scenes are painted across the main eighty-foot pictorial section. Red "tapestry" bands zigzag in a *Saltillo Sarape* pattern to boldly divide the main panel into six major sections and frame the vignettes. Artist Daniel DeSiga struggled with designs for several weeks before serendipitously arriving at the idea of a Mexican blanket motif to manage the long, narrow space that would be filled with landscaped sky, mountains, fields, and 103 separate human figures in the foreground. He chose a creamy oil-based sign paint for its consistency and colors.[21]

Describing how he created the broad landscapes of Yakima Valley's alluvial floodplains planted with sugar beets, potatoes, asparagus, tomatoes, hops, and apple orchards, DeSiga acknowledges the influence of Maxfield Parrish, and explains,

> When I do my skies, first my brush strokes span a number of feet in a large mural. I start at the bottom of the sky with a light blue and paint a 6-inch wide ribbon across the wall. Then I come back to the left and add a little darker paint in my coffee cup or can the next time (always from the left to the right), then I start another ribbon each time blending the one color into the next. I have been asked so many times, "Do you use an air brush to get that blend so perfect?" I say, "No, I did it by hand." The blends are my signature, I use blends on all parts of my work. First the skies, then the mountains, then the plains, then the people, always —never using the color black until the people and the foreground.[22]

Taking in the mural as a whole, the viewer's eye is pulled to the top-center section, for its central position in the composition, for its stark simplicity, and for the story it tells. Here stands a tall older farmworker, a weary, determined expression on his face, poised upright, cultivating the crops with a long-handled hoe. To his right and left are six other laborers dressed in blue work clothes, bending over to hoe or to harvest, forming a human pyramid or triangle. *El Sarape's* hidden transcript resides in this grouping.[23] Latinos and others familiar with the suffering and struggles of organized farmworkers from the time of the first mini-bracero program of the World War I period through the time of Cesar Chavez and UFW organizing can read this hidden transcript. It reveals that the bracero workers of the 1940s were contracted to do the most arduous seasonal "stoop work," and were subjected to the growers' racializing beliefs that they were physically, inherently, suited for such labor. Historian Erasmo Gamboa explained that in the eyes of local farmers the Mexican workers were a "welcome blessing" because,

> even during the years of labor surpluses local workers shunned stoop labor. The contracted workers were ideal, declared a representative of the growers, because "the cutting of weeds is done with [short] hoes and the Mexicans are declared to be adept to that class of work." Other farmers were of the opinion that "whites" did not make good sugar beet thinners because it was "back-breaking work for taller persons, and those of shorter stature work best."[24]

El Sarape's design acknowledges the thousands of unnamed Mexicans who worked under these conditions, and also the changes brought about by organized farmworkers' struggles of the 1960s and 1970s for a more humane working environment as the two laborers at top center-right employ two notorious tools of the bracero's trade: one holds the razor-sharp beet-cutting instrument or "weapon" and the second the infamous short-handled hoe (*el cortito*) that required workers to stoop over all day, close to the ground, in order to weed the fields.[25] Their faces obscured by straw hats, they are the only figures in the mural whose faces are hidden from the viewer.

Depicting the brutal working conditions imposed by the use of the short-handled hoe is not entirely new to artist Daniel DeSiga, himself the son of a migrant farmworker family born in Washington State. His best-known painting *Campesino* (1976) depicts a worker in golden yellow and khaki clothes bending over a rich loamy field, pulling weeds with a short hoe, posed against a vast blue sky. The viewer sees the round top of his straw hat, a triangular stooped silhouette—his face hidden.[26] The artist notes that the principle of the triangle form underlies the 1976 painting, and it appears on the top-center panel of *El Sarape* as well (see cover illustration).[27]

Fig. 6.3. El Sarape mural depicting Mexican Braceros (with self-portrait) in Toppenish, Wash. (photo courtesy of Daniel DeSiga).

The American flag appears at the left top corner with profiles of World War II soldiers, including one Mexican American in uniform. The Mexican flag appears on the top right corner flanking four *campesino* men, one of them a self-portrait of the artist (see Fig. 6.3). Other vignettes illustrate 1) an official announcing the state's bracero program in front of Washington's capitol building in Olympia [top right]; 2) braceros arriving on a 1942 steam engine locomotive [lower left]; 3) braceros cooking beans over a fire in front of a "tent-city" labor camp;[28] 4) a farmworker carrying a sack of potatoes to a table where clerks calculated wage rates—the table marked with signs "Chief Yakima Ranches," "Cal Peas," and "Del Monte"; 5) factory hands receiving instructions from a foreman (Jim Dukes) in front of the U and I Sugar plant [right]; 6) community members attending a "fiesta parade" (the only panel that includes women); and 7) Daniel DeSiga's nineteen-year-old son who died in an auto accident a year before the mural project began, depicted as a young worker harvesting tomatoes.

Beyond work in the fields, the mural portrays Latinos who served in the military, but does not encompass other aspects of family life, support for local churches, and small business ventures of Latinos in the mid-twentieth century. Every mural that portrays families and "daily life" focuses on European Americans. The portrait of Mexican American men in uniforms of the American armed forces is a significant theme shared by the *Adelante* mural of Sterling, Illinois, and the *El Sarape* mural of Toppenish despite the miles between them. According to *Toppenish from Sagebrush to 1997*, a photographic history book published by the local Historical Society, about nine Spanish-surnamed men served in World War II, two in Korea, and about ten in the Vietnam and post-Vietnam period.

The Historical Society volunteer selling the book in downtown Toppenish told me that they advertised in the local paper to seek oral histories of local residents in the 1990s. Society members providing an overview and a substantial number of photographs wrote some sections. Overall, the historical notes indicate a greater number of Japanese American than Latino veterans for World War II and Korea, and the book includes a section entitled "The Japanese." The family oral history section that makes up the bulk of the book includes several stories about African American families and many more about American Indian individuals, but no oral histories of current Asian American residents. Five stories about Mexican American families appear: Barrientos, Diaz, Fonceca, Macias, and Serna, none of whom arrived in Toppenish as braceros, although they settled mostly in the 1930s to mid-1940s. Mr. Fonceca lays claim to opening the first café that sold Mexican American food in the 1940s, and the Sernas bought the El Paso Restaurant in the 1990s. The fourteen-page section on Toppenish churches mentions ten churches with a substantial number of Latinos in their congregations.[29] In the preface, the Historical Society editors note that not only was the town established on land ceded from Yakama Indian allotments through marriage to Anglos, but that the town has a multicultural history:

> Later on, various other ethnic groups came, liked what they saw, and took up residence here. The German, French, Japanese, Chinese, Filipino, Black, and Hispanic people brought a rich cultural diversity to the area, which has contributed to its further growth. Toppenish became a veritable "melting pot" of the valley.[30]

A fuller recounting of these diverse histories could provide themes for many more public murals and "mural-in-a-day" celebrations.

The mural *El Sarape* emerged out of a complex process: (1) Latino community and Toppenish Mural Society collaboration for a mural on local Mexican American history; (2) identifying the theme, the artist, funding, and location; (3) local participation with the artist to gather oral narratives, family snapshots, and contemporary photos for a mural that represented community memory; (4) negotiating with the Mural Society for results that would comply with its by-laws, yet satisfy the artist's vision and community stories he managed to collect. The social context for

185

this process, however, has been the demographic transformation of Eastern Washington and the region's dependence upon Mexican labor for its labor-intensive agriculture, a matter of key significance in a state where agriculture is the largest business.

Although local mural themes and details must fall within the parameters set by the Toppenish Mural Society that oversees and approves all murals in the town, *El Sarape* not only manages to convey the significance of the Bracero Program for the region, but also displays cultural, historical, and social themes broadly shared by Mexican Americans and other Latinos across the country. One omission, from the artist's perspective, was the decision not to include women working in the fields, because the Society members pointed out that only male laborers arrived through the official bracero agreement between Mexico and the United States. Nevertheless, local people recall that women from Mexican families who lived in the Valley before 1942 joined male workers in farm work (see Fig. 6.4).[31] Indeed, during World War I, workers were recruited from Mexico to work in Northwestern states as well as the Northeast and Midwest. Utah-Idaho Sugar, the Mormon-owned sugar beet company which built a plant in Toppenish in 1928, had recruited Mexican workers to Salt Lake City as early as 1918.[32] The Mural Society waived the stipulation that murals should not include portraits of living persons, perhaps because *El Sarape*'s design required so many more individual figures than previous murals, while early photographs of Mexican Americans were not readily available. DeSiga took photo snapshots of local community members who stopped

Fig. 6.4. *Quitando (sic) La Sizaña, 1973, private collection.*

186

by to see the mural, as well as dignitaries from the Mural Society board including the Society president. These photos were transposed onto the wall to represent people of the past who were lost to historical memory.[33]

Differences of opinion arose about whether most braceros arrived by train, and whether there really had been a "fiesta parade" like the one in the upper right mural section. Former braceros did not remember a parade, but Mural Society members recalled that "they were given a parade." The term *Fiesta de Caballeros* on the banner seems to reflect the reinterpretation of the past within an elite "Spanish" tradition, a reinterpretation that has been common to the tourism industry of California and the Southwest.[34] The term *caballeros* is not found in *16 de septiembre* or *5 de mayo* fiesta traditions common to immigrant communities— thus, the celebration depicted may have been organized by employers or an official welcoming committee of the town rather than through grassroots efforts. This is one of many questions that requires additional research through oral history methods. The local museums such as the Toppenish Hops Museum and Railroad Museum have not given Mexican local ethnic history the attention that European American and Yakama Indians have received, so local documentary sources appear limited.

In regard to the artistic style envisioned for a bracero mural, Daniel DeSiga reports that the Mural Society initially envisioned the adoption of designs from the urban- or barrio-style that some members were familiar with from the California Chicano tradition, but the artist sought a design more in keeping with his own Northwestern roots.[35] The actual *location* of the mural was a decision external to the artist and community, and some controversy surrounds the location at the back of a grocery store where delivery and garbage trucks move in and out during the course of a week. The street is certainly not a main thoroughfare that a tourist cannot miss on a walking tour in the downtown area. On the other hand, the location did have the ample wall space that the artist sought for his panoramic vision, and the street has other public amenities such as a park and a fire station.

187

Clearing the Land, painted in 1989 to celebrate Washington's centennial year, was the first Toppenish mural, depicting a bearded farmer plowing the soil. The idea of public murals evolved from meetings of the Centennial Committee formed in 1987, consisting of European American townspeople and representatives of the Yakama Nation Heritage Cultural Center. They researched and planned events, such as holding historical lectures and creating a number of murals depicting early Indian and pioneer activities. The group received a $500 local grant for a mural project from the county. When the group disbanded, the Toppenish Mural Society formed as non-profit organization, supported by businesses and individuals "who believe in the mission" and share the vision of the Society, without any governmental financial assistance.[36]

A newspaper article in 2001 pointed out that various plans for local economic development to offset economic decline had been discussed since the 1979 closing of the U&I sugar plant, and eventually the idea of murals with a Western theme became the major focus.[37] Locals hoped to revitalize the community and attract tourism. According to the Mural Society, Toppenish had fallen on hard times in the 1980s and a real sense of apathy, discouragement, and frustration had taken root. Industry was leaving the area; farming, the mainstay of the valley, was in a slump; and "people seemed to be moving out of Toppenish almost daily." Pride in the community was at an all-time low.[38]

Taking this portrait of social disarray a step farther, a *Seattle Post-Intelligencer* photographer writing in 2003 describes the Toppenish of 1989 as a town in decline. In the article, "Short Trips: Murals of the Past Brightened the Future," he cites not only "a lack of identity" but also that "signs of decay were everywhere." In contrast to national Census data that indicate continual population growth in Toppenish, this writer accepted a one-sided version of local demographics and repeated that this "was a small town getting smaller." Adopting the perspective of white residents not coping well with the growing ethnic diversity of their town, he writes that this "mainly agricultural town had deteriorated to such a degree that one woman told me she was scared to even drive downtown."[39] Thus, a period of economic slowdown combined with a growth in the Latino population is represented by regional journalists through a discourse of "decline," "decay," "deterioration," and even fear. The proposed remedy for such ills gained popular and financial support among the local elite: a visual celebration of the "good old days" when white settlers won the West by conquering the harsh terrain and the native peoples.

The "Mural-in-a-Day" concept allowed for the rapid expansion of murals on storefronts and buildings facing the town's small central district. Each year, about fifteen artists would gather to complete an entire mural on the first Saturday in June, with spectators watching from portable bleachers set up on the street.[40] The murals added to other tourist attractions that have undergone substantial remodeling in recent years such as the Yakama Nation Cultural Center, the American Hops Museum, the Northern Pacific Railway Museum (formerly the Yakima Valley Rail & Steam Museum), and the annual Powwow and Rodeo. But the public display of more than sixty oversized, high-quality murals across building fronts in the historical downtown area distinguishes Toppenish from other western towns. By the late 1990s Toppenish was attracting tourists from all over the globe.[41]

Proclaiming itself the town "Where the West Still Lives," Toppenish invites visitors to take a walking tour or a lively horse-and-buggy ride led by tour guide "Cowboy" Jim Dukes, who appears on the *El Sarape* mural as a boss giving orders in front of the sugar plant, a role he actually played for U & I Sugar. DeSiga tells about their daily performance:

> Every day a covered wagon came by with a load of tourists. The driver... is Jim Dukes, a classic looking big Cowboy! And every time he came by we would do this act as if it were the first time I saw him... We would laugh because it was so funny to

us! We became the best of friends. I wanted to show reality (back in those) times. Yes, they had Spanish interpreters but they used the "*Patrón* System." So I painted Jim as my *Patrón*. You see him talking to a number of Mexican men and him giving orders. What's so funny is that he was a real *Patrón* at that time!... (This) became part of our "spiel" each time we talked to the tourists... No one knew why we laughed so much.[42]

Overall the theme of constructing the "Old West" — a benevolent take on "Manifest Destiny" — pervades the town murals, focusing on cowboys and Indians, pioneers and settlers, ranchers, farmers, and early technological developments in dredging the swamps, opening the railroad, and the arrival of electricity and newer farm equipment, cars, and airplanes. The emphasis on American Indian themes is appropriate for a town carved out of Yakama Reservation land, although institutions of the Yakama Nation emphasize different aspects of regional history in their own arts and storytelling. For example, the Yakama Nation recalls on its Web site:

The original land claimed by the Yakamas was 10.8 million acres. The reservation was set aside for the Yakamas by the Treaty of 1855 negotiated at Walla Walla between the United States Gov. Isaac Stevens and our people. All of the remaining land was ceded to the United States Government. Today the reservation is comprised of 1.4 million acres, still one of the largest in the state.[43]

The Toppenish murals that deal with settler-Yakama relations do not focus on land or treaties, but on a few specific events, folktales, the PowWow and Rodeo, and agricultural labor. One mural highlighted in tourist brochures and travel Web sites is a panorama of a defeated army colonel who retreated from a battle with Yakama Indians in 1855 (*Haller's Defeat* by Fred Oldfield). Other murals that receive particular emphasis have cowboy or townspeople themes such as *Christmas at Logy Creek* by Fred Oldfield, *The Old Saturday Market* by Robert Thomas, *When Hops Were Picked by Hand* by Robert Thomas, and *Rodeo* by Newman Myrah. At least six murals focus on women, and about a dozen on American Indians (European American women, children, together with American Indian people appear in a number of other murals about everyday life). Murals with Native American themes include historical scenes, traditional life, folktales, and customs, some painted by Cameron Blagg who is a "history buff" and "collects western and Indian artifacts" — but an American Indian artist painted none.

No mural is dedicated to the Japanese American farmers who migrated to the area before World War I, settled in town as workers, opened small businesses, or leased reservation land for planting, so the saga of families being taken to internment camps during World War II does not yet appear on the town's walls.[44] However, two significant Toppenish murals were painted by an Asian American artist, Ju-hong "Joe" Chen, who was born in China, feature important local women. *The Old Lillie Mansion* portrays "The Mother of Toppenish" Josephine Lillie, whose story hints at the complex layers of race and gender relations that built the town of Toppenish. Because her mother belonged to the Klickitat Tribe, Josephine received a land allotment of eighty acres under the Dawes Act in 1905, half of which she partitioned and sold as parcels. After the sale, this area was incorporated as the city of Toppenish. A second mural by Chen, *Estelle Reel Meyer*, portrays the first woman Director of Indian Education for the Bureau of Indian Affairs (1898) who later married a Toppenish farmer.[45]

In 1993 the Mural Society extended the historical period for its murals beyond the original period of 1850 to 1920 to include the 1920–1950 era. This change made recognition of Mexican Americans through a "bracero" mural possible.

Overall, the town's Anglo population has created a tourist haven in its own image, with a version of history that does little to explain the town's contemporary demographic realities. The "imagined community" created across Toppenish's public spaces since 1989 shows a town built by European Americans with dramatic backdrops of the natural environment and an Indian past. The present social reality of a town where Latinos comprise nearly 76 percent of the population with whites comprising just over 15 percent is nowhere implied nor explained on the town's walls. A perceptive Washington State University student who researched the discursive formation of local power in Toppenish murals similarly argues that the community "memories" reflected on local walls are selective and largely exclude perspectives from people of color in a multicultural community.[46] This is the situation that Daniel DeSiga aptly refers to as "hidden in plain sight":

> What a lot of Anglo people forget is that when they divided Mexico and the U.S. many Mexicans stayed in what's called "Aztlán": Texas, New Mexico, Arizona and California. Over the years we have expanded to the entire U.S. We are the fastest growing minority group in the U.S. and soon to be the largest. I feel Latinos are a group of people that are just not noticed, I call it "hidden in plain sight." Sometimes ashamed, you see us doing jobs that no one else wants to do. You see us as the "domestic help," like servants, waiters, gardeners, dishwashers in restaurants, cooks, farmworkers, and so on...We are everywhere but no one wants us "out front" so to speak. That's ok! Times are a-changin'![47]

Thus far, the majority population in the community can see themselves in only one mural—*El Sarape*—physically isolated from the geographic center of town, behind the "Marketplace" grocery store on West 2nd Street. A *Seattle Times* editorial commented:

> For a long time, historic murals throughout Toppenish, Yakima County, had only white and Native American faces, reflecting a particular period of the town's history. Last year, a new mural was painted reflecting the contribution of workers from Mexico. It was overdue.[48]

When the Toppenish Mural Society celebrates the revitalization that the multiple-mural project brought to the town since 1989, is their proclaimed "pride in the community" intended to include or exclude the presence of a majority Latino population?[49]

Official town descriptions point out that the Bracero Program coincided with World War II, a specific, bracketed period of time. Ongoing contributions to Northwestern agriculture going back to the turn of the century and continuing until the present is not mentioned in the local literature, even though it is implied in the mural *El Sarape* itself. Without the workers, Washington's agricultural sector could not function, as stated in a recent newspaper interview:

> "If you want to demonstrate the dependence the industry has on Mexican immigrants, it is very, very clear," said Mike Gempler of the Washington Growers League, which represents about 800 agricultural employers on labor issues. "They are the work force."[50]

Not surprisingly, the contemporary political picture in Toppenish, the Yakima Valley, and Eastern Washington region in general parallels the underrepresentation of Latinos in mural images, yet gradual inroads are being carved. The County of Yakima elected its first Hispanic County Supervisor (Jesse Palacios-R) in 1998, who was also the first Latino county supervisor in the State of Washington.[51] Gradual inclusion in local institutions has occurred in Toppenish as well. This includes the hiring of Julian Torres, the son of migrant workers, as Assistant Superintendent of Schools and the election of two Latino city council members by 2000 -- including Clara Jimenez as the first elected Latina councilwoman in 1997 and as the town's mayor in 2003.[52] With Latino Catholics becoming the majority in many parishes, the Yakima diocese appointed a Mexican American bishop in 1997.[53] Catholic bishops of the region voiced support for ecological sustainability, Yakama Indian rights, and social justice for Latinos in its pastoral letter:

> Our region is blessed with peoples of diverse cultures who, as individual citizens and cohesive communities, enrich the social fabric of our lives while contributing their labor to promote societal well-being. We are particularly concerned about the situation of Hispanic workers who sometimes receive low wages, endure unhealthy working conditions, and suffer discrimination. We need to celebrate the contributions of all the diverse peoples of the Columbia Watershed, and to explore joint projects for economic justice and ecological conservation.[54]

In conclusion, although Latinos have not yet gained political and social influence in keeping with their demographic growth, progress has been made. Demographically, Toppenish continues to grow, with no recent decline in the white population. In Yakima

County as a whole (as in Midwestern states), the white population has declined as Latino numbers increase. Census 2000 showed the County population at 212,300, with a Hispanic population of 78,731, or 37 percent, which is a 24 percent increase since 1990. As diversity grows, the white population is numerically smaller in Yakima County, down from 139,514 in 1990 to 119,652 in 2000.[55]

Visiting Toppenish in spring 2003, I noticed a large wooden sign set up along West First Avenue in front of the Yakima Valley Farm Worker's Clinic announcing—in Spanish—that there would be a community meeting (*Junta*) there the following Thursday. Such public signs are another way of demonstrating that a formerly excluded group is now defining themselves in the public sector in their own language, forging their own political agendas and claiming social space. In the words of William Flores, Renato Rosaldo, and other Latino social scientists, they are expressing their "cultural citizenship" as Latinos in the United States and opening up their own "social and political discourse."[56]

In keeping with Carlos Vélez-Ibáñez's analysis on the social significance of Chicano/a, Latino/a and Mexican American murals,[57] I have argued that *El Sarape* invokes a community's history, shared experiences, struggles, celebrations, and communal identity. Claiming a "space on the wall" as a community is a step closer to achieving a sense of belonging within a social context of historical exclusion. Recent analyses by Latino scholars have focused on the importance of "claiming identity, space, and rights" through group actions that have a cultural as well as a political component: "community is essential to survival, not only in terms of neighborhood or geographic locale, but also in terms of collective identity," and thus a "struggle for the right to control space and to establish community is a central one."[58]

Daniel DeSiga and other mural artists are doing their part by claiming a space on public walls, by remembering the past and forging a vision for the future—carrying out this work with joy.[59] As Daniel expresses it,

When Aztlán became part of the U.S., we did
too! We love this homeland, we will defend it to
the end. I am so happy to be here at this point in
time of history. I love being an artist and able to
be a visual contributor, not only for the future of my
culture but to show and document to our
young and to preserve their beautiful past.[60]

The artist dreams about painting new murals to represent the
growing Latino community, such as a scene from his childhood of
a campfire alongside a worn-out station wagon with a farmworker
family "on the road" huddling together, wrapped in *sarape*
blankets,[61] or further tributes to Mexicans and other marginalized
groups who built the West and Northwest:

I would love to paint a mural around that
railroad documentation of Mexicans working
alongside of the Chinese and the Afro Americans,
it happened throughout the United States. Another
fact is that the first cowboys were Mexicans on the
Haciendas run by the Spaniards (who brought the
horses), they were called "*Vaqueros.*" That's another
great mural.[62]

Is there room in Toppenish for an expanded sense of
community and a broader depiction of its multicultural history, or
will the town function as two distinct communities, living side by
side, but without a shared sense of place?

Endnotes

1. "De 'El traque' o de 'El lava-platos,'" María Herrera-Sobek, *The Bracero Experience: Elitelore versus Folklore* (Los Angeles: UCLA Latin American Center Publications, 1979), 89. Herrara-Sobek's translation (p. 91): "When I got tired of 'El Traque' (railroad labor) he invited me again / To pick tomatoes and to hoe beets. / There I earned indulgences crawling on my knees, / Bowing down for three, four, and five miles. / What poorly paid work / For working on one's knees!"

2. David R. Maciel and Maria Herrera-Sobek edited a recent volume that analyses the extensive "cultural or artistic works that have Mexican immigration as their major theme": *Culture Across Borders: Mexican Immigration & Popular Culture* (Tucson: University of Arizona Press, 1998).

3. Gilberto Garcia and Jerry Garcia, introduction in *The Illusion of Borders: The National Presence of Mexicanos in the United States* (Dubuque, Iowa: Kendall/Hunt Publishing, 2002).

4. Erasmo Gamboa, *Mexican Labor & World War II: Braceros in the Pacific Northwest, 1941–1947* (Seattle: University of Washington Press, Seattle, 1990), 1–31.

5. Newspaper articles regarding the growing Latino population in Toppenish and other Washington and Illinois towns appear in the *Seattle Times*, http://seattletimes.nwsource.com/mexico/, Wednesday, June 21, 2000, and the *Chicago Tribune*, featuring a story about Mexican immigration into Sterling, Illinois, where the historic "Adelante" mural was recently painted: Teresa Puente and Bob Kemper, "City Population Bounces Back: Urban Area Isn't the Only Place Latinos Make Mark," *Chicago Tribune*, Mar 15, 2001. See note 35 for DeSiga comments.

6. Carlos G. Vélez-Ibáñez, *Border Visions: Cultures of the Southwest United States* (Tucson: University of Arizona Press, 1996), 244.

7. "With a Bachelor of Fine Art Degree obtained from the University of Washington, DeSiga is among the most prominent Mexican American painters in the Northwest. His artwork has been exhibited in many forums such as the Denver Art Museum, the San Francisco Museum of Modern Art and the Wight Art Gallery at the University of California in Los Angeles... Daniel has painted about 20 murals; among them is the mural located at El Centro de la Raza (Seattle), the Locks in Ballard, 'Seagull Fly in the Sky,' in Rainier Valley, 'The Olympic Mountains' in Lynwood and a series of murals that he painted for the Washington State Labor Department in various offices throughout the state." *Latino Northwest Magazine* 3, no. 5 (August-September 2001): 6. He was also a member of the Sacramento, California, art group "Chicano Royal Air Force" in the

MARGARET VILLANUEVA

1970s; and the Smithsonian Institution American Art Museum collection (http://www.nmaa.si.edu) has his two paintings *Colegio Cesar Chavez, Mt. Angel, Oregon* (1975) and *Dia de los muertos* (1985). Evergreen State Collage features twenty of DeSiga's paintings, including the *El Sarape* mural as well as biographical and contact information, (accessed June 6, 2005).

8. I carried out a brief field study during June 2001 while Daniel DeSiga was drawing and painting the foreground details onto the background design and landscapes he had worked on since November, 2000, and made a second visit in July 2003. Subsequent information was compiled through e-mail interviews with the artist, telephone interviews, *Latino Northwest* magazine, newspaper and online articles, as well as the Mural Society newsletter and Historical Society book. Unless otherwise noted, the interpretation of the mural's themes and related historical data are my own.

9. Written communication from Daniel DeSiga, Dec. 4, 2001. Erasmo Gamboa wrote the principle historical account of braceros in the region: *Mexican Labor and World War II: Braceros in the Pacific Northwest, 1942–1947* (Austin: University of Texas Press, 1990).

10. Gamboa, *Mexican Labor and World War II*.

11. Margaret Villanueva, "Claiming Space on the Walls: Latino/Chicano Murals and Historical Discourse in Illinois and Washington Communities," presented at the Race in the Humanities Conference, University of Wisconsin-La Crosse, Nov. 15–17, 2001; David G. Gutiérrez, "Ethnic Mexicans and the Transformation of 'American' Social Space: Reflections on Recent History," in *Crossings: Mexican Immigration in Interdisciplinary Perspectives*, ed. Marcelo M. Suárez-Orozco (Cambridge: Harvard University Press, 1998), 311; Vicki L. Ruiz, *From Out of the Shadows: Mexican Women in Twentieth-Century America* (New York: Oxford University Press, 1999), 127–46; Vélez-Ibáñez, *Border Visions.*, 244–64; Margaret Villanueva and Sylvia Fuentes, "Chicana Claims to Socio-Cultural Space: Interdisciplinary Perspectives on Creating *Nuestra Comunidad*," presented at the *Midwest National Association for Chicano Studies (NACS) Conference*, University of Minnesota-Twin Cities, Nov. 11–12, 1994.

12. Ruiz, *From Out of the Shadows* 128.

13. Gutiérrez, "Ethnic Mexicans," 310–11.

14. William V. Flores, "Citizens vs. Citizenry: Undocumented Immigrants and Latino Cultural Citizenship," in *Latino Cultural Citizenship: Claiming Identity, Space, and Rights*, ed. William V. Flores and Rina Benmayor (Boston: Beacon Press, 1977), 263–64,.

15. Vélez-Ibáñez, *Border Visions*, 263–64.

16. "I was raised in a small city like Yakima near Toppenish but it was not until I started Collage at the University of Washington that I really became politically aware of what was going on with the United Farm Workers

movement, even though I came from a farmworker background. I knew before starting collage that I wanted to major in art, which I did but it wasn't until I became educated about what was going on in the world that I wanted to commit my work to what might be called social commentary art. A major turning point in my life and my first exposure into the national arena of the Chicano art movement was my involvement in a school takeover in Seattle in 1972. It was there that during that takeover of an old abandoned school I painted my first big mural. A group of artists and an art collective came from Sacramento during that takeover and gave us a workshop in developing a Centro. What we started is now called El Centro de la Raza, (a civil rights and one stop service center for many social issues). There I met the art collective called the Royal Chicano Air force (RCAF). I became an associate member, and later in my career moved to Sacramento to become an official member. They influenced me a lot..." Written communication from Daniel DeSiga, Dec. 3, 2001.

17. Vélez-Ibáñez, *Border* Visions, 245.
18. DeSiga acknowledges the advice of Drs. Erasmo Gamboa and Ricardo Favela in this project, as well as the long-term influence and support of Chicano scholars and other art historians such as Esteben Villa, Tomás Ybarra-Frausto, and Shifra Goldman, and the Armand Hammer museum in Los Angeles. Written communication, Dec. 3, 2001.
19. Vélez-Ibáñez, *Border* Visions, 245.
20. Ibid.
21. Written communication from Daniel DeSiga, Dec. 3, 2001.
22. Ibid., Dec. 4, 2001.
23. In *Domination and the Arts of Resistance: Hidden Transcripts* (New Haven: Yale University Press, 1992), James C. Scott describes "hidden transcripts" as activities of oppressed groups that take place outside the public spaces dominated by more powerful groups. In the case of public murals like *El Serape* or *Adelante* in Sterling, Illinois, the images hold meanings that suggest how Latinos have survived and overcome past oppression or exclusion through labor organizing or building independent ethnic-based organizations, for example. These meanings are not accessible to the viewer who is unaware of Latino perspectives on local and regional history.
24. In *Mexican Labor and World War II*, Gamboa defines the hidden transcript as those activities that happen just beyond public visibility that oppressed groups use to deflect, survive, and reject the demands of the power (54–55).
25. According to the Farmworker's Web site: "The During the 'Bracero' Program the short handle hoe was widely used. The 'braceros' still remember the all day long bending, thinning sugar beet fields with this tool. The use of the short-handle hoe is now illegal in most of the states,

although you still find farmworkers using it specially in south Texas and in New Mexico," www.farmworkers.org/shorthoe.html (accessed Dec. 7, 2003). The video "The Fight in the Fields" documents the UFW's efforts for better conditions and eliminating this tool: "El Cortito, 'the short one,' was a hoe that was only twenty-four inches long, forcing the farmworkers who used it to bend and stoop all day long—a position that often led to lifelong, debilitating back injuries," http://www.paradigmproductions.org/voices/voices.html (accessed June 8, 2005).

26. *Campesino* by Daniel DeSiga 1976 (oil on canvas, 50 1/2 x 58 1/2 inches); see painting online at Autry Museum site: http://www.tfaoi.com/newsmu/nmus2c.htm. Suzanne G. Fox, *Culture y Cultura: Consequences of the U.S.-Mexican War, 1846–1848*, Autry Museum of Western Heritage, 1998; Max Benavidez, "Cesar Chavez Nurtured Seeds of Art," *Los Angeles Times* (N/D); Richard Griswold del Castillo, Teresa McKenna, and Yvonne Yarbro-Bejarano, eds., *CARA – Chicano Art: Resistance and Affirmation 1965–1985* (Los Angeles: UCLA Wight Art Gallery, 1991), Cat. No. 65, 54.

27. "During my schooling at the UW I remember in one of my Art History classes that many of the old Masters would use the formula of the Triangle in their work. I was also into that 'power of the pyramids' at that time and that was the formula I used in that now famous painting *Campesino* published in the CARA exhibit. A lot of artists produce a lot of work but are only catapulted into history by one painting and that one is mine." Written communication from Daniel DeSiga, Dec. 3, 2001.

28. Canvas tents set up on concrete blocks were a commonplace form of housing for braceros, even though the workers were expected to stay until the beet harvest in November when cold weather conditions prevailed. Gamboa notes: "Six workers lived together in a sixteen-by-sixteen foot tent, furnished with folding cots… During the summer, the men were often driven from the tents by 100 degree temperatures, and in the fall and winter the fabric structures offered little protection from the inclement northwestern weather." *Mexican Labor and World War II*, 96.

29. Toppenish Historical Society, *Toppenish: From Sagebrush to 1997* (N.P.: Color Press, 1997).

30. Toppenish Historical Society, 1.

31. Fieldnotes, June 2001. Toppenish was an important site on the migrant circuit of Washington's Mexican farmworkers and settlers in the 1940s and 1950s, and by 1952 Toppenish had a Spanish-speaking Catholic priest (see Jerry Garcia, "Mexican Migration, Labor and Community Formation: A Case Study of Quincy, Washington, 1943–1980," 106–107 and Gilberto Garcia, "Mexican Communities in the State of Washington: The Case of

Othello, Washington," 122, in *The Illusion of Borders*. Additional information regarding the Mexican musical tradition in Washington State is available at http://www.nwfolklife.org/P_REC/NyS_info.html and photos of braceros in Oregon during the World War II period are available through the Oregon State Archives at http://arcweb.sos.state.or.us/osu/osuintwork.html.

32. Fernando Saúl Alanís Enciso, *El Primer Programa Bracero y el Gobierno de México 1917–1918* (San Luis Potosí, Mexico: El Colegio de San Luis, 1999), 22–26. The authors show 139,922 workers admitted in 1917.

33. A perusal of Washington's historical photo collection of railroad, canal, and apple industries reveals few discernable Latino or Asian faces, even though historians of Washington's ethnic past point out the importance of these groups in the state's labor history. For example, see Yakima Valley's extensive online photo collection at http://ww.yakimamemory.org/index/html. One of the few photos of bracero workers in Washington is available on the Web site "Columbian River History," along with numerous photographs of Asian American communities, (accessed June 6, 2005).

34. In *Latino Metropolis* (Minneapolis: University of Minnesota Press, 2000), authors Victor M. Valle and Rodolfo D. Torres refer to a "fantasy legacy" and "Hispanicizing nostalgia" that extend from "Spanish" architecture to restaurant menus and local "fiestas," as a parallel reality to actual working class Latino/Mexican life and culture (76–77, 85–86). The Toppenish Historical Society and Mural Society theme "Where the West Still Lives," coined in the 1980s can be interpreted as a similar attempt to create a parallel historical vision that fails to explain the actual demographic reality of the town and the region.

35. "That strikes a nerve with me because every time we see any Latino lifestyle represented of us 'Latinos' we see that same stereotypical scene of an L.A. barrio type mural. Yes! Many of my artist friends in California produce that type of mural. I just feel there are many Latinos throughout the U.S. and we all don't live like that and look like that. Many like me come from a farm, country, rural profile. I don't think the east coast city (murals) like Chicago barrios look like that. I knew I needed to design collages or a montage of many different ideas like an L.A. style mural but I didn't want to put the thoughts one on top of each other." Written communication from Daniel DeSiga, Dec. 5, 2001.

36. Toppenish Historical Society, "Toppenish State Centennial Committee" and "Toppenish Mural Society," (73–74), *Toppenish: From Sagebrush to 1997* (N.P.: Color Press, 1997). Some photos from the book are posted at http://www.toppenishhistory.com (accessed June 8, 2005).

37. Ross Courtney, "Toppenish's 60th Mural Pays Homage to the WWII Braceros," *Yakima Herald-Republic*, Thursday, Aug. 2, 2001.

38. "Toppenish Mural Society"; "History" on the Mural Society Web page, http://www.toppenishmurals.org (accessed June 2, 2005).

39. Jeff Larson, "Short Trips: Murals of the Past Brightened the Future," *Seattle Post-Intelligencer*, Thursday, July 31, 2003, http://www.seattlepi.nwsource.com/getaways/132986_shorttips31.html (accessed Dec. 7, 2003).

40. "Toppenish Mural Society." On my first visit to Toppenish in June 2001, I was not aware of this yearly event and missed it by just a day or two. I later learned that Daniel DeSiga joined other artists that summer to paint that year's mural-in-a-day. First, the lead artist paints an outline on the wall to be filled in with a large number of volunteers the next day, completing the work before sundown.

41. See Web sites on Toppenish tourist attractions: http://www.ohwy.com/wa/topmural.htm, the railroad museum http://www.nprymuseum.org and murals on http://www.yakima.net/toourism/murals.php. The Toppenish Murals homepage had an internal link to "Sarape" during 2002, but that Web site is no longer available online. Several Toppenish murals appear at http://www.toppenish.net/index.html and http://www.aviewofamerica.com/Washington/Attraction/ToppenishMurals/toppenishmurals.htm (accessed June 8, 2005), and on the local Chamber of Commerce Web site, http://www.toppenish.net/index.html (accessed June 8, 2005).

42. Written communication from Daniel DeSiga, Dec. 4, 2001.

43. Web site with information on Yakama Nation: http://www.critfc.org/text/yakama.html; http://www.yakamamuseum.com (accessed June 8, 2005).

44. "The Japanese," *Toppenish: From Sagebrush to 1997*, 76.

45. Information on murals and this version of local history were available on an interactive Web site hosted by a businessman in Spokane and later by the Mural Society, but since December 2003, toppenishmurals.org/index.html has not appeared online.

46. The racial-ethnic breakdown of the Toppenish population in 2000 was as follows: 8,946 total; 2,816 white; 50 black; 707 American Indian; 33 Asian; 6,774 Latino, of which 6,066 are Mexican descent (Washington Government Web site: http://www.ofm.wa.gov/census2000/profiles/place/1605371960. pdf, accessed June 2, 2002). "White" includes Latinos who identify themselves this way on Census forms. Washington calculates the "not Hispanic or Latino" population in Toppenish as 2,172 or 24.3 percent of the population, while "White Alone" comprises 1,398 persons, or 15.6 percent of the population. Regarding local power structure in Toppenish and "community choices" about mural themes controlled by the "Mural Society" and "Historical

Society," see Majel Boxer, abstract for McNair Scholar Research Paper: "The Murals of Toppenish: Markers of Selective Memory and Control Within a Multicultural Community," http://www.wsu.edu/~mcnair/mcfolder/symposium02.htm, (accessed June 10, 2005), and her article "Re-creating the "Old West": The Cultural Politics of Murals in Toppenish, Washington," *McNair Journal* 2 (Fall 2003).

47. DeSiga adds, "…We are in those low pay positions because we didn't have the education to hold those more skilled jobs. Now with this incredible change, we are becoming mainstream, assimilated. We are a large economic base. We are becoming educated to get those jobs we didn't hold in the past. We are like a slow moving train. No one is going to be able to stop us. I feel that those people who don't jump on the train with us 'are going to be left behind.' One of the greatest assets we have is we take our time to get it done right! Sometimes people see it differently, and call it lazy, our cultural lifestyle to us is different than to others." Written communication from Daniel DeSiga, Dec. 6, 2001.

48. *Seattle Times,* "A Portrait of Diversity," Editorial, Thursday, Mar. 15, 2001, http://seattletimes.com (accessed June 25, 2002).

49. The *Seattle Times* raised these questions in an impressive series of articles about the impact of the Mexican presence in Washington entitled "Under Two Flags: Mexican Workers in Washington Fields," including close-ups on immigrant life in Toppenish. The photo images accompanying the story are vivid enough to inspire a number of new murals; see http://seattletimes.nwsource.com/mexico (accessed June 8, 2005).

50. Lynda V. Mapes, "Needed but Often Illegal, They Pick Our Crops, Pine for Home," *Seattle Times*, Sunday, June 18, 2000.

51. *Yakima Herald* article online: http://www.tri-cityherald.com/vote98/primary/story1.html (accessed May 30, 2002). Articles on Yakima Valley race relations appear in the Herald's "Race in Yakima Valley," https://www.yakima-herald.com/race.php (accessed June 8, 2005).

52. Barbara A. Serrano, "Latinos Try to Boost Role in Politics," *Seattle Times*, Sunday, Nov. 30, 1997, http://www.seattletimes.com archives (accessed June 15, 2002.); Lynda V. Mapes, "Farmworkers Arriving from Mexican Don't Plan to Stay, But They Do," *Seattle Times*, June 20, 2000, http://www.seattletimes.com archives (accessed June 15, 2002).

53. David Wasson, "New Yakima Bishop Tours Cultural Site," *Seattle Times*, Jan. 7, 1997. http://www.seattletimes.com archives (accessed June 15, 2002).

54. Columbia River Pastoral Letter Project, online at http://www.columbiariver.org/main_pages/Watershed/WORD/english.doc (accessed Dec. 30, 2003).

55. Sandy Summers, "Some are Striving to Make Sense of Changes," *Yakima Herald-Republic*, Dec. 10, 2000, (accessed Dec. 7, 2003). Examining 2000 Census Bureau figures closely, it is clear that some "Hispanic/Latino" respondents identify themselves racially as "white," and thus appear to be counted twice: once as Hispanic and once as White. Statistical tables available to the public account for this by calculating the "White Non-Hispanic" population, but data has appeared in some reports without this correction. Online demographic information for Toppenish in 2003 that also reports in a manner that over-represents the "White" population by not specifying Non-Hispanic White under residents counted by "race" appears on http://www.epodunk.com/cgi bin/genInfo.php? locIndex=25031 (accessed June 8, 2005).

56. William V. Flores, William V. Flores, "Citizens vs. Citizenry: Undocumented Immigrants and Latino Cultural Citizenship," 263–64.

57. Chicano and Chicana mural artists began their collective art movement in California and the Southwest in conjunction with the Chicano Movement of the 1960s, in bold styles reminiscent of the Mexican muralists (see the Web sites http://www.sparcmurals.org:16080/sparcone/index.php and http://www.chicanoparksandiego.com/index.html as examples.) Chicago, Minneapolis, and smaller Midwestern communities exhibit many murals that follow the Chicano tradition, as well as Latino murals focusing more broadly on pan-Latino immigration and local community histories (see the Web sites http://www.americas.org - "Mosaic Mural" link (Minneapolis, MN) and http://adelantesterling.tripod.com (Sterling, IL).

58. William V. Flores with Rina Benmayor, introduction to *Latino Cultural Citizenship: Claiming Identity, Space, and Rights* (Boston: Beacon Press, 1997), 16.

59. I love the latest "politically correct" word to identify us, *Latino*, because it not only is about Mexicans, it includes Puerto Ricans, Cubans, South Americans, and so on and so on. Our strength is expanding. When I say strength, I don't mean threatening! What is so great, we don't want to take over anything! We are not threatening to any security of this great nation. We just want to contribute and we want to be acknowledged for those contributions. We also want equal representation and our share of the great "American Pie." Written communication from Daniel DeSiga, Dec. 6, 2001.

60. Ibid.

61. Ibid., Dec. 5, 2001.

62. Ibid., Dec. 4, 2001.

Testimonio de un Tejano en Oregon: Contratista, Julian Ruiz

Carlos Saldivar Maldonado

Introduction

People of Mexican descent have been part of Northwest history for a long time. However, the decades of the 1940s and early 1950s witnessed the significant migration and subsequent settlement of Chicanos in that region. Many Chicano families who made the trek north during these decades pursued their livelihood in the bountiful fields and orchards there. While some Chicano families journeyed to the Northwest on their own accord, others were recruited by farm labor contractors already established in the region. Presently, published sources do not exist that highlight the role labor contractors played in the historical migration and subsequent settlement of Chicanos in the Northwest. The story of farm labor contractors in Oregon is important within the general context of Chicano Northwest history. Farm labor contractors who actively recruited Chicanos to the region offer a unique historical glimpse into the migration and settlement of Chicanos there. It is critical that the story of these early farm labor contractors be documented to augment the Chicano Northwest historical record. This task is most urgent since some of the early farm labor contractors are advancing in age and may not be available to researchers as an important historical source. Such research would likewise be useful for conducting comparative analysis of farm labor contracting and Chicano migration and settlement in other regions.

The purpose of the following oral narrative is to tell the life story of Julian Ruiz, a Tejano farm labor contractor in Oregon's Willamette Valley. Julian played a role in the migration and settlement of Chicanos in Oregon during the early 1950s. The narrative will illuminate the evolving experience of a farmworker turned labor contractor. Likewise, Julian's story will highlight farm labor contractor practices he used to recruit Tejano families to Oregon's Willamette Valley. Julian's story will illustrate how labor contracting has changed over the years, will reflect cultural sensibilities among Chicanos, and lastly, will underscore the notion that his singular life is linked to a collective Chicano experience. This oral or life history narrative is presented in the "testimonio" tradition. A brief discussion focusing on the historical development and characteristics of the testimonio tradition will be highlighted in the first section. Whereas traditional testimonios generally provide only a direct life story, this testimonio will end with a brief identification of themes that emerged from the narrative.

Methods

Prussian philosopher-historian Wilhelm Dilthey stated that one "penetrates more deeply into the structure of the historical world by sorting out and studying individual contexts. The most fundamental of these contexts is the course of the individual life in the environment by which it is affected and which it affects; it is present in the memory of the individual."[1] Dilthey goes on to say that the individual's memory represents the "germinal cell of history" and that "individuals are as much the logical subjects of history as communities and contexts."[2] This view of history resonates well with the testimonio tradition that often illuminates a collective history through the memories and experiences of an individual life. According to testimonio scholars, the testimonio genre first emerged in Cuba shortly after the Cuban revolution. Miguel Barnet, considered one of the precursors of the testimonio form, documented the life story of Esteban Montejo, a former slave in colonial Cuba. Montejo's life story or testimonio was published in 1966 in Cuba under the title of *Biografía de un Cimarrón*. In 1968, it was published in several languages including English under the title *Autobiography of a Runaway Slave.*[3] *Biografía de un*

Cimarrón illuminates Montejo's life within the context of slavery, the abolition of slavery, and the war of independence. *Biografía de un Cimarrón* was unique in that it gave voice to those marginalized in society and absent in recorded history. The testimonio narrative soon spread to the rest of Latin America during the late 1960s and 1970s.

The spread of the testimonio tradition became closely linked to the popular social revolutionary movements of Latin America, particularly Central America. Thus, testimonio became recognized as narrative of resistance in the context of the Third World. Social science and humanities scholars throughout the world including the United States soon became attracted to these emerging narratives of resistance. Scholarly questions regarding the nature and parameters of testimonio narrative soon became the focus of discussion. John Beverley contributed to this discussion by defining testimonio as "a novel or novella-length narrative in book or pamphlet form told in the first person by a narrator who is a real protagonist or witness of the events he or she recounts, and whose unit of narration is usually a "life" or a significant life experience. The testimonio may include, but is not subsumed under, any of the following textual categories, some of which are conventionally considered literature while others are not: autobiography, autobiographical novel, oral history, memoir, confession, diary, interview, eyewitness report, life history, novella-testimonio, nonfiction novel, or factographic literature."[4] Other important features of the testimonio tradition include the notion that the testimonio is an act of communicating the subaltern status of a class or group of people. While the testimonio premises an individual's story, it is simultaneously a singular and collective story. The testimonio is characterized as history from the bottom or everyday person. The testimonio tradition also involves a mediated narrative where a narrator tells his/her story to another who records, writes, and edits the account. So the oral tradition, the first person, and the role of an interlocutor are central to the testimonio tradition.

CARLOS S. MALDONADO

Testimonio represents an excellent tool for conducting oral and life history work to expand Chicano historiography. The testimonio has several qualities that compliment the Chicano experience. First, testimonio provides opportunity to recover history through those who have been historically absent from the mainstream historical record. Second, testimonio resonates with the oral tradition dominant in the Chicano community and culture. Third, testimonio narrative is historically present in our community's historical experience reflected in the "cronicas", diaries, and other southwest Spanish colonial writings. Fourth, the testimonio tradition serves as an alternative to traditional methods of historical inquiry in Chicano historiography.

According to historian Mario Garcia, "scholars of the Mexican American experience have not utilized oral history to construct autobiographical texts along the line of the Latin American testimonio." Recent works by Garcia including *Memories of Chicano History: The Life and Narrative of Bert Corona* (1994) and *Luis Leal: An Auto/Biography* (2000) are useful examples of the testimonio genre. Garcia's effort to link testimonio and Third World struggles to minorities in the U.S. has provided an opportunity to augment Chicano historical discourse.[5]

The following testimonio narrative is based on a series of oral or life history interviews with Julian Ruiz, a Tejano labor contractor who was directly involved in recruiting Tejano families to Oregon beginning in the 1950s. As such, he was part of Chicano Northwest history and the migration and subsequent settlement of Chicanos in Oregon. These interviews were videotaped, transcribed, and edited to render a testimonio highlighting his life history that clearly reflects a fragment of the collective Chicano experience in Oregon.

"Hijo de Troqueros y Campesinos Tejanos": Historia de Julian Ruiz

My grandparents on my father's side were Tejanos. My mother's parents came from Mexico but I don't know where in Mexico. I grew up with my grandfather Susano Ruiz in Asherton, Texas. He was born in 1884. My grandfather was a strong patriarch of the Ruiz extended family. He was a stern-looking man who didn't tolerate bad language and disrespect. In fact, in the mornings we would greet him with a "Buenos dias" and a kiss on the back of his hand to show respect. My grandmother Nasaria was born in 1890. My grandparents had three sons and two daughters. My father Juan Ruiz was born in 1912 in Laredo, Texas, and my mother Anastacia was born in 1913 in Palacio, Texas. My grandfather Susano built a home in Asherton that we called "La casa grande." My parents and "tios," some with their own families, lived at "La casa grande" with my grandfather. My grandfather Susano did trucking, labor contracting, and farm work. As a trucker and labor contractor he bought row crops from small local farmers in the Asherton area and hired crews to harvest the crops. He then trucked the produce to the packing houses in San Antonio, Texas. He also supplied workers to farmers and even toiled in the fields as a farmworker in Texas, Montana, Arkansas, and Louisiana. The Ruiz sons followed my grandfather's trucking and agriculture related livelihood.

I was born in 1930 in Asherton, Texas in my grandfather Susano's "La casa grande." I was my parent's first born. My parents had eleven children. I remember growing up with my grandfather Susano, "tios," and some cousins in "La casa grande." My grandmother, Narsaria, died in 1932 so I don't have any memories of her. Growing up in "La Casa Grande" I became very close with my "Tia Catarina," who remained unmarried. She became like a second mother to me. She practically raised me until I was about thirteen years old (see Fig. 7.1).

Growing Up in Asherton

I have good memories growing up in Asherton, Texas. Asherton was like other Texas towns in south Texas. The town was divided into the Americano side of town and the Mexicano barrio. The Americanos controlled the town. The Americano sheriff held local power for many years. Local farmers supported the sheriff and other Americanos in power. The farmers used their power to pressure their Mexicano workers to vote for the farmer's candidate. It wasn't unusual for the

Fig. 7.1. Young Julian Ruiz, 1942 (photo courtesy of Ruiz Family collection).

farmer to pay their workers' poll tax. The workers oftentimes felt that their jobs would be in jeopardy if they voted otherwise. Schools in Asherton were segregated. We had a grade school for the Mexicanos. It wasn't until the fifth grade that Mexicanos went to school with the Americanos. I remember that all my teachers were Americanos. I was an outgoing student. In grade school I liked singing in front of the class. I sang both English and Spanish songs. One song I remember singing went, "Voy a escribile a mi Santa Claus, para que me traiga una morenita, y si puede, que me traiga dos." One particular teacher liked me and would bring lunch for both of us. She brought sandwiches. This is how I came to know mustard. You know Mexicanos don't use mustard in their food. Growing up, I also remember going to a home school of a Mexican woman in town who taught Spanish to the Mexicanitos. I think she used to charge like 25¢ a week for the lessons. This is where I begin reading and writing a little Spanish.

In the late 1930s, my grandfather, Susano, remarried and life at "La casa grande" changed. My parents and uncles all sought out their own homes in Asherton. During the early 1940s, my grandfather Susano stopped trucking and started a small meat market and a mill for making corn tortillas in Asherton. My father and uncles continued trucking and doing agriculture related work. My Tio Joaquin and other close family members worked out of a small produce packing house run by my Tio Joaquin in Asherton.

As I said earlier, my parents and tios also earned a living as farmworkers. In 1942, when I was twelve or thirteen years old, my father and my Tio Joaquin took their families to Ferriday, La., to work in the cotton fields. They had traveled to Louisiana in 1941 with my grandfather Susano. A man who worked on a plantation in Louisiana came to south Texas to recruit cotton pickers. My grandfather agreed to take several Tejano families to Louisiana who had been picking cotton with him. At first, my grandfather and the other Tejano families just picked cotton. They returned to Louisiana the following year as cotton sharecroppers. My grandfather Susano traveled around. One year he traveled to Montana to thin and weed the sugar beets. Later he also worked in Arkansas.

In Louisiana, we worked as sharecroppers alongside the black people. My father and uncle also did some trucking for the cotton gin. I even remember that one year my Tio, Joaquin, took a truckload of fruit from Texas and set up a fruit stand in Ferriday. We worked for a man named Johnson at the Panola Plantation near Ferriday. We traveled to Louisiana between 1942 and 1946. The Panola Plantation had housing for about twenty sharecropper families. The majority of the sharecropping families were black. Eight were Tejano families. My father, mother, and seven of us kids lived in a two-bedroom plantation house. The house was simple. It had wooden floors and a jack pump for water. The house had several beds and a hairdresser. We had our very own radio. You know very few workers had radios in those days. We started planting and cultivating the cotton fields. We then moved on to weeding and finally picked the cotton. We stayed in Louisiana for about six months and worked until November to finish the picking season.

One year, I noticed that Mr. Johnson had an old 1932 Ford truck on blocks in one of the plantation sheds. The truck didn't have tires and looked like it had not been driven for years. I told my father about the old truck, but he didn't pay too much attention to me. I asked Mr. Johnson if he would sell the truck. He laughed and said that the old truck would probably not even run. I think that he also laughed because here was a scrawny thirteen-year-old kid trying to deal for the old truck. I persisted. He finally told me that he would give me the truck. I ran home and told my father about the truck. My father was bewildered and said, "What do you mean he gave you the truck?" My Tio, Carlos, who knew a little bit about engines, got the old truck running. We soon bought some tires. The truck needed four rear tires, but because things were tight during the war we only installed two rear tires. I didn't want to be a picker so I drove into the black neighborhood in Ferriday and recruited a small cotton picking crew and ran them around in the old 1932 truck. This is how, at the age of thirteen, I began my early farm labor recruiting.

I liked going to the black neighborhood in Ferriday. They had small restaurants and a dance hall. I liked to hear the blacks play the blues and see them dance the jitterbug. I recall one particular song the black musicians played was called the "Ration Blues." The song went like this, "Oh baby, baby, baby. What wrong with Uncle Sam? He is cutting all my sugar, now he is messing with my ham. I got the ration blues. He gave me but only forty ounces of any kind of meat. These little forty ounces won't last me a whole week. I got the ration blues." The blacks got along with the Tejano families. The Americanos discriminated greatly against the blacks. The local sheriff warned us about mixing with the blacks. He didn't want us to go into the black neighborhood. The Americanos threatened us by telling us that if we mixed with the blacks we would be treated like the blacks. Even the local sheriff warned us about mixing with the blacks and going into their neighborhood. I remember that blacks attending the local movie theater were restricted to the theater's balcony area. We were allowed to sit in the main floor but the Americanos would at times threaten to put us in the balcony if we mixed with blacks. This discrimination made me think about Texas, particularly west Texas where we would see signs in the restaurants that read, "No Mexicans allowed, Whites only." These signs angered me, but you couldn't do anything. I recall Mexicano veterans got so angered at these signs that they would tear up such places. They of course ended up in jail or fined.

Mi Casamiento

In early 1946, at the age of sixteen, I met my future wife at a dance. We knew each other for about three months before we married. One night a friend of mine and I walked her home late from the movies. I thought that she was going to get in trouble with her parents for returning home late. We stopped by her house and talked. I told her that I would stick around to see if she did get in trouble. After waiting awhile and seeing that nothing happened my friend and I walked away. Looking back toward her house I suddenly saw my wife and her younger sister come out of their house. I walked back toward her home. I asked her if she had gotten into trouble. She said that everything was fine. All of a sudden her mother came out of the house and saw us. We bolted. My future wife and I ran one way and my friend ran another way. We didn't even know where to run. We aimlessly walked around Asherton. My friend ended up at my grandfather's house and told him what had happened. My grandfather Susano came looking for me. He found us and sent me to my parent's house and he took her to his house for several days. Several days after this, my father returned from a trucking trip from San Antonio and got the news.

He got real mad and gave me tongue-lashing. By this time it was socially impossible for my wife to return home. You know things like this were more delicate back then. There was nothing else to do but get married. My parents went to her parents and formally asked permission for us to get married. A justice of the peace married us at my grandfather's tortilla mill and little meat market. We went to live at my father's house, very much like my own father who lived with my grandfather in "La casa grande."

After getting married I stopped going to school. My father didn't want me to leave school, but I did not want to be made fun of at school for being married and having my father financially support me. I told my father, "I want to work, give me work." This was the last year my father and tios traveled to Louisiana. My new wife and I joined them to Louisiana. Returning back to Asherton, I began trucking for the Ruiz brothers. I initially drove the Ruiz brothers' trucks to the San Antonio produce market. The Asherton area produced big crops of carrots, spinach, onions, turnips, and other produce that we trucked to San Antonio. I soon learned the ins and outs of the buying and selling taking place at the market. I would usually drive out of Asherton with a truckload of produce and spend several days traveling and selling the load at the Rios Brothers or the Fernandez Produce Houses in San Antonio. The market was always busy.

Being so young and being in charge of selling the truckload of produce created some initial problems for me. Once I remember trucking a load of onions to the market. After I made the sale I was given a check and I went to the local bank to cash the check. The bank cashier looked at me and asked, "Is this your check? Are you Julian Ruiz?" I was about 16 years old, short, and probably weighed no more than 115 pounds. I had to stand on my toes because the bank counter was a little high for me. I answered, "Yes." Since the check was for a large amount, the cashier decided to call one of the Rios brothers to verify my story. As she spoke on the phone, she asked, "Did you give a big check to a little bitty guy?" She soon said, "okay" and hung up the phone. When I returned to the produce house, one of the Rios brothers yelled out, "Here comes the little bitty guy." Thereafter, the Rios brothers and the guys at the produce house would tease me about the incident and began calling me "El Little Bitty" or simply "Bitty." The name stuck and, in fact to this day when I visit Asherton, some of my old friends still call me "Bitty." Even my oldest son, who was born in 1946, was nicknamed "El Bitty Chiquito" by my friends.

On another occasion, my cousin Juan Ruiz, who was about my age, drove with me to Homestead, Florida, to buy a truckload of tomatoes. Sometimes we had to drive long distances to get truckloads of produce because an early freeze in south Texas would wipe out the row crops. In Florida, produce house workers dumped tomatoes into wooden crates weighting about fifty pounds. The tomato crates were stacked about six or seven high. Being so short, I had to use an empty crate to reach the top crate stack to check the quality of the tomatoes. Once I asked a produce seller what a crate of tomatoes was selling for. He took a long look at me and asked, "Where is your father?". I exclaimed, "I am the one who is buying!" At first it seemed like he didn't want to believe me. I took one of the tomatoes and sliced it and checked the inside of the green tomato. I recall the guy just looked at me and soon realized that I knew what I was doing. I checked the seeds of the tomato to see how much color they had. I had to correctly judge the tomato so that it would reach its peak of ripeness within four to five days. This was the ideal condition that the produce houses would buy the tomatoes. I soon made a deal and had them load about 300 to 350 crates on to my father's truck for the long journey back to Texas. We generally drove day and night on our return trip. In Asherton, my Tio Joaquin had a small packinghouse near his house where we repacked and graded the tomatoes and other produce into smaller boxes. In a couple of years, the sellers and buyers at the different produce houses got to know me and I didn't have too many problems after a while.

CARLOS S. MALDONADO

By 1950, I had saved enough money from trucking to put a $700 down payment on my own truck. It was a green cab Chevrolet truck with dual rear wheels that I bought in Carrizo Springs. I think I paid about $4,000. My monthly payments were $80 a month. I told my father that I would either start my own trucking operation or join him. He told me that since I already knew the trucking business, the buying and selling taking place at the San Antonio market, and had developed some relationships with produce buyers, it would be good if I stayed with him. Since my father did not speak English, my association with him would also be advantageous.

Nuestro Viaje al Norte

During the early 1950s the trucking business began slowing down and competition became very heavy. Some of the produce packinghouses started moving to other areas of the state such as Hereford, Houston, and Dallas. Agriculture in the Asherton and surrounding area also lessened. This affected the local trucking business. By this time, my father and uncles had decided to split off and do their own trucking. A compadre of my father, who earlier had traveled to the Northwest, told my father that farmers in Oregon were in need of workers. The compadre gave my father a name of a farmer he had worked with in Independence, Oregon. My father made contact with the farmer and decided to make the trek to Oregon in the spring of 1950. He took his family as well as other families and drove north to work in the hops in Independence, Oregon. I stayed behind with one truck tending a struggling trucking business.

My father returned to Asherton, Texas, after the harvest season. That year he told me that I should join him in making the trek to Oregon the following spring. He suggested that I go to Oregon a month or so earlier before him. The plan was for me to make a labor contracting deal with the Independence farmers. Meanwhile my father would line up Tejano families in Asherton to make the trek north to Oregon. I agreed and, in early February 1951, I drove to Oregon. I drove my father's 1945 Chevrolet car with my sister, her husband and two kids, and my uncle, Leo. My wife stayed behind in Asherton waiting to come up later with my father. We had many car problems on the road. Something happened to the car's electrical system and it burned up several batteries and generators. By the time we got to Burbank, California, the car had broken down again. By this time we had also run out of money. My Uncle Leo, who had worked in Moses Lake, Wash., for a Japanese farmer, decided to call him and ask for an emergency loan. The farmer wired him the needed money. When we finally got to Oregon, I went to Independence to talk to the farmer my father had directed me to. It turned out that the Independence farmer had decided not to farm his hops because of low prices. By this time, I was no longer thinking about making labor contracting deals with Oregon farmers. The immediate need was to at least find work. I called my father and explained the situation. I then went to St. Paul, Oregon, and met with other families from Asherton who worked for a farmer named Ed Davidson outside of St. Paul. I talked to the farmer and he gave me work and camp housing for my family and my father and his family. This is how my travels to Oregon began.

La Vida en los Campos

In mid-March, my father drove his truck to St. Paul, Oregon. One of my other relatives followed my father and drove my 1950 truck. Soon my father, his family of nine, and my wife and four young children arrived at the Ed Davidson labor camp. Since I had experienced some problems getting situated in Oregon, I was glad that I had decided earlier that I didn't want my wife and family with me until I had things set up for them. The cold and rainy March weather greeted the weary travelers to our new temporary Oregon home. My wife didn't much like Oregon or the labor camp. Some of her first words after arriving at the camp were "Pos,

217

que esto?" (What is this?) However, she never asked to return to Asherton or complained about wanting a better place to live. She didn't like it, but quickly resolved to make the best of things. This was very supportive of her. My family brought very little with them. They didn't bring any furniture, just blankets, clothes, dishes, a washtub and washboard, and other limited personal things. This was the first time my children had traveled outside of Texas. The Davidson camp had three large faded grayish cabins. Each large cabin was divided into two family living units. Each family living area had two large rooms. One room was the kitchen and dining area and the second room was the bedroom. So things were a little tight, particularly for my father and his large family. The cabins had running water and a wood stove. The camp had a community shower and restroom in one of the end cabins. The cabin's floor was concrete. Davidson didn't charge the people for the camp housing or utilities, but expected them to work in his farm. I soon put my eldest son in the St. Paul grade school.

Early on it was difficult adjusting to Oregon. The most difficult thing was that Mexican foods were not found in the local grocery stores. This meant no fresh or canned chiles or other Mexican spices, pan dulce, chorizo, or tortillas. In fact we resorted to using "Fritos" to make "migas," a traditional Mexican breakfast dish made with fried corn tortilla wedges and scrambled eggs and topped with salsa. We had to adjust to not having Mexican foods that were readily available in the local stores in south Texas. The Oregon spring weather was cold and rainy, a big difference from south Texas. We had to split firewood for heating and cooking. Cooking with green or wet firewood gave us some problems. Our cabin would, at times, become filled with smoke. Cooking on a woodstove was difficult for my wife. This wood heating and cooking situation was a big change from our lives in Asherton.

It was also challenging for me to go from trucking contracting and being my own boss to working for someone else as a farmworker. Having our home in Asherton and living in the labor camp meant that my wife didn't have some of the basic household things we took for granted. We built a kitchen cabinet out of old wooden apple crates to store our food. We bought used mattresses and used scrap materials to divide the large bedroom into bedrooms for my kids and my wife and me. We washed and cleaned the cabin to make it more livable. Another thing that we missed were the Mexican dances, movies or other entertainment. Even though our initial stay was only temporary, we still missed the cultural things we had in Texas. The Davidson labor camp was about four to five miles out of St. Paul. This was different than living in town in Asherton. My wife stayed at the camp and cared for our three younger children while everyone else went out to work in the fields. Even though several Tejano families lived at the camp, it was different living in an area where Mexicanos were few. Those families who stayed year-round in Oregon felt this isolation even more.

The first year in Oregon we worked in the hops, strawberries, pole beans, and other row crops. By early fall, work in the Willamette Valley began to slow down so we soon headed to Prineville and Madras in eastern Oregon to pick and truck potatoes. The potato harvest was the last crop in the harvest season. By late October we would be anxious to head back to Asherton until the following spring. We followed this routine for several years until I decided in 1954 to stay in Oregon for good. Talking about our annual return trip to Asherton from eastern Oregon reminds me of a funny story that happened to us one year. My youngest brother Beto, who was about nine years old, liked to car hop. He would start the trip with my father, then hopped in my truck, and soon hopped on another family car. This particular year, the caravan of trucks and cars returning to Asherton stopped at Burns, Oregon, to eat and gas up. When we were ready to leave we yelled out if everyone was on board. The drivers of each truck or car shouted back, "Si, vamonos." So we took off not realizing that Beto was not on board. Each truck or car assumed that my carhopping brother was riding with someone else. Soon the different trucks and cars heading to Asherton became separated on the road.

Several days later, the different trucks and cars began arriving in Asherton. When the last truck arrived in Asherton, we realized that we had lost Beto. We all figured that the last time we had all seen Beto was back in Burns, Oregon. My mother was sick about it and began screaming for Beto. I, too, was very worried because it was late October and already cold. I imagined my little brother walking in the cold night along the highway. I went to the Carrizo Springs sheriff's office and explained the situation and using a map we retraced our route from eastern Oregon back to Asherton. We didn't know where we had lost Beto. We called the highway patrol to ask if they had seen a young boy on the road. We thought that maybe we had left Beto behind in one of the many bathroom stops we made on the side of road. We finally called the Burns sheriff's department and told him about our lost brother. The sheriff asked us to describe Beto and what he had been wearing. The sheriff said, "Yes, he is here." Beto stayed at the local jail the first night and then the sheriff took him home to be with his family. Soon we had Beto on the phone. Beto was angry for being left behind. The next day the Burns sheriff put Beto on the bus to Asherton all dressed up and toting a small suitcase. Several days later Beto arrived back home in Asherton. The whole incident was scary, but funny after we knew he was safe and sound.

El Principio de Mi Trabajo Como Contratista en Oregon

During that first year in Oregon, I met Ralph Case, a farmer who lived across the street from the Davidson labor camp. We soon developed a friendship that continues to this day. Back then he encouraged me to head a crew for him during the hop harvest. I agreed and during the hop harvest I ran a night crew and drove a tractor for him. He paid me $2 an hour. This was great because the going hourly wage was 80¢ an hour. I also hired out my truck for the hop harvest. I would drive my truck during the morning and then hire a driver for the afternoon. I was working about 15 hours a day during the hop harvest. Case liked my work and later asked me to recruit workers for him for the following year. I was hesitant at first. I didn't want to misinform people about coming from Texas to work in Oregon. My own experience was still fresh in my mind. Oregon was too far for them. I told him that he didn't have enough harvest work. I was concerned about workers being idle. He told me that he would talk to fellow farmers in an effort to keep workers busy. He told me that toward the end of the harvest season we would talk with other farmers and come up with a plan for recruiting Tejano farmworkers.

At the end of the harvest season, Ralph Case called me to his house to meet with him and a couple of other farmers. The other farmers included Bill McKay and Dick Spurup. At the outset of the meeting Bill McKay said to me, "You are going to be a contractor next year." They discussed their plan and toward the end of the meeting Ralph Case brings out a box of cigars and hands each one of us a cigar in a gesture of closing a deal. I can still remember the emotions I had that night when Case pounded his desktop and said to me, "From now on, you are going to be a big shot!" In anticipation of meeting with you today, I called Case and I asked him if he remembered that night. That night in 1951 was still vivid to him after all these years. He told me, "You have come a long way."

My labor recruiting and contracting in Oregon began that night. Thereafter, every year I signed up other area farmers. I initially ran four small labor camps but this increased. Two of the largest camps that I ran had 30-35 cabins. Each of the cabins housed a family of five or six. "El campo verde," so named because it was painted green, was one of the larger camps I operated outside of Woodburn. As I gained more farming contracts, the number of workers I contracted also increased. My contracting went beyond San Pablo and even into Independence, Brooks, Gervais, and Woodburn. In the beginning, there weren't any legal requirements to be a labor contractor. During the early 1950s you simply went about your business. It wasn't until the early 1960s that we started feeling the pressure in Oregon to get a state contractor's license. We also had to register with the federal government. During the 1950s there were very few of us working as labor contractors. I was the only contractor that recruited families from Texas. The other contractors simply hired workers that came to Oregon of their own accord.

By 1955, after returning yearly to Asherton, Texas, once the crops were harvested, I decided to stay year-round in Oregon. In fact, my younger brother Primitivo and his family were the first ones of the Ruiz family to stay year-round in Oregon, and he was the first Mexicano to live in St. Paul during the winter. I decided to stay year-round in Oregon to keep from having to take my children out of school to make the trek to Oregon each spring. By this time, I had also lined up more farmers for whom I recruited and contracted Tejano families. I anticipated that the decision to stay in Oregon would further help me establish and develop stronger relationships with area farmers. A farmer named Ben Dyke provided me with an old two-story farmhouse during my first Oregon winter in 1955. Moving out of the labor camp and moving into a regular house made my decision to stay in Oregon easier. During the winter I worked part-time. The savings I made during the harvest season helped us make it through the first cold winter in Oregon. The grocery store in St. Paul where we had set up credit for Tejano families also provided credit to me. By 1957, I bought my house in St. Paul. I lived in this house until the early 1970s.

Reclutamiento de la Gente

I started recruiting Tejano families for Willamette Valley farmers in 1952. I had not yet decided to stay in Oregon for good. Before returning to Texas in 1951 for the off season, I explained to Case, McKay, and Spurup that the people I would be recruiting would need money to make the long trip from Texas to Oregon. I also mentioned to them that the people would need some support to buy food and other needs once they arrived in Oregon and before they would start working. The farmers agreed to lend me advance money that I would, in turn, use to make loans to the recruited families. I had to pay back the farmers' advance recruitment money at the end of the harvest season. This meant a major financial risk for me. Each of the farmers pitched in money to the recruiting pot. One year I had $10,000 to recruit workers. The farmers also helped me establish credit for the families at the local grocery store. I returned to Texas that winter knowing that camp housing, jobs, and travel loan money for the families would help me recruit Tejano families to Oregon.

I first started recruiting families I knew from Asherton, Carrizo Spring, and Crystal City. Later on I went to Raymondville, La Sara, Monte Alto, Alamo, San Benito, and other communities in "El Valle." I made direct visits to families. After several years of directly visiting interested families I began to recruit out of the local employment office. Soon people would anticipate my annual recruitment trips. Families that I recruited to Oregon came for varying reasons. These included the hard economic conditions in Texas, particularly in farm work, and higher wages in Oregon than in Texas. Camp housing and work also enticed families, and the loan support I provided served as an incentive too. Families who had previously traveled to Oregon helped encourage others. The call to "Vamonos al norte" was enough to stir the interest among some families. Some families, who annually traveled to west Texas or New Mexico, simply extended their trek to Oregon. Oftentimes, one family would lead me to another family who had expressed an interest in making the trek north to Oregon. Depending on the size of the family, the condition of their vehicle, and money they had in hand, I would estimate the amount a particular family would need to make the trip to Oregon. The loans I made to the families usually ranged from $300 to $500. These loans were based on verbal agreements. It was expected that the families would pay off the loans as they worked. The usual travel expenses included gas, mechanical repairs and tires, and food expenses on the road. My return trip to Oregon took place in early March. This coincided with the annual car license renewal in Texas. It never failed; this needed expense was usually part of our travel loan negotiations. Some families, afraid of getting lost or breaking down on the road, followed me to Oregon. They felt that if they did break down on the road they had me to depend on for the needed money for repairs. I would often lead a caravan of cars and pickups to Oregon. Once I recruited an entire extended family named the Benavides from Monte Alto, Texas. The extended family included three brothers, and their young families, and an unmarried sister who cared for their elderly mother. One of the brothers accompanying my caravan somehow got lost on the road. We finally realized that we had lost him. The sister went looking for him and luckily found him. I also recall one particular family of seven who wanted to make the trip with me, but didn't have a car. The family was poor and was living in another family's garage in Raymondville, Texas. I had another person with me to help me drive so all nine of us made the trip to Oregon in my pickup. Because of limited space, the family riding with me brought very few things with them. Some families scheduled their departure at a later date. Several families took the loan money and never showed up in Oregon.

On our trip to Oregon, we would usually stop in some small town on the road to gas up or buy food at a grocery store. It always amused me how the clerks at these stores looked amazed at the hoard of Mexicanos entering their store to buy a loaf of bread, baloney, cans of pork and beans, and other food to prepare a meal on the side of road.

In the beginning, I took a route through Utah to reach Oregon. However, the snow conditions in Utah in early March forced me to change my route through California. Once in Oregon, I directed the families to different labor camps where they got assigned a cabin. Most of the time, each family got a cabin but, once in a while, a large family needed two cabins. Since the cabins were fairly close to each other, separating a family into two cabins wasn't a problem. The families brought very little with them so one of the first things the families did was go to local second-hand stores to buy mattresses, pots and pans, and other basic household items. Several families arrived at the labor camp and didn't like the situation or the rainy spring weather. Once in a while the camp would awaken in the early morning and realize that a particular family had left in the middle of the night. Word of a family's departure quickly spread throughout the camp. I would at times drive out to find them, particularly if I had advanced them a travel loan to Oregon or they had taken credit at the local grocery store under my name. Efforts to find them generally proved futile.

Most of the families would generally work with me for several years. They kept busy throughout the spring and summer working in the strawberries, cucumber, pole beans, hops, and other crops. By fall, farm work slowed down in the Willamette Valley so I would extend my trucking and labor contracting to the potato harvest in Prineville and Madras in eastern Oregon. I started doing this in 1952 and continued for many years. I was only one of several labor and trucking contractors that worked the potato harvest in eastern Oregon. Others included Manuel Caudillo and Chavel Ruvalcaba. Chavel was originally from Asherton, but did trucking out of Sunnyside, Wash. Some families I recruited from Texas followed me to eastern Oregon to pick and truck the potato harvest. I basically worked out of Prineville and Madras, Oregon. In Prineville, I had about five potato farmers that I supplied with workers and trucking. In Madras, I contracted with another six farmers. Housing for the workers in eastern Oregon was limited so I would arrange housing through local motels and apartments. Several weeks before the potato harvest began I drove to eastern Oregon and secured housing for the workers by putting down a rental deposit. In Madras, I housed about ten families and in

Prineville I had about seven families. In Madras, I usually arranged housing with the Madras Motel. The workers were responsible for paying their own housing.

Some families returned to Texas after the potato harvest only to return the following spring. Other families who had decided to stay in Oregon returned to the Willamette Valley. A few of the families that returned to the Willamette Valley remained in the labor camps during the winter. One particular farmer was concerned about this since the camp cabins were made of plywood sheeting and not insulated for winter use. Some of these families later sought out housing in town. Some of the families I recruited to Oregon helped establish the early Mexicano communities in Woodburn, Gervais, and St. Paul.

It was one of these years in eastern Oregon that my father died from a heart attack while working in a potato cellar in late October 1962. The day my father died we had to work late to truck in all that had been picked during the day. We were concerned that the potatoes would freeze if we left them in the field. My father was overseeing the unloading of the trucks at a potato cellar. Earlier that day my father had complained of heartburn, but attributed it to drinking the night before. I was driving around checking with the loaders in the different fields and then drove to the potato cellar. As I neared the cellar, I noticed that a station wagon was parked on the cellar's unloading ramp. I yelled out telling one of the workers that the car needed to be moved out because we had another truck ready to unload. The worker walked toward me and told me, "Julian, your father died." I responded, "What the hell is with you? What are you saying?" By this time the attending doctor whose station wagon was parked on the unloading ramp came over and confirmed my father's death. I yelled at the doctor, "Where is my father?" "We took him to the mort [mortuary]," he answered. I argued, "Why? You should have taken him to the hospital; maybe he is not really dead." The doctor said, "No, I tried to give him oxygen, but he was already gone." The doctor tried to console me and gave me a shot to ease my shock. Several days later we took my father to St. Paul in the Willamette Valley where we had his funeral and burial. My father was a very young man when he died. He was only fifty years old. My mother still had three kids living with her when my father died. My mother stayed with me for several months but then decided to return to Asherton.

Business Ventures and Changes in Contracting

During the following years, I continued labor and trucking contracting but I also established several businesses. One particular effort was staging Mexican dances in the Woodburn area. The dances began in the early 1960s and were only seasonal when the harvest was in full swing. In fact, the first band that I hired was a family from Phoenix that I had recruited among others. One day when I was at their camp he told me that his family were all musicians. He invited me to come by after work to their cabin and listen to them play. This is how the idea of sponsoring Mexican dances came about. The family worked for me as pickers Monday through Thursday and on Friday I paid them to practice and play for dances on the weekend. They called themselves "Los Atomicos." I began renting halls in Broad Acres, Hubbard, and Woodburn. In downtown Hubbard, I rented the Grange Hall and in Woodburn I rented the Belle Passe Hall next to 99E. The interest and need for the dances by the Mexicano community was clearly there.

The first real business besides my labor and trucking contracting was a small gas station in Gervais, Oregon. I started the gas station in 1964 after I realized that in doing trucking I would often drive through Gervais and by this small corner gas station. So I decided to take it over and use it for gassing up my trucks. "El campo verde," one of the large labor camps that I ran, was also between Gervais and Woodburn. In 1967, I took over a rundown tavern near Hubbard on 99E called the Play More Park. I ran it for several years until the state forced me to renovate it. I renovated the tavern by expanding it to include a restaurant, bar, and a dance hall. I called it "El Acapulco." I ran "El Acapulco" until 1972. In the early 1970s, I bought a small grocery store between Gervais and Brooks on 99E. I moved my family from St. Paul to a small house next to the business. I called it the Rancho Market. I sold Mexican grocery products as well as curios and tacos. I began distributing Mexican foods to area stores including corn tortillas. In 1998, my son Jeff took over the duties of the store and redirected it to concentrate on nursery plants and Mexican garden accessories and pottery. We renamed the business the Rancho Gardens. This was the period when the nursery industry began to take off in the Willamette Valley. During this time I continued to do labor and trucking contracting. My older son Jerry began to assume more of my contracting duties. The contacting business has changed over the years. The first change I saw was the increase in state government regulations relating to labor contracting. The wage, safety, and reporting requirements have grown significantly. Second, most of the farmworkers coming into the Willamette Valley are single Mexican males. In fact, most workers we hire are no longer families from Texas. The single men generally come on their own accord from Mexico and California. I haven't had to actively recruit workers for many years. Third, new labor contracting opportunities have opened up. One of these has been the Christmas tree industry. This also includes tree planting as well. This has provided farmworkers a job during the winter months. We are very much involved in contacting workers for the Christmas tree industry. Another area is the plant nursery business. We also provide workers for the growing nursery business in the Willamette Valley. In fact, our Rancho Gardens business reflects this growth in the nursery business. Fourth, my own trucking business has pretty much disappeared. In fact, I sold my trucks because many of the farmers I contracted with began buying their own trucks. And sixth, my contracting business is being assumed by one of my sons who is more prepared in the business and state government aspects of labor contracting as well as computers. Seventh, labor organizing has become more evident through the union work of Pineros y Campesinos Unidos del Noroeste-Tree Planters and Farm Workers United of the Northwest (PCUN). PCUN has been active fighting against bad contractors but this not affected our labor contracting very much. I feel that Cesar Chavez did much for farmworkers but I also believe that he negatively affected workers as well. My sons will further develop the Ruiz labor contracting and Rancho Gardens nursery business. My hopes are that my sons will be successful. I learned a lot from my father and grandfather. Their trucking, labor contracting, and spirit of risk taking and success influenced me and helped me in my work and personal life. My sons represent the fourth generation of Ruiz labor contractors (see Fig. 7.2).

Narrative Themes

Whereas the traditional testimonio is the direct story as told by an individual, I have elected to include a segment that compliments Julian's testimonio. The following segment highlights several thematic points that emerge from Julian's testimonio.

First, Julian's testimonio provides a strong cultural element. Specifically, his testimonio illustrates the extended familial pattern of living together where grandparents, parents, and their children live together to form a close-knit extended family. Susano Ruiz's "Casa Grande" served a social and an economic purpose. Susano

Fig. 7.2. Julian Ruiz at one of his Oregon cabins, 2000 (photo courtesy of Ruiz Family collection).

centered the Ruiz extended family's trucking and agricultural related livelihood. The grandfather's role clearly underscored Susano's continuing authority and status as the patriarch of the Ruiz extended family. The formal greetings bestowed on Susano illustrate the reverence and respect afforded to the grandfather. The sense and importance of family, the trucking and labor-contracting legacy left by Susano Ruiz, and the spirit of risk taking in journeying beyond Texas to Louisiana, Montana, and Arkansas to make a life certainly influenced Julian's own life. Julian struck out for the north from Texas to establish a new life in Oregon. He established himself as a successful labor contractor in Oregon's Willamette Valley. He now serves as the patriarch of the Oregon Ruiz family. Several of his sons and daughters direct his labor contracting and nursery business. Julian was very much influenced by his grandfather and father. He in turn is influencing another generation of Ruizes.

A second thematic point that emerged from Julian's testimonio is the issue of race and discrimination. Working and living as a farmworker in Texas and Louisiana exposed Julian to issues of race and discrimination. He attended a segregated school and lived in an ethnically divided community. He witnessed firsthand businesses that displayed "No Mexicans, Whites only" signs. His family worked and lived with black sharecroppers and witnessed firsthand the race relations between blacks, whites, and Mexicanos. He recognized the power structure in his own local community of Asherton that placed Mexicanos at the bottom and Americanos on top. He likewise recognized the manipulative power that Americano farmers had over Mexicano workers in the electoral process.

A third thematic point that emerged from Julian's testimonio is the life of migrant farmworkers. Julian's travel to Oregon substantiates the unpredictable life of farmworkers. The experience of journeying to unknown and far away places to make a life is clearly illustrated by Julian's own travels to Oregon. Labor camp housing and the associated challenges experienced by migrant farmworkers in such camps are underscored in Julian's testimonio.

A fourth thematic point that emerged from Julian's testimonio is the adjustments that farmworkers are forced to make in culturally isolated areas such as Oregon. The absence of cultural foods and social outlets contributed to Julian and other farmworkers' needs to adjust to new cultural settings. Julian's testimonio also reflects his and others' proactive efforts to recreate cultural opportunities in Oregon for the emerging Mexicano community. The staging of Mexican dances, establishing Mexican cultural businesses, and other efforts reflect this cultural recreation in Oregon.

A fifth thematic point that emerged from Julian's testimonio is the development of a labor contractor in Oregon. The symbiotic relationship between farmers and Julian as a labor contractor is illuminating. For example, Julian's labor contracting experience and contacts along with the farmers' capital resources created an indispensable relationship critical in recruiting farmworkers to Oregon.

Sixth, the whole aspect of recruiting Tejano families to Oregon was quite revealing. Julian's testimonio highlights the diverse reasons Tejano families had in making the journey to Oregon.

A seventh thematic point that emerged from Julian's testimonio is the historical changes in labor contracting. Initially, Julian experienced few state regulations regarding labor contracting and the welfare of workers. Today, state laws governing labor contracting business reflect the labor protection needs of farmworkers. These state laws include provisions for tightening legal expectations for labor contracting, including fines for operating an unlicensed labor contracting business. Labor contractors are required to carry a $10,000 bond to pay for any labor contracting violations. Legal requirements for farmworker housing either owned or operated by labor contractors have also been strengthened. State labor camp laws have also focused on protecting farmworkers from being discharged and evicted as a

CARLOS S. MALDONADO

result of filing a labor complaint against the labor camp operator. The active role of Pineros y Campesinos Unidos del Noroeste (PCUN) has been important in advocating for legislation protecting workers. While new legal requirements in Oregon have impacted labor contracting, new labor contracting opportunities have also developed. The change of row crop employment to new labor needs including the emerging Christmas tree and nursery industry has expanded labor-contracting opportunities.

And eighth, Julian's testimonio illuminates the role he played as a labor contractor in establishing the Chicano community's presence in Oregon's Willamette Valley. I speculate that similar experiences took place in other regions of the United States. Presently, there exists a dearth of sources that document the role labor contractors played in the recruitment, settlement, and labor of farmworkers in Oregon and the Northwest. Julian Ruiz's testimonio premises a particular life experience that certainly illuminates the lives of many Tejano families who came to Oregon and began to establish a sense of community in various Willamette Valley communities. It is important to further document the experiences of farm labor contractors to expand our understanding of the Chicano/Mexicano presence in the Northwest.

Endnotes

1. H.P. Rickman, ed. *Wilhelm Dilthey, Pattern and Meaning in History: Thoughts on History and Society* (New York: Harper & Row, 1961), 89. The quotation is a translation of the texts taken from volume vii of Dilthey's works published by Teubner Verlag, Stuttgart.
2. Ibid., 79.
3. Esteban Montejo, *The Autobiography of a Runaway* Slave, ed. and trans. Miguel Barnet (New York: Pantheon Books, 1968).
4. John Beverley, "The Margin at the Center: On Testimonio (Testimonio Narrative)" in George M. Gugelberger, ed., *The Real Thing: Testimonio Discourse and Latin America* (Durham: Duke University Press, 1998), 24.
5. Mario T. Garcia. *Bert Corona, Memories of Chicano History: The Life and Narrative of Bert Corona* (Los Angeles: University of California Press, 1994), 21. See also Garcia's *Luis Leal: An Auto/biography* (Austin: University of Texas Press, 2000).

Mexicanos and the Catholic Church in Eastern Washington: The Spokane Diocese, 1956–1997

Gilberto Garcia

Historically, the Catholic Church has played an important role in the Mexican communities in the United States. In the Southwest, the relationship between the predominantly EuroAmerican Catholic Church and the Mexican population began in the aftermath of the military takeover of the area. According to Chicano historians, the relationship was forged in conflict exposing the ethnocentric and racist tendencies of the institution. When *Mexicanos* moved into areas outside the Southwest, the institution saw them just like other immigrant groups, and expected the eventual assimilation of the population into the mainstream of the Catholic Church. Without the historical legacy Mexicans inherited in the Southwest and as newcomers in the region, more recent developments forged the relationship between the institution and the Mexican origin population in the Northwest. From 1956 to 1997, the struggle between conservative and progressive forces within the institution affected the relationship between the Mexican origin population and the Catholic Church. The struggle of these forces must be seen against the background of the reform movement of Vatican II, the theology of liberation movement, and the new conservatism of Pope John Paul II. While this struggle affected the structure and policies of the Catholic Church, Latino Catholics responded with various theological models, thus revealing a heterogeneous population. However, an analysis of the external forces reflected in the changing demographics in the community played an important role in the relationship. In the late 1940s and early 1950s, the Catholic Church in Eastern Washington encountered a small but growing Mexican population that posed a challenge to a predominantly white institution. While at that time the size of the population and the economic and political powerlessness in the Mexican community was not a threat to the white English-speaking population in the region, by the 1980s the dramatic demographic growth of the population had shaken the foundations of the institution and exposed the ethnic racial divide within it. In some communities in the Spokane Diocese, the relationship was strained, leading to conflict and separation and raising questions of ethnic and racial discrimination in the Catholic Church. This was particularly the case in Othello where beginning in the 1980s, the population growth affected the schools, the political system, public service agencies, and the Catholic Church. Upon close examination, the conflict and crisis between the Catholic Church and the Latino Catholic parishioners was a microcosm of the problems in the larger society. This essay presents a review of the literature on the Catholic Church and the Latino community in the United States. It follows with a chronological examination of the history of the relationship between the largely Mexican origin population and the Catholic Church in the Spokane Diocese in Eastern Washington from 1956 to 1997.

The Catholic Church and the Latino Community

Research on the Latino Catholic Church in the United States provide the insights necessary for understanding the relationship of the Catholic Church and the Latino community in the Northwest region. Any discussion on the nature of the American Catholic Church must begin with one of the early studies on the institution. *The Mexican American People* by Leo Grebler, Joan W. Moore, and Ralph C. Guzman presented one of the first serious analyses of the Catholic Church and its relationship to the Mexican origin population in the United States. The study, titled "Dynamics of the Catholic Church: From Pastoral to Social Concern," examined the reasons for the failure or failures of the American Catholic Church in the Mexican and Mexican American community in the United States. Author Patrick H. McNamara concluded that the meager resources available to the Church in the Southwest and the need to spend the scarce resources in pastoral concerns explained its failure in the region. The entrance of more Mexican immigrants who mixed traditional and folk Catholic practices with pagan (Indian) rites exacerbated the problem facing the institution. McNamara argued that with "no firmly structured church" to deal with the encounter of Mexican and Anglo cultures, "ruling over isolated settlements with no financial support," "a shortage of clergy," and to make things worse, a church under the control of "foreigners" rather than "American" priests retarded the assimilation of the population.[1] Needless to say, ethnocentric and assimilationist perspectives influenced this assessment of the nature of the Catholic Church in the Southwest. Several years later, the same author reconsidered his previous research and provided a response to the critics of the new generation of Chicana/o scholars. Patrick McNamara's "Assumptions, Theories and Methods in the Study of Latino Religion after Twenty Years" raised important theoretical and methodological issues on the study of the Catholic Church and the Latino community in the Northwest region. McNamara assessed the limitations of the research published in the classic study *The Mexican American People* and reviewed the theoretical orientation in the early research on the Church. He acknowledged the influence of an assimilationist bias in the study: "Given the comparisons with Gunnar Mydal, it is not surprising that a kind of functionalism with assimilation as a major motif formed the underlying intellectual ground of the study."[2]

While acknowledging the problems inherent in the early research, McNamara failed to move the discussion into new theoretical directions. Instead, he concluded that a new paradigm must "balance institutional analysis with a cultural approach focusing on enduring elements of folk religiosity both Catholic and Protestant."[3] Nevertheless, the questions raised in the essay reveal the weaknesses of studies that continue to promote a research agenda based on the European immigrant model. Such a view is widely accepted among mainstream scholars and the Church hierarchy in communities outside the Southwest. More recently, historical studies that examine the experience of Latinos in the American Catholic Church reflect changes in the assumptions and interpretations guiding the research. Moises Sandoval's *Fronteras: A History of the Latin American Church in the USA Since 1513* is an anthology of the Catholic Church from the beginnings to the present. The book includes studies on the history of the institution in the Southwest as well as an examination of the Church in the Midwest and East. While focusing on the Mexican origin population, the study examines the Puerto Rican experience and the role of Latino Protestantism in the United States. Sandoval's chapters on the Catholic Church from 1946 to the present are especially useful in understanding the importance of the Chicano Movement and Church structures for Latinos.[4] Sandoval's *On the Move: A History of the Hispanic Church in the United States* presented his own historical synthesis on the Latino church in the United States and expanded and updated sections found in the first study.

In the last study, a liberationist perspective defined and guided the examination of the Latino church in the United States, a perspective that emphasized what he calls "the Church of the Poor." Several insights found in the study are useful in the historical interpretation of the Catholic Church in the Northwest region. The study clearly identified the differences in the experience of European immigrant Catholics and the experience of Latino Catholics: the important role of racism and discrimination inside and outside the church. Secondly, the class differences between the church and the community further separates the two entities. A third important reason for the social distance between the institution and the Latino community is the notion of an "uprooted people, which includes documented and undocumented immigrants, political refugees, and the urbanized Latino population."[5]

Besides the national histories discussed above, important regional historical interpretations on the Latino Catholic Church in the United States offer insight on the issue. *Mexican Americans and the Catholic Church, 1900–1965* by Jay P. Dolan and Gilberto Hinojosa provides the researcher with three studies on the relationship of the Mexican origin population and the Catholic Church.[6] Gilberto Hinojosa's *"Mexican American Faith Communities in Texas and the Southwest"* and Jeffrey M. Burns's *"The Mexican Catholic Community in California"* present interesting interpretations of the Mexican origin Catholic experience in the Southwest, and useful sections on the history of the Church's activities in the post-1940s era. However, within the context of communities located outside the Southwest, the studies are limited by an interpretation grounded on the centrality of the community's Spanish and Mexican roots prior to 1836–48[7]. In spite of the Southwest centric approach of previous historical studies, researchers on the Church and the Latino community include the experience of communities beyond the Southwest. David A. Badillo's "The Catholic Church and the Making of Mexican American Parish Communities in the Midwest" examined the relationship of the Mexican origin population and the Catholic Church in communities outside the traditional Mexican Southwest. Badillo captured the essence of the historical experience of the Church and the Mexicano communities in the Midwest: "Mexican Catholicism in the Midwest emerged quietly, without the symbolic artifacts of Spanish missions or a legacy of colonial Catholicism. It matured within the changing context of United States urban and social history as a distinctive regional component of the Mexican American experience. However, it remained tangled in an antiquated framework of European immigration."[8] For researchers on the Latino Catholic Church in the Northwest, the above observations are instructive for an understanding of the historical experience in the region. Mexicans in the Northwest like their counterparts in the Midwest lacked a legacy of "colonial Catholicism" and were subjected to "an antiquated framework of European immigration." Placed within the larger context of the United States, Northwestern communities developed as "a distinctive regional component of the Mexican American experience"

Alberto Lopez Pulido's "Conflict and Struggle in Mexican Catholics" examined the history of the Mexican community and the San Diego Diocese by focusing on power relations and ethnic/racial conflict in a religious institution. A central idea in the study examined conflict and power struggles as manifestations of the competition over "symbolic resources (that is, sacred beliefs and practices) that embody racial and ethnic identities and traditions."[9] While the study examined the history of a diocese in California, it offers a framework that goes beyond historical periods and geographical boundaries. Regardless of geographic location in the United States, conflict and power struggles between Latino Catholics and the institution manifest themselves as competition over "symbolic resources." Recent studies on the Catholic Church contribute to our understanding of the issue of gender and the activism of Chicanas/os in the institution. Lara Medina's *Las Hermanas* examines the history of Chicana/Latina religious activists in the U.S. Catholic Church and provides one of the best studies on the interconnections of race, ethnicity, and gender in a religious institution. However, in spite of the inclusion of women activists from throughout the United States, it is plagued with the same southwest centric perspective of the history of Chicana/Latinas in the U.S. Catholic Church.[10]

The above discussion on the literature of the Latino community and the Catholic Church reveals a paucity of studies on the history of the Catholic Church in the Northwest region. Wilfred P. Schoenberg's *A History of the Catholic Church in the Pacific Northwest, 1743–1983* presented a brief historical overview of the Latino community and its relationship to the predominantly white Catholic institution. Unfortunately, the study revealed the biases of Euro-American scholars who apply stereotypical references on the character of Latina/o culture. For example,

Schoenberg described one of the priests working in the Northwest: "He had the macho image and the endowments of the heart of the Mexicans and the gift-of-gab of the Irish."[11]

A second flaw of the study is the application of a simplistic framework based on the experience of the Church with European immigrants. This perspective common among traditional American historians fails to see the differences in the historical experience of the white European immigrants and Mexican immigrants. In reference to the report on the Yakima Valley Mexican Catholic community, Schoenberg used a simplistic "just like the" Europeans model and remarked, "This report reveals the repetitious nature of immigrant problems for the northwest church; first the Irish, who could speak English, then the Germans who could not, then the Italians. What was happening to the Hispanics had happened before."[12] Needless to say, the study is incomplete, covering the work of the Catholic Church in fewer than eight pages, most of it based on a report on the conditions of the Mexican Catholic community in the Yakima Valley.[13] Nevertheless, the short history provided a point of reference to the focus of this study on the Spokane Diocese. According to Schoenberg, the Catholic Church in the Yakima Valley, which attracted the largest number of Mexicans, failed to undertake an organized program until 1968. He found very little institutional interest in the Spanish-speaking Catholic community in the Yakima Valley; priests came and left, with no permanent and consistent pastoral work prior to 1968.[14]

Schoenberg included only part of the report; a complete copy of the original report is located in the archives at Gonzaga University. Yet, in the Spokane Diocese, the church established an organized structure beginning in 1956 by appointing Spanish-speaking priests who took care of the pastoral needs of the Mexican origin population in the region. Finally, in Patricia Brandt and Lillian A. Pereyra's *Adapting in Eden: Oregon's Catholic Minority, 1838–1986*, the treatment of the Latina/o community is limited to a few pages in the history of the Catholic Church. In spite of the number of interviews conducted for the chapter, the historical overview is superficial.

While acknowledging the initial "cultural conflict" between the Mexican origin population and the institution, the authors conclude: "In Woodburn, it took some time to overcome hostility between the Anglo and Mexican American communities, but gradually resentment diminished and St. Luke became a bicultural parish, as many others have since, with Masses celebrated in both English and Spanish."[15] Such is the status of research on the Mexican origin population and the role of the Catholic Church in the Northwest.

Thus, the literature on the Catholic Church and the Latino community forces the researcher to consider several alternative approaches and considerations. First is the need to reject interpretations of the nature of the American Catholic Church and the Latino community in the Northwest based on assimilation models. Second is the recognition that issues of race and racism play an important role in the social dynamics of communities in the region. Third, the examination of diverse and heterogeneous responses from the Latino community to social institutions in the United States presents a complex and changing reality. Finally, without the colonial legacy of the Catholic Church in the Southwest, it is imperative that researchers highlight the distinctive contribution of the Latino Catholic experience in areas beyond the traditional Southwest, within the context of a national framework.

The Mexican Population and the Diocese of Spokane: First Contacts, 1956-1964

The Diocese of Spokane came into existence by papal decree in December 1913, covering 30,000 square miles of Eastern Washington and serving sixteen counties.[16] From the 1900s to the 1940s, the population in the communities located in the diocese was predominantly white. Due to the shortage of labor during

World War II, Mexican braceros entered several of the small communities within the boundaries of the diocese. In the Walla Walla area braceros arrived as early as 1943, worked in the pea farms in the area, and continued to arrive until 1947, but were gradually replaced by domestic workers from Texas and California.[17] By the 1960s, the Mexican population had dispersed to other areas including Pasco and Othello.[18] An organized plan to reach the Mexican Catholic population began in 1956, and by 1964 the entrance of Mexican and Mexican American migrant workers into the region extending from Walla Walla to Othello set the stage for the first contact of the EuroAmerican Catholic Church and the Mexican community.

The philosophy and policies of one of the most progressive bishops in the history of the diocese shaped the first years between the Catholic Church and the Mexican population. Bishop Bernard Topel of Helena, Mont., took over the reins of the Spokane Diocese in 1955. In the Vatican, major changes were about to take place that led to some of the most important reforms in the history of the Catholic Church. Catholic theologians and historians saw the end of "the Tridentine Era of the Church and the whole fortress mentality characteristic of the Roman Catholic Church since Trent."

Under the rule of Pius XII, the institution gave power to the Curia and weakened the influence of the bishops.[19] After his death, the Church underwent a major historical transformation through the work of Pope John XXIII and Pope Paul VI: Vatican Council II (1962–1965).[20] Most historians agree that the proceedings inside the Vatican Council revealed the struggle between the traditionalists and the progressives in the Catholic Church. In the end, the progressive forces were victorious in producing major changes in several areas of the Catholic Church.[21] During the Vatican Council reforms the Curia (the central administrative body of the Catholic Church) contained the most conservative and traditional sector of the Catholic hierarchy. Most significant, these reforms provided the basis for action-oriented Catholics.

The preface of the *Pastoral Constitution on the Church in the Modern World* stated that "the joys and hopes, the grief and anxieties of the men of this age, especially those who are poor or in any way afflicted, these are the joys and hopes, the griefs and anxieties of the followers of Christ."[22] Promulgated by his Holiness, Pope Paul VI on Dec. 7, 1965. This progressive stance from the Catholic Church influenced the hierarchy of the Spokane Diocese on the treatment of the ever- growing Mexican population in the area.

Ordained in 1927, Bishop Topel earned his doctorate degree in mathematics at Harvard, and later taught at Carroll College. Whether this influenced his thinking or not, his father supported socialists before World War I.[23] More than likely, influenced by the Vatican II reforms, Bishop Topel paid close attention to the plight of Mexican workers in the communities located in the boundaries of the diocese. Bishop Topel is remembered as a sort of St. Francis of Assisi; he lived in an old house with no heat, no phone, and little or no food in the icebox.[24]

In 1956, the number of Spanish-speaking workers from Texas and Mexico grew in the Walla Walla area, pressing the diocese to assign priests in several labor camps. More than likely, the local clergy alerted the diocese of the need for priests who could take care of the growing Spanish-speaking population. Initially, the Spokane Diocese assigned English-speaking priests who offered masses and religious instruction in the auditorium of the labor camp. A Mexican American high school student translated Mass to Spanish for the benefit of around 120 persons. The church conducted masses in the labor camp in the evenings as well as in the hall of the Pea Growers' Association, previously the Walla Walla Air Base. This labor camp housed single workers. It is difficult to ascertain if these workers were domestic workers or the few braceros that made it into the Northwest in the 1950s.[25] While the entrance of braceros practically came to an end in the Northwest in 1947, some entered communities in the Columbia

Basin in the early 1950s.[26] Moreover, Mexican American farm migrant workers brought their families to work in the region.[27] In preparation for the following year, the Spokane Diocese bought a building, formerly a Baptist Church, for a mission church to serve the needs of Touchet.[28] As the population grew in the area during the harvest season, the diocese brought the first Spanish-speaking priest to Walla Walla. By August 1957, the Spokane Diocese announced the assignment of Father Da Lio as a chaplain to St. Mary's Hospital in Walla Walla. Born in Italy and educated in the Pontifical Gregorian University in Rome, Father Da Lio was fluent in several languages including Spanish. Before his assignment to Spokane, he worked as a teacher in the Ruben Dario College and in the Academy of Fine Arts in Nicaragua.[29] Between 1957 and 1964, Father Da Lio served the growing Mexican population in the area, offering masses, religious instruction, and the celebration of traditional Catholic rituals.[30] In 1958, Bishop Topel visited the Walla Walla area and observed firsthand the impact of a Spanish-speaking priest in the community. During this visit, the deplorable conditions of the Mexican laborers convinced him of the need for a socially active church. In a report on the visit, Bishop Topel was critical of the prosperity of the larger community and the deplorable conditions in the labor camps. Bishop Topel stated the following in the report, "The over-all impression of the Mexican camp is this. Have you a mental picture of the shacks that housed the slaves in the South 100 years ago, the congestion, and the primitive conditions? I have. And this is what I saw when I looked at this Mexican camp south of Walla Walla."[31]This visit convinced him of the necessity for a labor union and an advocate for the needs of the Mexican laborers. Bishop Topel said, "When I saw how bad these conditions are, I realized anew the necessity of unions."[32] Thus, Bishop Topel embarked on a project that included the pastoral needs of the community as well as a social action project.

A Pastoral and Social Action Project: The First Mexican Priest in the Spokane Diocese, 1964–1972

The completion of the Columbia Basin Irrigation Project expanded the capabilities of the agricultural economy to extend into areas beyond Walla Walla. Of the communities located in the boundaries of the Spokane Diocese, Pasco, and Othello attracted a large number of Mexican workers. The entrance of Mexicans in the area coincided with the completion of the East Columbia Irrigation District. The construction of the O'Sullivan Dam in 1948 prepared the stage for the distribution of water through the Potholes Canal. In 1953, the first farmers in the Othello area received water from the irrigation district.[33] From 1956 to 1968, Othello's agricultural economy expanded, requiring the need for workers in labor intensive crops, especially sugar beets. Farmers in the county requested irrigation water for a total of 39,587 acres in the biennial 1964–1966 and 12,904 acres in the biennial 1966–1967.[34] The growth of the Mexican population convinced Bishop Topel of the necessity of a native Spanish-speaking priest, and he invited Father Victor Briones, a volunteer with the Guatemala Mission, to help the diocese in the Walla Walla, Pasco, and Othello area. Father Victor Briones, the first Mexican priest in the history of the diocese, played an important role in the early years of contact between the Catholic Church and the Mexican population in the region. In his first year, Father Briones compiled a census of the Spanish-speaking Catholic community in the region and reported on the needs of the population in 1964. The report provided glimpses of the early Mexican community in the diocese and recorded the growth of the population. Walla Walla recorded the highest number of Mexicans with 463, followed by Othello and Pasco with 375 and 185, respectively. A high percentage of the total population was young with around 63 percent under the age of eighteen. The English skills of the population varied from to city to city; in comparison to Pasco with 18.4 percent, Othello at 33.6 and Walla Walla at 24.7 recorded a higher percentage unable to speak English. In addition, other issues reported in the census convinced the hierarchy of the need for a more active Catholic Church. The low level of attendance at Mass in the Mexican community concerned the hierarchy in the Spokane Diocese, in spite of a low percentage of converts to Protestantism. The *Inland Register* confirmed the importance of the new assignment in the diocese: "Speaking a common language, sharing a common racial heritage, Father Briones has been able to reach these people as no North American priest possibly could."[35] The original report was not found in the Spokane Diocese Archives (see Fig. 8.1).

To reach the Mexican Catholic population, Father Briones utilized the cursillo movement to incorporate them into the predominantly white institution. The cursillo movement originated in Spain in 1947 and was introduced to the United States ten years later. During the cursillo, lay persons and priests usually meet for three days of intense religious study and dedication. The objective is to train an active leadership within the Catholic Church.[36] In 1965, the diocese organized the first Spanish language

Fig. 8.1. Mexican ensemble of Spanish-speaking parishioners attending the first Spanish-language Cursillo of the Spokane Diocese performed hymns and liturgical songs. Lay participants were members of the Latin American Club in Othello, Wash., 1964 (photo Courtesy, Inland Register).

cursillo in Othello with the participation of people from Walla Walla, Pasco, Eltopia, and Othello. According to the *Inland Register*, the participants of the cursillo heard the first Spanish mass in the Spokane Diocese.[37] While on the one hand, the cursillo movement gave the Mexican origin community an organizational structure needed in the development of a leadership; on the other hand it had a negative counterpart. *Cursillistas* are Latino Catholics (clerical and lay) "who think of the world and the church as hierarchical structures." Moreover, their Christian life places importance on the church mission and worship as well as the solidification of church authority. This theological model contained the seeds of conflict that later clashed with other Latino Catholics in the diocese.[38]

During Father Briones' assignment in the diocese (1964–1972), he was actively involved in various community issues, and especially advocated for the improvement of the conditions of farmworkers in migrant workers committees in the state. Bishop Topel's unconditional support for the activities of the Mexican priest clearly came from his support of the socially active Church promoted by Vatican II reforms. In fact, in 1969, Bishop Topel donated $3,000 from the sale of his house in organization seed money for the establishment of a credit union.[39] According to the history of St. Patrick's Parish, Father Briones is credited with the celebration of the first Spanish masses in Pasco and the formation of the first Spanish language church choir.[40] In 1971, he was the chair of the Health and Housing Committee subcommittee of the Governor's Advisory Committee on Mexican American Affairs.[41] Thus, the progressive stance of the Catholic Church hierarchy, influenced by Vatican II reforms, validated the activist role of the first Mexican priest in the diocese.

The Maturity of the *Cursillo* Movement in the Spokane Diocese: Community Gatherings in Othello in the 1970s

The growth of the Mexican population in Othello convinced the Catholic Church of the need for more Spanish-speaking priests in the diocese. Bishop Topel's agenda helped in bringing in several Latino priests that included priests from Colombia and Mexico. Father Maria Jose Pelaez was born in Colombia and assigned to the Othello area. Othello's Mexican descent community recorded high levels of activism during Father Pelaez's tenure in the local parish. The cursillo movement established in the early 1960s continued to have an impact in the 1970s. Besides organizing cursillos for the Mexican community in the Columbia Basin region, Father Pelaez supported the organizational efforts in the area by promoting community gatherings and the celebration of cultural events. Eventually, other Latino priests in the Spokane Diocese such as Father Villabona and Father Pedro Ramirez joined him.[42] In Othello, the cursillistas staged the first Mother's Day Fiesta in 1971, attracting around five hundred people from Washington, Idaho, and Oregon to the event.[43] Utilizing the traditional Mother's Day holiday in combination with the religious image of the Virgin of Guadalupe, in 1972 the same organization staged the second annual Mother's Day Fiesta. The fiesta began with a mass officiated by Father Pelaez followed by a traditional Mexican barbecue, Mexican dancing, and other fiesta activities. The organizers were successful in drawing more than one thousand persons to the Mother's Day Fiesta. Photographs in the Othello newspaper show people dressed in charro outfits as well as people holding the American and Mexican flag and surrounding the image of the Virgin of Guadalupe. Some of the men in the photographs are shown wearing American Legion caps: former G.I.s who fought in World War II. Other photographs show Fiesta participants in a musical program on stage and game booths in the background.[44] By 1973, the organization was successful in attracting an even larger audience to the Mother's Day Fiesta. The event in 1973 followed a similar format, but added a dance to conclude it.[45] These early community gatherings in the 1970s illustrate the visibility of the Mexicano and Mexican American population in the area. More important, it is likely that the cursillo movement influenced a new generation of active Catholics. According to Hinojosa, the cursillo movement across the United States "validated the importance of ordinary men as individuals and as members of the community. In fact the movement appealed to the poor and the common man (see Fig. 8.2).

Toward the late 1970s, the Latino Catholic community in the area showed signs of change: while many were part of the cursillo movement, others began to articulate a different theological model. The proponents of this model emphasized a search for equality without implying conformity and sought cooperation with all in the struggle for justice and peace in society, with the hierarchical nature of the church not as important except as a "sign." In other words, "The Church is a kind of sacrament of intimate union with God and of the unity of all mankind; that is, she is a sign and instrument of such union and unity." Latino Catholics who articulate such a model are known as "pastoralists."[46]

A New Generation of Latino Clergy and the Church of the Poor

The Chicano Civil Rights movement and the Latin American Liberation Theology movement affected a new generation of Latino clergy committed to social change in the community. In spite of Vatican II reforms, some

Fig. 8.2. *Gazing at La Virgen de Guadalupe. Organizers of the 1970s Mother's Day Fiesta meeting with Father Pelaez, Othello, Wash., circa 1970s (photo courtesy of Othello Outlook).*

communities struggled with conservatives and traditionalists who refused to accept change. At the national level, two organizations began a movement inside the Church that addressed social and political concerns of the Mexican origin population in the United States, PADRES (Priests Associated for Religious, Educational, and Social Rights) and Las Hermanas. After the first meeting of PADRES in 1969, the resolutions demanded a more active Catholic Church in the solution of problems in the Latino community. The resolutions included a demand for more Latinos in the Church hierarchy, the appointment of more Latino pastors in large Spanish-speaking communities, the use of the Church's finances in social and economic programs in the communities, the application of a Catholic liturgy sensitive to the cultural roots of the Latino communities, and the expansion of programs designed for the recruitment of Latino priests in seminaries.[47] PADRES played an important role in the transformation of the Catholic Church hierarchy and in refocusing attention to the needs of the growing Latino Catholic laity. Similarly, by 1971, religious sisters established a national organization dedicated to the concerns and problems of the Latino population and named it Las Hermanas. Some of the priorities of Las Hermanas focused on leadership development in the barrios and the demand for a better use of nuns in pastoral ministry in the United States. The organization supported the farmworkers movement, the need for Latinos in the Church hierarchy, and the Mexican American Cultural Center. More importantly, the religious sisters played an important role in establishing *comunidades de base* (grass roots Christian communities) throughout the United States.[48] The cultural center in San Antonio, Texas, and the growth of comunidades de base were outgrowths of the influence of the liberation theology movement. The center attracted important theologians and promoted an activist Church involved in the issues of the poor. Socially minded clergy and lay people participated in the activities of the center that in turn shared their experiences throughout the United States.[49]

In the Northwest region, the movement affecting the Catholic Church made an impact until the mid-1970s. A new generation of Latino clergy and religious sisters entered the region that was influenced by developments at the national level. The new generation of religious leaders supported a more active Church in the solution of the problems facing Latinos. Not surprisingly, the entrance of the new clergy was the work of the progressive Bishop Topel who invited them to the diocese. Within the diocese several priests contributed in making the Church more sensitive to the needs of the growing Latino Catholic population. When Father Pelaez left the Othello area, the Catholic Church recognized the need for Spanish-speaking priests and assigned Father Pedro Ramirez Alejos, the second Mexican priest in the history of the Spokane Diocese. Father Ramirez was ordained for the Spokane Diocese in his hometown of Juventino Rosas, Guanajuato, Mexico, in 1974. In 1972, Father Ramirez studied theology at Mt. Angel, Oregon. On his return to the Diocese, he celebrated a Mass at Sacred Heart Church in Othello.[50] While serving the Othello community, Father Ramirez promoted the cultural and religious life of the Mexican population through activities such as *Las Posadas* (the reenactment of the Holy Family's search in vain for a room at an inn).[51] Eventually, Father Ramirez became diocesan director of the Spanish Speaking Apostolate. Active in the community, he participated in regional and national *encuentros* (meetings), and promoted an agenda of the Latino Catholic community in the region. In the diocese, he was involved in the production of three separate radio programs for broadcasts in Eastern Washington on Sunday mornings.[52] Father Ramirez moved to St. Patrick's Parish in Pasco from 1980 to 1988 as an associate pastor, and in 1991 he became pastor. In 1996, he was named a monsignor. He represents the pastoralist vision in the clergy. Other priests in the diocese included people connected with the progressive movements in the Latino clergy. Father Filiberto Gonzalez Moreno was ordained as a priest in 1976 at St. Patrick Parish in Pasco. Born in Tejalpa, Mexico, Father Gonzalez began studies for the Spokane Diocese at Mt. Angel in 1972. He held a philosophy degree from the Superior Institute of Ecclesiastical Studies in Cuernavaca, Mexico, and attended a special pastoral program at the Mexican American Cultural Center in San Antonio. This center was the training grounds of the new clergy dedicated to social change in the Latino community. According to the historical records of St. Patrick Parish, as the resident priest for the Latino community (1976–1980) "he initiated Spanish bible studies, formed St. Patrick's Hispanic organization and the Hispanic Liturgy Committee."[53] Father Gonzalez played an active role in the regional and national encuentros, in 1977, as the regional Northwest representative for the NCCB/USCC reported in the Second National Spanish Pastoral Encounter.[54]

Las Mujeres and the Catholic Church

In the Northwest, a group of religious sisters formed a chapter of Las Hermanas who participated in various community meetings to promote the interests of the Mexican population. Sister Carmelita Espinoza RGS was among the religious sisters. At the start of her pastoral work in the area, she had just completed two years in the National Coordinating Team of Las Hermanas, a Latina National group of religious sisters. Trained at the Instituto Pastoral Latino Americano in Quito, Ecuador, Sister Carmelita brought a socially active philosophy into the region.[55] Sister Carmelita Espinoza RGS joined an interdiocesan pastoral team that included Father Ramirez and Sister Maria de Jesus Ybarra ODN.[56] Sister Carmelita explained the interdiocesan pastoral team in the following way, "Because Bishop Topel was nationally respected, he was able to pull political clout among his brother bishops in the Northwest. We started working inter-diocesan *sin fronteras* (without borders) and we worked as a mobile pastoral team. We covered Othello, Pasco, Walla Walla (Spokane Diocese), and Moses Lake, Warden, Royal City, Quincy (Yakima Diocese), and Hermiston (Baker, Oregon, Diocese). At that time we had access to all these parishes and we worked with the grassroots. We developed, determined, and implemented pastoral programs unique to the Hispanic. The in words pastorally speaking were *pastoral de conjunto* (pastoral team), *comunidades de base* (base communities), *conscientizacion* (raising consciousness), *pueblo de Dios en marcha* (the people of God marching)."[57] Sister Carmelita and many of her religious brothers and sisters, influenced by the ideas in Vatican II reforms as well as those in liberation theology, worked energetically in the struggle for social justice in the Latina/o community. According to Sister Carmelita, one of the most important priorities of the pastoral work among the Latino population was the rebirth of cultural pride, especially among the youth. This was done through encuentros similar to the English-speaking Search Program for Youth. Sister Carmelita was well known at the national level in the Las Hermanas organization.[58]

The Liberationists: The Encuentro Movement in the Northwest Region

As the new religious leadership developed in the Northwest, a theological model that emphasized a different vision of the Catholic Church affected the various communities in the diocese. While agreeing with pastoralists on some issues, the liberationists view "the church's incorporation into social movements rather than on sign value. This model views the role of the church "not in terms of presence but of effects."[59] A liberationist model formed at the national level via the encuentros and eventually reached the Northwest region. The Encuentro movement began in June 1972 when hundreds of people met in Washington, D.C. to discuss a pastoral plan for Latinos. A central issue of the first encuentro was to challenge the assimilationist tendency of the church for a more pluralistic approach in dealing with the Latino community. Later in August 1977 the second National Encuentro was held again in Washington, D.C. In comparison to the first meeting, however, this time the laity played a larger role and the meeting focused on workshops rather than presentations. Also, the Spanish language was used in the proceedings of the encuentro, giving the participants more opportunities for input in the final set of resolutions. The last encuentro was organized in 1985.[60] Both the national and regional encuentros brought together a diverse group of Catholics from the cursillistas and the pastoralists to the liberationists. Regional meetings were organized in Washington, Oregon, Idaho, Utah, and even in Minnesota. Some of the areas stressed in the *encuentros* included the Spanish language, popular religion, education, and social justice.[61] Other goals of the pastoral work of the new generation of religious activists focused on the transformation of the Catholic Church by getting an indigenous priest, deacon, or lay woman as a community faith facilitator for every Latino community. However, the struggle for social justice within the institution was not free of conflict. Sister Carmelita confessed the following on her work in the community, "As I reflect upon our pastoral work, the hierarchy was very supportive mainly because we were doing the work the Anglo priests (even though some spoke Spanish) were unable to do, bring the people to the Catholic faith. But our problems were almost always with the foreign-born Irish priests. They were racist at times, ignorant, and definitely failing in their call to pastor all peoples regardless of race and language difference. There were parishes in which the team was not permitted to enter with our programs."[62]

During the 1970s the Encuentro movement energized the Latino Catholic community in the Pacific Northwest by giving them a chance to transform the Catholic Church. As early as 1971, discussions noted the need for a northwest regional section within the United States Catholic Conference Division for the Spanish Speaking West Coast Office. In 1975, religious leaders met with Northwest bishops to discuss the needs of the Latino Catholic community in the region. Topics included informal religious education through prayer, catechisms with special emphasis on the bilingual and bicultural reality of the Latino community, and important liturgical moments in the religious and social life of the Latino community.⁶³ Regional meetings were held in various parts of the Northwest and brought national religious leaders in the Latino community to the region. Members of PADRES and Las Hermanas played an important role in organizing the conferences and bringing attention to the problems of the growing Latino communities in the Northwest. In 1976, the Northwest Religious Education Congress meeting held in Yakima on Oct. 23 and 24 brought together around fourteen hundred participants. The conference presented topics on human rights and justice, the role of the Latino people in the United States, alcoholism, drug addiction, and sexuality.⁶⁴ In preparation for the second encuentro, religious leaders outlined the basic themes focusing on evangelization, ministries in the Latino community, human rights and the Latino person, integral education, political responsibility, and recognition of the pluralism in the Latino population.⁶⁵ On Oct. 15 and 16, Latinos analyzed and examined the conclusions of the Second National Encuentro. Participants concluded that the region lacked priests and formulated the formation of a mobile religious regional team to address the issue. They proposed to continue in the formation of Christian communities throughout the region. Once again national religious leaders participated in the conference, including Virgilio Elizondo, a well-known Chicano theologian.⁶⁶ The following year, the Northwest Religious Education Congress met in Spokane and presented workshops on the contribution of Latino Culture to Christian spirituality in the United States, intercultural values, and the role of parents in the religious education of children.⁶⁷ The activism produced by the National Encuentros continued into the 1980s. During Feb. 17–19, 1984, the diocese held a workshop of one hundred participants from Connell, Othello, Pasco, Walla Walla, and Spokane to prepare for Encuentro III. The topics examined included family, religion, economics, politics, and culture. Bishop Welsh participated in the workshop and legitimized the community efforts to transform the Catholic Church.[68] In 1985, regional meetings were held in Connell and Ellensburg, Wash. On Mar. 23, 1985, Connell participants prioritized the issues around evangelization, education, social justice, youth, and formation of leaders. Over 150 participants composed of lay, religious leaders, and clergy from the region met to analyze the resolutions from the various dioceses represented in the meeting. Thirty representatives from the Spokane diocese participated in the meeting. The group concluded with resolutions on evangelization, education, social justice, youth, and leadership. In education, the participants demanded more bilingual and religious education classes and courses on the rights of immigrants. Participants wanted the Church to take a stronger stance on racism, a more active role in resolving the problems affecting Latino youth, and train more lay leaders for prominent roles in the Church.[69] Two years later, the diocese attempted to apply the process developed at the Third National Encuentro by holding a workshop at Fort Wright College where participants observed, prioritized, and planned strategy for specific parishes in the diocese.[70]

In conclusion, the activism of the regional and national encuentros in the 1970s and 1980s heightened the community's awareness of their role in the Catholic Church. The meetings raised consciousness, political awareness, and a more confident Latino Catholic community in the diocese. By the 1980s, the demographic growth of the Latino community in Eastern Washington affected the relationship between the Latino community and the Church. The non-Latino white population responded with fear to the growing Latino populations in their parishes. A combination of the two factors above led to conflict and crisis within the Spokane Diocese.

GILBERTO GARCIA

Conflict and Crisis in the Spokane Diocese:
El Centro Guadalupano de Othello, Washington, 1981–1997

In the decade of the 1980s, social, political, and economic issues affecting the Mexican origin population resurrected the hostility of the dominant Anglo population toward the Mexican community in Othello. In previous decades, the population was small, constituting no more than one third of the total population in 1970. However, the demographic growth of the Latino population in the 1980s affected relations between the two groups. Even though in the 1980s the Latino population constituted 33 percent of the total population in the city of Othello, by the end of the decade, the 1990 census reported that the Latino population had grown to 46 percent of the total population in the city. By far the largest national origin group in Othello is of Mexican origin and in 1990 constituted 94 percent of the total Latino population. In reality, the Mexican population represented an even higher percentage, since a large number of people lived on the outskirts of the city limits. An examination of the social and economic characteristics of the community revealed the ethnic-racial divide between the white and Latino population. An important social indicator illustrative of the historic inequality between the Euro American population and the Latino population is in the area of education. In 1980, the Latino origin population recorded low levels of education with 60.8 percent of the age twenty-age five and over population completing fewer than eight years of schooling. Only 16 percent of the Latino population completed four years of high school, in contrast to 32.7 percent of the white population. Although the 1990 census information is not comparable, it nevertheless illustrates the educational differences between the Euro American and Latino populations. In 1990, the Latino population age twenty-five and over, 22.7 percent completed less than a fifth-grade education in comparison to 2 percent of Euro Americans. Latino descent high school graduates and higher recorded only 23.1 percent, in contrast to Euro

Americans who recorded 85.3 percent. This difference is replicated in the college and university level; Latinos recorded 11.2 percent and Euro Americans 48.8 percent. The following economic factors expose the interconnections of race, class, and gender in the study of inequality. The income differences illustrate the economic subordination of the Latino community: in 1980 the median income of the Latino community was $15,174 and by 1990 it increased to $20,189, while the median income of the white community in 1980 was $19,653 with an increase to $28,333 by 1990. While the income levels show improvement for the Latino community, it is clearly below the levels of the white population in Othello. In fact, the median income of the predominantly Mexican origin population changed insignificantly when it is examined as a percentage of the white median income. In 1980, the median income of the Latino population was 77 percent of the median income of the white population. By 1990, it barely improved to 71 percent of the median income of the white population in Othello.

A more telling indicator of inequality is found in the poverty levels of the Latino community. While the percent of white families below poverty decreased from 13.4 in 1980 to 6.9 in 1990, the percent of Latino origin families below poverty grew from 25.8 in 1980 to 37.1 in 1990. Perhaps, the most important indicator of the social and economic subordination is in the distribution of the Latino origin population in the occupational structure. Between 1980 and 1990, the occupational structure revealed the economic inequality between the Latino population and the white population in Othello. The white population monopolized the higher-paying jobs in the managerial and technical occupations, while the Latino population remained overrepresented in the lower paying jobs in the operator, laborer, and farming occupations. In the 1990 census, white employed persons age sixteen and over reported high percentages of 23.6 and 26.6 in the managerial and technical occupations; by contrast, Latino employed persons age sixteen and over recorded percentages of 6 and 14 in the same occupations. In the working class occupations, 42 percent of the operators and 18.5 of the farming employees were Latinos, while white workers recorded percentages of 14.5 for operators, 16.8 for precision, and 9.8 for farming occupations[71] (see Table 1).

Table 1: Employed Persons 16 Years and over by Race and Latino Origin, Othello, Washington 1990

	TOTAL WHITE Percent of Total White	TOTAL LATINA/O Percent of Total Latina/o
Managerial	23.6	6
Technical	26.6	14
Service	8.4	9.8
Farming	9.8	18.5
Precision	16.8	9.5
Laborers	14.5	42

Source: 1990 Census of Population. General Social and Economic Characteristics Washington, Section 2 of 2

According to Chicana/o social scientists, labor market segmentation-dual labor market analysis explains the inequalities of the Latino population in Othello, Wash. The theory explains inequality through an analysis of the position or location of the Latino and white population in a primary and secondary labor market. The primary labor market includes those "jobs, which offered security and stability, good pay and working conditions, the possibility of advancement, and a stable set of procedures in the administration of work rules."[72] The secondary labor market exhibits the opposite characteristics and it is a market relegated to minorities and women workers. In this analysis, the specific characteristics of the dual labor market determine the social and economic position of the Mexican origin population. Further examination of the data reveals segmentation along race and gender lines, thus, the analysis adds to the complexity of the experience of Latinas/os in a small community in the Northwest. For example, this is applicable in the analysis of the occupational breakdown in the community of Othello. The census presents a domination of white males and females in the managerial and technical occupations, but a small percentage of Latinas/os also forms part of the same occupations. The same observation applies to the distribution of Latino and white workers in the various categories of farming, precision, and operators. Latinas/os constituted a higher percentage in the farming and laboring occupations, while white males represented a higher percentage in the precision occupations. White females are hardly visible in the farming, precision, and laboring occupations[73] (see Table 2).

Even though data for the city of Othello is not available, information gathered from The Statistical Abstract of the United States: 2000 illustrates the inequality of the earnings between male and female workers at the national level. Higher median weekly

Table 2: Employed Persons 16 Years and over by Race, Sex, and Latina/o Origin, Othello, Washington 1990

	WHITE MALES Percent Total White	WHITE FEMALES Percent Total White	LATINO MALES Percent Total Latina/o	LATINAS Percent Total Latina/o
Managerial	11.7	11.9	1.5	4.4
Technical	10.5	16.2	3.9	10.0
Service	2.6	5.8	3.3	6.5
Farming	8.6	1.2	16.7	1.8
Precision	15.6	1.2	8.6	--.--
Laborers	9.4	5.0	23.3	18.6

Source: 1990 Census of Population. General Social and Economic Characteristics Washington, Section 2 of 2

earnings were reported for the managerial and technical occupations, while lower weekly median earnings were found in the farming and laborer occupations. The inequality of the weekly median earnings is clearly seen between males and females. These factors directly impact the class formation in the small community of Othello and it is reflected in the struggle inside the Catholic Church.[74]

Consequently, their position in the labor market presents a diverse and heterogeneous class formation composed of white and Latina/o workers differentiated by occupation and earnings as well as the formation and presence of a white and Latina/o bourgeoisie. This diverse social and economic position of Latinos and Euro Americans was reflected at the political and ideological level in the conflict between the Church and the Latino community in Othello. Thus, the growth of the Latino population and the social-economic inequalities tested the viability of the white institutions and its capabilities to resolve the social issues affecting the community.

Unlike previous decades, Latinas/os challenged the power of the white English-speaking population in the small community of Othello, Wash., in a wide spectrum of social and political arenas. Reflecting a national trend, and in many ways resembling the scenario presented in *The Burden of Support: Young Latinos in an Aging Society*, the predominantly white population responded with fear to the dramatic population growth in the Latino community.[75] This climate of fear and conflict affected the social, cultural, political, and economic arenas in the small city in the Columbia Basin. An important challenge occurred in the educational institutions when a group of Latinas/os questioned the failure of the school district to hire qualified bilingual-bicultural teachers. Hispanos Unidos, a grass roots organization, confronted the inability of the school district to respond to the growth of the Latina/o student population in the area. Newspaper articles and editorials reflected the friction between the white English-speaking population and the Latina/o population.[76] By the end of the 1980s,

Latina/o students constituted 51.57 percent of the district's total student population. The growth was visible in the elementary schools, where the percentages ranged from 52.01 percent in Scootney Springs Elementary to 54.90 percent in Hiawatha Elementary School and 55.23 percent in Lutacaga Elementary School.[77] Yet, the administrative and educational makeup of the institutions reflected the predominance of a white professional class and an almost invisible presence of Latina/o professionals.[78] A second area of friction emerged in the distribution of public resources for senior citizens. Latina/o senior citizens complained of racial and ethnic discrimination in the local community center.

After a period of friction, the Mexican elderly formed an organization to defend the rights and privileges of senior citizens and eventually established the Latin Senior Citizen Center.[79] In both cases, the demographic growth of the Latina/o population sparked the friction between the two communities. Published opinions reflected the divisions in the white community as well as the large Mexican origin population in Othello. At another level, the Latina/o community was responding to the social and economic reality of the population in the political arena. In 1988, several grass roots organizations united to improve the living conditions of Latinas/os in Othello. According to the coalition, among the serious issues affecting the Latina/o community several warranted attention: access to local school boards and more bilingual counselors, youth employment and training programs, city and county services for Latina/o neighborhoods, and the lack of Latino police officers. The organization began a voter registration drive and encouraged Latinas/os to question political candidates in special forums.[80]

The Catholic Church, an important institution in the life of the Latina/o community, was affected by the changes occurring inside and outside the institution. Structurally, the policies of a new leader in the Catholic Church affected the relationship between the growing Latino population and the religious institution. In 1978, John Paul II[81] was installed as the new Pope of the Catholic Church. Like his predecessors, he launched an attack on the popularity and influence of liberation theologians. Prior to the Puebla meeting, the Curia in the Vatican engaged in a political campaign to exclude important Latin American theologians and fill the conference with conservative religious leaders.[82] Beginning in 1979, in his visit to Mexico, John Paul II criticized the movement: "We find 're-readings' of the Gospel that are the product of theoretical speculations rather than of authentic meditation on the word of God and a genuine evangelical commitment." He added an even stronger attack on the movement when he stated, "In other cases people purport to depict Jesus as a political activist, as a fighter against Roman domination and the authorities, and even as someone involved the class struggle. This conception of Christ as a political figure, a revolutionary, as the subversive of Nazareth, does not tally with the Church's catechesis."[83] This philosophical and religious stance eventually reached every Catholic community in the world, including the small community of Othello. In the diocese, the progressive Bishop Topel resigned from his position in 1978 and Lawrence Harold Welsh became new bishop of the Spokane Diocese. Welsh was the son of Irish and Italian parents who grew up in mining camps. Bishop Welsh entered the seminary at St. John's Collegeville and while living there allegedly spent some of his vacations in the Red River Valley in North Dakota. Bishop Welsh learned Spanish while working with Latina/o migrant workers in the area, which probably was a factor in his appointment to a diocese with a large Latino population. Only a few years after his installation, Bishop Welsh faced a serious crisis more damaging than the closing of Marycliff High School.[84]

 After fifteen years of contact and interaction, Latina/o Catholics were far from being homogeneous. Some Latino Catholics belonged to the traditional cursillistas movement, others evolved into pastoralists, and yet others represented the liberationist movement. All of these groups played an important role in the conflict between the Catholic Church and the Latino

Catholic community. In the 1980s, a segment of the Mexican origin population questioned the practices of the predominantly white Church. After a series of clashes, the Latino community established a separate religious community center under the name of the El Centro Guadalupano. The following is an overview of the major players and issues in a crisis that divided the small Catholic community in Othello.[85] At the center of the conflict was Father Dan Wetzler, the supporters of the Catholic Church (the Latino cursillistas and the white Catholic parishioners), and the members of the El Centro Guadalupano (pastoralists and liberationists) who represented a counter-hegemonic force in the struggle. The symbol of the opposition and the representative of the aspirations of the Church of the Poor was Father Jesus Oliva, a Mexican priest appointed to work with the local Latino community.[86]

On Oct. 25, 1981, the Catholic community in Othello celebrated the 25th Anniversary of Sacred Heart Parish. It was a festive moment for the community, with special guests including Bishop Welsh of the Spokane Diocese and two Mexican priests, Father Pedro Ramirez and Filiberto Gonzalez, who had previously served in the parish. In recognition of the large Mexican Catholic community in Othello, Bishop Welsh gave a large picture of Our Lady of Guadalupe. The celebration served two purposes. First, it was a day to celebrate the addition of a new building to the parish in its 25th Anniversary in the diocese. Just as important, Bishop Welsh announced the appointment of Father Jesus Oliva as the new associate pastor. Father Oliva served previously at Holy Family Parish in San Antonio. Born in Mexico, Father Oliva completed his training in the Diocese of Shreveport. Bishop Welsh stated, "Father Jesus Oliva will be associate pastor with specific concern for the Hispanic people in the parish."[87]

Father Oliva arrived in Othello in November 1981. Once in the parish, he began a campaign to bring the Spanish-speaking Catholic parishioners into the Church. According to Geronimo Coronado, Father Oliva visited families in Othello and invited them to be more active in the church. He reminded them that the church was not there just for baptisms or weddings. As a result of this approach, the attendance of Spanish-speaking parishioners grew in the Church during mass.[88] Other activities in the community included working with the Catholic youth in Othello through the organization of "Semillas de Dios."[89] The youth group staged plays and a Lenten walk in which participants challenged the oppression of the community. A newspaper story documented this activity and the explanation given by the participants: "The purpose of the march was to mark Lent by proclaiming Christ as their leader, making reparation for past personal failures and to protest what they see as sinfulness in society today, including discriminatory practices and causing hunger among the poor."[90] Others articulated a critique of American foreign policy and the dehumanizing treatment of all people in the world.[91] As a result of his work and activities, the priest became the center of the conflict between the white community, segments of the Mexican American community, and the Mexican immigrant population. Parish activist Ray Ramirez reflected on the work of Father Oliva. "He wanted all of us to be a 'church' and that we should share and live like brothers. When he came to the parish, he wanted to know what we wanted as Mexicanos. He wanted more freedom to use the basement of the church and for the Hispano community to have more freedom to use the facilities for activities in the church."[92] According to Ramirez, "Father Oliva wanted more activities in the church such as bible study classes, catechism and other activities."[93] With the rise in the number of Latino Catholics in the parish, conflict arose between the Anglo and Mexican parishioners. Ramirez added, "The Anglo community was not very supportive and many times criticized our functions. We were accused of leaving the facilities dirty and that made us feel uncomfortable. When we demanded equal access to the facilities in the church, they told us they were the owners of the church."[94]

In addition, the conflict concerned other issues, particularly finances. Latino parishioners requested information on the financial support from the diocese for the "Hispanic Ministry." The response was never to the satisfaction of the Latino members of the parish council who were always outvoted in meetings. The parish council and the priest responded that it was not enough to run the Church. "When a decision had to be made that would affect both communities, the vote would always be 7-4, which is not the way it's supposed to work."[95] The conflict escalated and the diocese decided to change the pastor and associate pastor. Ramirez remembers how the decision to remove Father Oliva angered the Mexican parishioners. According to Ramirez, the removal of the two pastors revealed the unequal treatment of the Mexican priest. "The diocese gave Father Oliva three days to depart from the parish, while the white pastor was given 30 days to leave the Church." Beset by the inability to change the decision of the Church hierarchy to remove Father Oliva, the problems between the Mexican parishioners and the Anglo parish council members escalated further in the parish. Father Oliva lasted seven months in the parish but left an imprint in the Mexicano population. He represented the new school of thought that emphasizes a more humanistic and committed Church against racism, poverty, and inequality. Stated in another way, he favored a pluralistic and egalitarian Church and rejected assimilation, intolerance, and the subordination of the Mexican community. Father Oliva's ideas and active role in the parish resonated among the Mexican parishioners who had been affected by the regional and national *encuentros* of the 1970s.

Disregarding the concerns of the Mexican parishioners, the diocese appointed a white priest to the local parish. Father Dan Wetzler was assigned to Othello on July 12, 1982. Before the arrival of the new priest, the disgruntled Mexican parishioners heard a rumor or statements attributed to the white priest. According to Ramirez, the rumor coming from Spokane was clearly racist in character. According to hearsay, the white priest commented to people in Spokane, "Dirty Mexicans—if they want to hear mass in Spanish they should go back to Mexico. I do not need the $100 they pay for mass." Ramirez related a story on the arrival of the new priest. "A week after his arrival, the group met in the basement of the parish and confronted the priest on the statement. He denied it and got very mad." In an attempt to resolve the problems in the parish, the white priest and the diocese supported the request to acquire more space for the activities of the parishioners. Thus, the diocese paid the rent for a building where the Mexican parishioners organized and conducted activities. According to Ramirez the situation got worse. "The white priest celebrated mass for about a year, but he did not like it. He informed the group that the mass in Spanish was canceled and directed them to a parish in Moses Lake."

In spite of the cancellation of Spanish mass, the Mexican parishioners continued to meet at 11:30 a.m. in the parish. Once in a while the priest checked the activities of the group, but only thirty to forty people attended the services. However, the number of participants grew to one hundred people, and finally the priest told the group that he needed the parish. The conflict climaxed in a vigil staged outside the Spokane Chancery, at that time Bishop Lawrence H. Welsh's residence. But the conflict was not just an Anglo vs. Mexican struggle, as a report revealed not only the division in the Catholic Church but also the various fractions in the community that emerged in the conflict. A group of Mexican Americans supported the position of the white Catholic Church and sided with the actions of the white priest. From the perspective of the activists, the supporters represented the most assimilated segment of the community as well as the beneficiaries of the policies of the white community in Othello. "Many of these people have been in Othello for many years and have been successful enough to own property or send their children to college. Ramirez and his allies accused them of denying their Mexican heritage and becoming "Anglicized."[96] The white priest, Father Dan Wetzler, explained the conflict differently, "Oliva, who was at Sacred Heart seven months was involved in 'political activities' and preached a brand of 'liberation theology' that contributed to the division within the parish."[97] Other conservative supporters of the mainstream Church stated their opinion on the conflict, "Father Oliva was sent home because he disobeyed the bishop. He was told to serve every Catholic, to serve the whole community."[98] Many of the critics of the Guadalupano group were old activists of the cursillo movement in Othello. Afterward, the group realized that it was time to move out from the parish. In 1985–1986, the Mexican parishioners decided to buy the building and established themselves as a non-profit organization. As with other communities in the United States, the parishioners used the symbol of the Virgin of Guadalupe and named the organization El Centro Guadalupano. The building of the organization served as a center of community organizing as well as a center for community-wide activities. Following the experience of communities in Latin America, the group organized El Centro Guadalupano as an *iglesia de base*, which emerged in Latin America due to the lack of priests. Sister Carmelita Espinoza and Sister Gregoria Ortega played an important role in the formation of El Centro Guadalupano as a community base religious organization. Both of them were part of the network of religious activists who advocated a "liberationist" perspective. Mexican priests were invited to El Centro Guadalupano and provided basic ministry to the community. Father Jesus Oliva visited the community several times at their request and the members of the center paid his flight and expenses from Mexico. He gave mass to the participants and encouraged them to continue the struggle for justice and equality. The basic thrust of his masses emphasized such ideas as the quest for social and economic equality and the centrality of a Mexican identity in the Catholicism of the participants in the Centro Guadalupano.[99]

However, as a separate entity, the activists of El Centro Guadalupano faced a continuous battle with the white priest. According to Ramirez, whenever the organization attempted to promote fundraisers on behalf of the Latino community, the Catholic priest informed radio stations and other community outlets not to support the organization activities. Facing a formidable foe, El Centro Guadalupano raised enough funds to buy a building that became the center of the organization activities. When the Latino community engaged in counter hegemonic politics in the larger society, El Centro Guadalupano joined and supported movements against the injustices in the educational and political system. For example, when the school district became the target of criticism by a new Latino organization, El Centro Guadalupano supported the demands for an improvement in the educational experience of Latinos. Also, when the same organization initiated a voter registration campaign in Othello, El Centro Guadalupano sponsored the event and allowed the use of the facilities for a community panel on the topic.[100] Other examples of the solidarity of El Centro Guadalupano with Latino organizations include the close relationship to and participation with the Othello Latin Senior Citizens. For example, El Centro Guadalupano provided the facilities for the preparation of food for the Othello Latin Senior Citizens as well as for organization meetings throughout the year.

The conflict extended over several years, but in the 1990s the appointment of a new bishop and of a Mexican pastor ended the affair. In 1990, Bishop William S. Skylstad of Yakima took over the reins of the Spokane Diocese. Born in Omak, Wash., in 1934, Bishop Skylstad studied for twelve years from high school until his ordination on May 21, 1960. Several years later, the bishop continued his graduate studies at Washington State University and Gonzaga. On May 12, 1977, he was appointed Bishop of Yakima and promised to learn Spanish to minister to the large Latino population in the diocese.[101]

A pastoralist by inclination, Bishop Skylstad supported the farmworkers in the valley and shared many similarities with the vision of John Paul II. Moreover, like most of his religious brothers in the Northwest Catholic Church, Bishop Skylstad brought an antiquated immigrant model to the predominantly Mexican origin population in the Yakima Valley and the Columbia Basin in the State of Washington. When Bishop Skylstad took over the diocese, he found himself embroiled in two community conflicts.

Besides the Latino community in Othello, a small Latino population in Spokane challenged the white hierarchy in the diocese. In his deliberations and political handling of the St. Joseph Parish conflict in Spokane, Bishop Skylstad utilized a white priest and a coalition of Central American and South American parishioners against a vocal and articulate group of Mexican Catholics. Ultimately, the policies of the new bishop forced the founders of the Spanish Mass in Spokane to organize outside the Church structure. Following the model of El Centro Guadalupano in Othello, the group formed La Comunidad Guadalupana de Spokane.[102] Faced with two communities in conflict, he wanted the immediate solution of the problem in Othello. In Spokane, the bishop opted to totally destroy the opposition through the old tactic of divide and conquer. In Othello, the solution required a different strategy: he announced the assignment of a Mexican priest in the Othello parish. However, whereas in the past, the power of the Mexican priests was relegated to a white priest, this time a Mexican priest was given full control of the parish. Sometime in September 1996, Father Eliodoro Lucatero began a reconciliation of the dissenting group. The new priest gave mass for around six months in the Centro Guadalupano. Eventually, he suggested the group join the local parish, and the battle between the Catholic Church and the Latino community came to an end.[103] El Centro Guadalupano continues to operate in the community through fundraising activities and other functions.

Conclusion

This study examined the historical relationship between the white, English-speaking Catholic Church in Eastern Washington and the Mexican origin population in the Spokane Diocese. After examining the history of the Mexican Catholic community in Eastern Washington and the institutional framework of the Catholic Church, the struggle between progressive and conservative forces shaped the relationship of the two entities. Initially, the Vatican II reforms and later the ideas of liberation theology supported a more socially active Catholic Church on behalf of the growing Latino population in the region. The politicization of the Latino community, which took place with the advent of progressive priests and the participation of the community in the Encuentro Movement, set the foundation for a more active Latino community in the Catholic Church as well as the basis for the conflict in the diocese. In addition, the dramatic Latino population growth was a major factor in the friction affecting the white English-speaking and Mexican origin communities in the region. The community no longer accepted being treated as second- class citizens and demanded equal treatment and respect from the larger society.

Endnotes

1. Leo Grebler, Joan W. Moore, and Ralph C. Guzman, *The Mexican American People: The Nation's Second Largest Minority* (New York: The Free Press, 1970), 450–52.
2 . Patrick McNamara, "Assumptions, Theories and Methods in the Study of Latino Religion after 25 Years," in *Old Masks, New Faces: Religion and Latino Identities*, ed. Anthony M. Stevens-Arroyo and Gilbert R. Cadena (New York: Bildner Center for Western Hemisphere Studies, 1995), 24.
3. Ibid, 31.
4. Moises Sandoval, *Fronteras: A History of the Latin American Church in the USA Since 1513* (San Antonio, TX: Mexican American Cultural Center, 1983).
5. Moises Sandoval, *On the Move: A History of the Hispanic Church in the United States* (New York: Orbis Books, 1990).
6. Jay P. Dolan and Gilberto Hinojosa, eds., *Mexican Americans and the Catholic Church, 1900–1965* (Notre Dame: University of Notre Dame Press, 1994).
7. See Gilberto Hinojosa, "Mexican American Faith Communities in Texas and the Southwest" in *Mexican Americans and the Catholic Church, 1900–1965*, ed. Jay P. Dolan and Gilberto Hinojosa. (Notre Dame: University of Notre Dame Press, 1994); and Jeffrey M. Burns, "The Mexican Catholic Community in California," *Mexican Americans and the Catholic Church, 1900–1965*, ed. Jay P. Dolan and Gilberto Hinojosa. (Notre Dame: University of Notre Dame Press, 1994).

8. David A. Badillo, "The Catholic Church and the Making of Mexican American Parish Communities in the Midwest" in *Mexican Americans and the Catholic Church, 1900–1965*, ed. Jay P. Dolan and Gilberto Hinojosa (Notre Dame: University of Notre Dame Press, 1994), 308.

9. Alberto Lopez Pulido, "Conflict and Struggle for Mexican Catholics," *Latino Studies Journal* (September 1994): 38.

10. Lara Medina. Las Hermanas: Chicana/Latina Religious Activism in the U.S. Catholic Church (Philadelphia: Temple University Press, 2004).

11. Wilfred P. Schoenberg, S.J., *A History of the Catholic Church in the Pacific Northwest, 1743–1983* (Washington, D.C., 1983), 695–96.

12. Ibid., 700.

13. The report and a scant file on the Mexican Catholic community in the Yakima Valley is found in the archives of Gonzaga University.

14. A History of the Catholic Church in the Pacific Northwest, 694. Schoenberg included only part of the report; a complete copy of the original report is located in the archives at Gonzaga University.

15. Patricia Brandt and Lillian A. Pereyra, *Adapting in Eden: Oregon's Catholic Ministry, 1838–1986* (Pullman, Wash.: Washington State University Press, 2002), 142.

16. Father Ted Bradley, *The Roman Catholic Diocese of Spokane: A Short History of the Diocese of Spokane,* http://www.dioceseofspokane.orghistory.htm.

17. On the impact of the braceros in the region, see Erasmo Gamboa, *Mexican Labor and World War II: Braceros in the Pacific Northwest, 1942–1947* (Austin: University of Texas Press, 1990).

18. The *Inland Register* (hereafter *IR*) reported on the growth of the Mexican population in the Walla Walla area in the 1950s and in 1961 published a series of special reports on the issue of migrant workers in the area.

19. Thomas Bokenkotter, *A Concise History of the Catholic Church* (New York: Doubleday, 1990), 355. Also see George Bull, *Vatican Politics at the Second Vatican Council, 1962–65* (New York: Oxford University Press, 1966).

20. Lawrence Elliott, *I Will Be Called John: A Biography of Pope John XXIII* (New York: Readers Digest Press, 1973); and Alden Hatch, Pope Paul VI (New York: Random House, 1966).

21. *A Concise History of the Catholic Church,* 356–67. During the Vatican Council reforms the Curia (the central administrative body of the Catholic Church) contained the most conservative and traditional sector of the Catholic hierarchy.

22. "Gaudium et Spes," preface to *Pastoral Constitution on the Church in the Modern World.* Promulgated by his Holiness, Pope Paul VI on December 7, 1965.

23. *A History of the Catholic Church in the Pacific Northwest,* 629–30.

24. For an expanded report on Bishop Topel see *A History of the Catholic Church in the Pacific Northwest*, 714–15.
25. The Bracero Program, a bilateral agreement between the United States and Mexico, began in 1942 during World War II and concluded in 1964.
26. See Jerry Garcia, "Mexican Migration, Labor and Community Formation: A Case Study of Quincy, Washington, 1943–1980" in *The Illusion of Borders: The National Presence of Mexicanos in the United States*, ed. Gilberto Garcia and Jerry Garcia (Dubuque, Iowa: Kendall–Hunt Publishing Company, 2002), 103–19.
27. For a discussion of the Mexican American migration into the Northwest, see Erasmo Gamboa, "Mexican Migration into Washington State: A History, 1940–1950," *Pacific Northwest Quarterly* 72 (July 1981): 121–31.
28. *IR*, July 20, 1956.
29. *IR*, August 2, 1957; May 2, 1958.
30. *IR*, July 28, 1958; Aug. 8, 1958; July 31, 1959.
31. *IR*, July 28, 1958.
32. Ibid.
33. *The Outlook and Ritzville Adams County Journal, Adams County Centennial Edition* (Othello, WA, 1983).
34. See Calvin F. Schmid and Stanton E. Schmid, *Growth of Cities and Town* (Olympia, WA: State of Washington, 1969).
35. *IR*, July 19, 1964. The original report was not found in the Spokane Diocese Archives.
36. For a brief discussion on the history of the cursillo movement and its introduction in the United States see Jeffrey M. Burns, "The Mexican Catholic Community in California," in *The Mexican American and the Catholic Church, 1900–1965*, ed. Jay P. Dolan and Gilberto Hinojosa. (Notre Dame, 1994), 222–24.
37. *IR*, Jan. 27, 1965; Jan. 31, 1965.
38. Antonio M. Stevens Arroyo, *Prophets Denied Honor: An Anthology on the Hispanic Church in the United States* (New York: Orbis Books, 1908), 176.
39. *IR*, August 10, 1969.
40. St. Patrick Parish History, http://www.rc.net/spokane/st_patrick/history.html.
41. Governor's Advisory Committee on Mexican American Affairs, Report on Recommendations, March 31, 1970.
42. *The Othello Outlook* (hereafter OO), Nov 2, 1972; Feb 8, 1973; August 8, 1974.
43. *OO*, May 13, 1971.
44. *OO*, May 4, 1972; May 11, 1972; May 18, 1972.
45. *OO*, May 3, 1973; May 10, 1973.
46. *Prophets Denied Honor*, 177.

47. *Fronteras*, 398; and *Prophets Denied Honor*, 139–40.
48. *Fronteras*, 405–409.
49. Moises Sandoval. "The Organization of a Hispanic Church," in *Hispanic Catholic Culture in the U.S.: Issues and Concerns*, ed. Jay P. Dolan and Allan Figueroa Deck, S.J. (Notre Dame: University of Notre Dame, 1994), 156–57.
50. *IR*, August 1, 1974.
51. *IR*, December 15, 1977.
52. *IR*, Nov. 10, 1982.
53. http://www.rc.net/spokane/st_patrick/history.html.
54. *The Inland Register*, July 28, 1977.
55. Sister Carmelita Espinoza to Gilberto Garcia, Feb. 26, 1998, in author's files. See "Las Hermanas," *The Handbook of Texas Online*, http://tsha.utexas.edu/ handbook/online/articles/view/LL/ix13.html. Also see *Prophets Denied Honor*, 141–42.
56. *IR*, April 24, 1975.
57. Sister Carmelita Espinoza to Gilberto Garcia, Feb. 26, 1998.
58. For a discussion of Carmelita Espinoza's religious political activism at the national level, see *Las Hermanas*, 55–56, 66, 70, 72,.
59. *Prophets Denied Honor*, 177–78.
60. *On the Move*, 79–84; *Prophets Denied Honor*, 313–33.
61. Sister Carmelita Espinoza to Gilberto Garcia, Feb. 26, 1998.
62. Ibid.
63. *IR*, April 22, 1971; April 24, 1975.
64. *IR*, Sept. 23, 1976; Nov. 4, 1976.
65. *IR*, July 28, 1977.
66. *IR*, Nov. 17, 1977.
67. *IR*, Sept. 7, 1978.
68. *IR*, Feb. 22, 1984.
69. *IR*, April 4, 1985; May 9, 1985.
70. *IR*, April 16, 1987.
71. The figures and percentages were drawn from the 1980 and 1990 Census of Population, General Social and Economic Characteristics in the State of Washington.
72. Mario Barrera, *Race and Class in the Southwest: A Theory of Racial Inequality* (Notre Dame: University of Notre Dame Press, 1979), 209–12.
73. Ibid. For a similar analysis, see Manuel Avalos. "Economic Restructuring and Young Latino Workers in the 1980s," in *Chicanas and Chicanos in Contemporary Society*, ed. Roberto M. de Anda (Boston: Allyn and Bacon, 1996), 35–39.

74. Even though data for the city of Othello, Wash., is not available, information gathered from *The Statistical Abstract of the United States: 2000* illustrates the inequality of the earnings between male and female workers. The 1990 figures at the national level reported males with the highest median weekly earnings for the managerial and technical occupations ranging from $567 and $502 in the Technical Support and Sales positions to $729 median weekly earnings for managerial positions. The median weekly earnings for males were in clear contrast to females in the same occupations. For females in the managerial occupations, the median weekly earnings were $510; in technical occupations, $331. In the service, precision, operator, and farming occupations, the inequality of median weekly earnings between male and female workers is clearly visible: median weekly earnings ranged from $317 (male) to $230 (female) in the service occupations; $486 (male) to $316 (female) in precision; $375 (male) to $261 (female) for operators; and $261 (male) to $216 (female) in farming occupations. U.S. Census Bureau, The Statistical Abstract of the United States: 2000 (U.S. Department of Commerce, Economic and Statistics Administration), 403.

75. David Hayes Bautista, Werner O. Schink, and Jorge Chapa. *The Burden of Support: Young Latinos in an Aging Society* (Stanford: Stanford University Press, 1988), 1–9.

76. OO, May 31, 1989; June 7, 1989; June 14, 1989; June 21, 1989; June 28, 1989.

77. Minority Enrollment Summary by School Building by District by County for Washington State School Districts for 1989–90 School Year. Report *1345A Public School Minority Enrollment Summary, 1989–90*. April 1990 (Olympia, WA: Office of Superintendent of Public Instruction, 1990).

78. *Statistical Analysis: Comparing Student Enrollment and School Personnel: Selected School Districts, Washington State, 1986–2001.* Information Pamphlet, Latino Educational Achievement Project. (no date).

79. Luis Garcia, interview by Gilberto Garcia, spring 1992.

80. OO, Aug. 17, 1988.

81. Mieczyslaw Malinski, *Pope John Paul II: The Life of Karlo Wojtyla* (New York: The Seabury Press, 1979.); Carl Bernstein and Marco Politi, *His Holiness: John Paul II and the Hidden History of Our Time* (New York: Doubleday, 1996). For a discussion of his ideas, see George Huntston Williams, *The Mind of John Paul II: Origins of His Thought and Action* (New York: The Seabury Press, 1981).

82. See Moises Sandoval, "Report from the Conference," in *Puebla and Beyond*, ed. John Eagleson and Philip Scharper (New York: Orbis Books, 1979), 28–43.

83. Pope John Paul II-Opening Address at the Puebla Conference, Jan. 28, 1979, http://www.catholic-forum.com/saints/pope0264hn.htm. In later documents, the Pope proposes two new statements on his critique of liberation theology. See *Instruction on Certain Aspects of the "Theology of Liberation"* Aug. 6, 1984, and *Instruction on Christian Freedom and Liberation*, Mar. 22, 1986. For a critique of his papacy, see Chip Mitchell, "The Catholic Clash: John Paul's Raucous Reign," http://www.americas.org/item_331.
84. *A History of the Catholic Church in the Pacific Northwest, 1743–1983*, 747–51.
85. See a local newspaper's report of the conflict in *Spokesmen Review*, Oct. 24, 1983.
86. Ibid.
87. *IR*, Nov. 4, 1981.
88. Geronimo Coronado, interview by Gilberto Garcia, spring 2003.
89. I want to thank Alma Coronado who provided information and materials on the group.
90. *OO*, Mar. 28, 1982.
91. *OO*, April 3, 1982.
92. Ray Ramirez., interview by Gilberto Garcia, Feb. 2, 1992.
93. Ibid.
94. Ibid.
95. *Spokesmen Review*, Oct. 24, 1983.
96. Ibid.
97. Ibid.
98. Ibid.
99. I had the opportunity to hear Father Oliva give mass in the Centro Guadalupano while preparing this paper on the Catholic Church.
100.*OO*, Oct. 19, 1988; June 14, 1989.
101.*A History of the Catholic Church in the Pacific Northwest*, 739–40.
102.This is a story for another paper. I have collected the letters and documents concerning this battle in St. Joseph Parish in Spokane.
103.Ray Ramirez, interviewed by Gilberto Garcia, spring 1998.

"As Close to God as One Can Get" Rosalinda Guillen, A Mexicana Farmworker Organizer in Washington State

Maria Cuevas

"Organizing… is about transforming the individual to value his or her work and to see the value they have in the whole food system. The transformation is not just with the worker; it is the transformation in the relationships to the land, to the community, to the grower, to other workers. To elevate the farmworker presence in the food production system is how we create and develop leadership and farmworker unity so that they can create the opportunities for change and develop perceptions of why we're here and exist."

—*Rosalinda Guillen, November 2004*

Introduction

This paper represents part of a series of interviews and discussions I have had with Rosalinda Guillen over the course of three years (October 2001–November 2004) as part of my dissertation research.[1] I first met Rosalinda in 1996 at Washington State University where she and her husband Joseph Moore presented a workshop on their work with the United Farm Workers (UFW) in the boycott against Chateau Ste. Michelle wineries. Rosalinda was instrumental in leading and organizing the members in a successful campaign[2] that resulted in the signing of a union contract that provided unheard of benefits to farmworkers in Washington State and the "best union contract for the UFW at the time" that consisted of increased wages, health benefits, retirement pension, arbitration and grievance process, and a pesticide investigation committee.[3] I was captivated by Rosalinda's description of the participation of the women in the campaign, many of them monolingual, Spanish-speaking farmworkers with families. Her vivid account of their activism countered what is often assumed about Mexican immigrant women: that they are submissive, family-oriented, and subservient. That they were family-oriented is congruent with research on Chicana activism[4] and provides a basis for the transformation of traditional gender ideology to one of a more "radicalizing" ideology, as Rose suggests. For example, ideas that place women in the home as the sole nurturer, caretaker, and martyr as in putting others before her are traditional views of women being submissive and subservient. However, U.S. stereotypes of Latinas also provide us with images of maids, domestics, and childcare providers, agricultural workers, or flashy "hot-blooded" Carmen Miranda types. In all but the last case do we not see Latinas confronting authority or unfair conditions, and in the latter it is with patronizing humor that assures the challengee that her real motive is to gain the attention or affections of the authority figure and not to be taken seriously. It is the purpose of this essay to look more closely at the life and leadership activities of one Mexicana involved in organizing and leadership in order to contribute to a redefinition and reframing of leadership and activist work. The importance of leadership and activism in Chicana/o[5] history cannot be overstated as the accomplishments and gains made by various individuals and organizations provided the means for successive generations to benefit, for example, in higher education, from expanded/improved social welfare policies and programs, and attention to health care needs. The dynamics of leadership activism and the power to create social change can help us to understand the transformative potential of organizing, particularly for this disenfranchised group of farmworkers.

Rosalinda is a testimony to female leadership and farmworker struggles. I wanted to investigate how and in what ways her perspectives and actions have challenged traditional leadership and labor organizing. How do we transform powerlessness to empowerment for farmworkers and women? To understand her work, I propose to use what Delgado-Bernal refers to as a Chicana epistemological framework.[6] Delgado-Bernal theorizes a Chicana "standpoint" that places Chicanas at the center of the research activity and that legitimizes the knowledge that arises from her "social, political, and cultural conditions." A Chicana epistemological framework challenges the notion of a universal body of knowledge that can be objectively identified and defined. Only when investigated further by asking questions of "whose conception of knowledge and for whom" can one begin to understand the nature of hegemonic domination.[7] Encouraged by other Chicana feminists to explore the ways that "conceptual frameworks of social significance"[8] must be redefined from Chicana experiences, Rosalinda's knowledge and experience inform us of a "model of leadership" manifested from her raced, classed, and gendered social location.[9]

The following examination of the history on Rosalinda, her thoughts and work on organizing, and her involvement in the Chateau Ste. Michelle boycott campaign seeks to detail a style of leadership that incorporates the notion of "justice and egalitarian ideals" not unlike other Chicana and Latina union organizers.[10] In the process, it is the social relationships developed around the goals of social justice, struggle, and social change that suggest differences in women's leadership and activism work.[11] In my analysis of traditional forms of male leadership I refer to Anne D. Gordon's "masculinist defined categories" of power that include "power, influence and visible authority in the world of politics and economic affairs."[12] In addition, I suggest the idea of a synthesis of public and private selves incorporated into "women's leadership" (as opposed to a separate public and private self that could be characterized as traditional male leadership,)[13] women's lives differ according to their particular social locations, and thus I refrain from calling this a "woman's model" of leadership. Women just as easily are "structured" into traditional male models of leadership. What I hope to show here is Rosalinda Guillen's unique leadership methods and beliefs as she works with both women and men toward goals of social justice that not only achieve their organizational objectives but also contribute to the transformation of workers' lives in unexpected ways.

Her (Story)

A youthful 53-year-old woman of Mexican descent, Rosalinda left California to return to her childhood home in northwestern Washington State to continue out her life's work as an organizer.[14] Rosalinda Guillen Herrera, the oldest of eight children, has three sisters and four brothers. Born on Dec. 28, 1951, to Jesus Guillen and Maria de Jesus Herrera in Haskell, Texas, her family was part of the Midwest migrant circuit traveling north to Nebraska, Minnesota, Wisconsin, and back again to Texas. Drawn by the available work in building the railroads of the Northwest and tired of the unsettled and unpredictable life of migrant work, her father settled his family in La Conner, Wash., near the Canadian border when Rosalinda was about nine years old.

Bordering the Swinomish Indian Reservation, La Conner is a town of predominantly Scandinavian immigrants who had settled into logging jobs. The daughter of an artist father and poet mother, the town provided perhaps an atypical environment for this precocious and inquisitive young girl. An artist's colony, La Conner was tucked away from the diversions of urban life, cultivating a bevy of bohemian artists and intellectuals who served as Rosalinda's mentors and teachers. As one of three Latino farmworker families in town throughout her childhood, Rosalinda recalls discussing politics with her parents and their eclectic group of friends. She was introduced to political theorists Karl Marx, Mao Tse Tung, and Lenin through these encounters. An enthusiastic reader in a family of avid readers, she was encouraged to argue and discuss her ideas with her parents and their friends. "Knowledge is power" her father taught her. This remarkable approach to childrearing most likely contributed to Rosalinda's sudden announcement to her unsuspecting parents that she was a communist and would begin her quest to liberate the poor at the ripe old age of fifteen. She ran away with her farmworker boyfriend to work toward liberating the downtrodden.

She married her boyfriend and had their first child, a son, when she was seventeen. Two years later her second son was born. Desiring to live and work in a more stable environment, Rosalinda found work with the Skagit State Bank in the Skagit Valley in the data processing department and remained there for sixteen years. She was active in community work at the same time and in the early 1980s became involved with the Rainbow Coalition to elect Jesse Jackson as the Democratic Party presidential nominee.[15] A critical point in Rosalinda's life occurred in the late 1980s when the workers with the Chateau Ste. Michelle Winery in central Washington sought and received the support of the Rainbow Coalition in the boycott against the winery. Sometime later, the workers asked her to assist them to lead the boycott. Rosalinda recalls thinking about this proposition as she was in her "prime" at the Bank, having led and developed their banking system's entry into the burgeoning field of computer technology. She had remarried and by then had three sons, the youngest of whom was ten years old.

One afternoon, as she was aimlessly driving around, she was compelled to stop at a local Catholic church. Not a practicing Catholic, Rosalinda had a spiritual epiphany when she decided to pray for guidance and was "led" to accept the position offered by the Ste. Michelle workers. She notes that La Virgen had been a spiritual guide for the farmworkers in the early days of the Cesar Chavez farmworker movement, and believes that faith in La Virgen and in a Higher Power leads many farmworker organizers to do the work they do.

In a move that was reminiscent of an earlier calling, Rosalinda quit her middle-class job at the age of forty to work with the farmworkers in central Washington. She says her extended family was ready to "commit her"; they thought she was crazy. Nevertheless, with her husband and children in tow, she moved to rural Sunnyside, Wash., about three hundred miles southeast of Skagit Valley.

Château Ste. Michelle Boycott Campaign

The battle to win major labor concessions with Chateau Ste. Michelle (CSM) Wineries took seven years to accomplish. The battle cannot be pinpointed to a particular moment in time but can be described as the culmination of farmworker frustration, the determination of a few devoted organizers, and tremendous community and allied support working to address the plight of agricultural workers in Washington State in the 1980s. Problems with management and work conditions (sexual harassment, lack of job security and grievance process, varying wages and benefits), led the CSM workers to seek help from an independent farmworker organization in Washington State in the late 1980s. The successful signing of the labor contract between the United Farm Workers of America, AFL-CIO[16] and the CSM management in December 1995 heralded the first labor contract for the UFW outside of California since 1972 and the most comprehensive and humane contract to benefit farmworkers in Washington State.[17]

Shortly before approaching Rosalinda to assist in the campaign, the CSM workers had been organized under the strategic guidance of a young scholar activist from Yale University, Kurt Peterson. Serious, thoughtful, and committed to a strong labor contract, Kurt opened his home to Rosalinda and her family so that she could join them in Sunnyside to help with the campaign. With little more than her books and notes on Cesar Chavez, Saul Alinsky's "Rules for Radicals," and the skillful advice of her third husband, Joseph Moore, a civil rights organizer, Rosalinda began immediately to organize the workers of Château Ste. Michelle Winery, "a tightly knit workforce from Michoacan, Mexico."[18] Together with the workers, they learned how to organize a boycott against one of the largest wineries in the state.

AS CLOSE TO GOD AS ONE CAN GET

When Rosalinda initially began working with the workers, they were predominantly men; women constituted about 30-40 percent of the winery workforce. Not accustomed to union work, women did not attend the early organizing meetings in 1993, although she asked them to participate. By the close of the boycott in late 1994, women and children were a regular part of the union meetings. The boycott had become their issue as well. As she explains:

> The workers had transcended gender—they did not see each other—me—as men or women; rather they saw themselves as workers, organizers, a community with common goals... I didn't go in with an agenda of forcing the men to work with the women or of forcing the women to stay for the initial planning meetings. Their "critical consciousness" sort of emerged organically...[19]

In this way, traditional Mexican men found themselves supporting women, their wives, and their friend's wives, to pursue traditionally "men's jobs" such as working the machinery or in other technical areas. Guillen continues:

> ...When the possibility of actually winning a good labor contract began to be realized, the men could see for themselves (by that time) the women being courageous and taking on responsibilities through union organizing which resulted in changes in all of their lives... changes in the way they would work with each other... changes in the way they related to each other at home.[20]

These ideological changes were similarly found in Zavella's cannery workers and Gutierrez De Soldatenko's garment workers who posit that the gender division of labor is simultaneously being "worked out at home" as well.[21] Although, how these complex relationships get worked out on a daily basis can be a difficult and painful one (as we will see later in this chapter), it is the opportunity to confront one's contradictions that contributes to the personal "transformation" that Rosalinda refers to. As Mendez-Negrete concludes in her study of Chicana leadership,

> While arriving at a Chicana consciousness, these activists and leaders have learned to engage leadership and activist processes anchored in relationships with those who, like them, are interested in pursuing social change regardless of leadership perspective.[22]

By late December 1994 the workers began negotiations for a union contract with CSM and signed the contract on Dec. 5,

Fig. 9.1. Estella Ferrer and Rosalinda Guillen at the United Farm Workers Office, Sunnyside, Wash., 1995 (photo courtesy of Rosalinda Guillen).

1995. The contract gave the workers the right to due process in the event of a grievance; questions about job security, retirement/ pension, and health benefits; and basic respect. Guillen was subsequently promoted to serve as the National Vice President of the United Farm Workers of America headquartered in Sacramento, Calif., in the late 1990s. She became one of the critical forces behind the farm labor mediation bill SB 1736 that was signed into law in the fall of 2002.[23] The farm labor bill would give growers and unions the incentive to conduct timely contract negotiations and is considered to be one of the most important pieces of farm labor legislation in decades.[24] (see Fig. 9-1).

On Organizing

> Consider this combination for power and wealth: Land, plenty of free water and plenty of cheap land. This is a most fantastic combination for anyone who wants to make money, create political influences and a keep a large number of laborers unorganized. Because of this combination, there are growers in California and the western part of the United States who are not only rich but are also very powerful.
> —*Cesar Chavez, A Union in the Community*

Organizing farmworkers is understood to be difficult work among labor organizers.[25] Their impoverished and powerless status proves a formidable obstacle when workers depend on daily work for survival. Attempting to rally forces against powerful agricultural interests who readily hire undocumented workers desperate for available work, when challenged by labor demands, can seem self-defeating. As such, the wonder and power of Cesar Chavez's Farm Workers Movement can be understood when union organizers were able to negotiate successful labor contracts with the powerful grape industry in California.

Washington State provided a much different political, agricultural, and demographic dynamic that has effectively worked to keep Latino farmworkers in a vulnerable position.[26] For example, the history of the social and physical discrimination targeting the bracero workers from Mexico during the 1940s resulted in the workers performing countless work stoppages and strikes to protest the inhuman work conditions typical of the agricultural industry in that state. The workers were adept at thwarting the attempts of growers to use migrant workers against their resistance such that the growers eventually gave up and opted to end the Bracero Program in 1947.[27]

Today, small family farms of less than 100 acres represent the majority of acreage in Washington State although they are losing ground rapidly to the larger "mega" farms of over 2,000 acres of land characterized by California's agricultural industry. Still, these mega farms represent only 5.7 percent of the farmland in the state in 1997.[28] And, although agricultural production overall is declining, farmers have fixed costs and must harvest their production, regardless of the availability and cost of labor. As agricultural production declines and more farms succumb to bankruptcy, demand for workers is surmised to decline, although recent years have seen complaints of a labor shortage.[29] Issues of housing remain a primary concern for farmworkers, in addition to steady yearly employment (as opposed to seasonal work), and worker benefits such as health care and retirement.[30]

The challenges of organizing can be understood when placed in the context of the power structures that exist to deny support for farmworker labor conditions. Recalling the particular difficulties within the agricultural industry, Rosalinda explains:

> Organizing is different with farmworkers (than
> with other labor groups). You use the same
> organizing principles and the basics are the same

but it is the level of fear that exists in the farmworker community itself that makes organizing this group so different. There is such an imbalance of power between the grower and the worker where they [farmworkers] are so powerless.

The fear they carry is the fear of losing their job… they are living paycheck to paycheck; there is the fear of being homeless in a rural area, without any support systems… it (the fear) is more intense. Lack of documentation intensifies this fear but really, we're talking about people who are living at or below the poverty line. This makes them extremely vulnerable.[31]

Maralyn Edid documents the history of "racism and xenophobia" that has plagued agricultural workers from the Japanese and Chinese in the West to Latino immigrant workers, citing the constant threat of job loss and potential violence that accompanies workers who attempt to improve their work conditions through labor organizing. Growers have also had at their disposal access to powerful "social, political and judicial allies" to further their union busting efforts.[32] Complicating this situation, Rosalinda explains that,

…in traditional unions, the worker pays dues. This is the return on the investment and effort taken by the union to organize the workers. But farmworkers cannot pay as much as other workers, so what is the return on the initial investment? Most unions won't work with farmworkers because of this. Agricultural work is also less than 3 percent of the workforce so it doesn't make practical sense to expend energy on this group (this also includes the fisheries and other related work).[33]

Furthermore, the "heterogeneous socioeconomic character" of farmworkers, the "chronic oversupply of farm labor," and the inevitable deterioration of union power and control as old workers retire and new ones replace them further serves to deter organizing this group of workers. Finally, farmworker organizers and leaders themselves differ on the kinds of strategies needed to permanently address their conditions.[34]

Additional concerns include the social relationships that tie the workers to the larger community. Consideration of these concerns demonstrates Rosalinda's attention to the complex social, economic, and political ties that characterize rural communities. Rosalinda states,

> What else makes this so much different than organizing other groups is that farmworkers have a family structure that supports a rural culture; that is, how people relate to each other and to the farmer (they work for) is quite complex. I mean, their children go to the same schools, they may attend the same churches, and they shop in the same food stores.[35]

This idea of the "family structure" supporting a "rural culture" speaks to the relational aspect of organizing and leadership. Here, Rosalinda understands the complexities and intricacies of power relations that intertwine workers' lives with growers' lives. Power may be centralized for the agricultural industry but for farmworkers, however frail and loosely organized their political and social networks to power structures, these relationships all lead back to the grower. Fear is one of the manifestations of these unequal social and power relationships. Moreover, her recognition of the importance of family was critical in her decision to pursue family members as key players in the campaign against CSM wineries. This strategy also targeted and dispelled the fear that the workers had by bringing family members into the decision-making process and thereby creating a more powerful sense of unity and force against the huge winery. Rosalinda continues on the aspects of organizing,

> What we're talking about is that this is near slave-like conditions that exist for the worker in terms of his relationship to the grower; it is this cycle of relating to each other in ways that are abusive. The abuse may be direct as in outright disrespect and labor exploitation; however, in many cases the grower is a "good guy" who tries to be fair; the reality is he still holds the power over the worker: power to decide how much and whether he gets paid, to decide whether he gets benefits, training, medical attention when he needs it; the worker may do all he can not to rock the boat and this work condition, this relationship, becomes "normalized. This is why it's like the plantation owner and slave worker—the relationship they have becomes a way of life so that many times the worker doesn't "see" the abuse (or unfairness).
>
> In this case, the grower is afraid of losing his well-trained worker and the worker is afraid of challenging his comfortable situation, losing his job, even when s/he knows that other workers are not faring so well.[36]
>
> This is where raising consciousness about the conditions of farmworker oppression and the lack of mobility for workers becomes important to the organizer. She must convey to the worker how they are benefiting while other farmworkers are losing. This is where you need to bring about unity. You do this gradually through dialogue. This is the importance of speaking "truth to power"[37] about the conditions of their work; this is where conflict arises

among the workers. But once they confront their fear and unite, their fear disappears and power is created.[38]

On Food Production-Food Justice

No issue can get people excited and interested in doing something about a problem as much as when personal dignity is involved. No injury is greater than not being looked upon as a human being. The deepest kind of hurt is when you find you're not welcome, when even by the tone of voice you are addressed, you know, that you are not considered to be anyone... The working conditions and the wages, the lack of drinking water, the lack of education, the lack of housing, all hurt but not so deeply as personal injury.
— Cesar E. Chavez, A *Union in the Community*

As an organizer who has won her fair share of labor battles, Rosalinda is only too aware of the limitations of labor union campaigns that focus on tangible and well-defined goals such as a union contract. Confronted with the always present conditions of poverty that farmworkers live with, winning contracts can seem to be a never-ending process. Rosalinda has evolved her knowledge of farmworker issues within the context of the agricultural global systems and food production. Agricultural sustainability programs focus on developing "softer" farming methods that are gentler on the earth and food but still render workers invisible in the process of food production and environmental sustainability discussions. Rosalinda is critical of this recent perspective:

Farmworkers are written off in the traditional agricultural model, and we only look at the farmworker as a charity case and offer our charitable efforts,[39] which assuages our guilt, but when we talk about the value of our food and food production then it becomes a different story. Instead of profit, we're also talking about equity. Instead of the bottom line in dollars, questions like what is equitable for workers? For growers?

Organizing in this context is about transforming the individual to value his or her work and to see the value they have in the whole system. The transformation is not just with the worker; it is the transformation in the relationships to the land, to the community, to the grower, to other workers. To elevate the farmworker presence in the food production system is how we create and develop leadership and farmworker unity so that they can create the opportunities for change and develop perceptions of why we're here and exist.[40]

Reframing the issue to that of food justice brings us to value the human, the individual, the work that s/he does in the system of food production.

We highlight the values of tenacity, endurance, perseverance, creativity, and by recognizing how this work is valuable and nothing to be ashamed of. These values are good values that come from our agrarian background... this way of life contributed to these values. When we think like this then we can understand why the worker must have a union contract; it gives them a sense of the value of their worth when they are paid well and can take care of themselves with a good labor contract. It becomes real in economic terms, which in turn, makes a difference in how they see themselves—with pride and respect.[41]

In the traditional model of food production that Rosalinda critiques, farmworkers are invisible, ashamed of the work they do, and seen as a sad by-product of the agricultural system. In fact, after a recent conference at Washington State University, held by the Children of Aztlan Sharing Higher Education (CASHE) organization, Rosalinda noted that the purpose of the conference was to provide career opportunities for immigrant Latino students to get out of the fields. Instead of viewing farm work as something to be respected and valued, it just becomes an embarrassing stepping stone to social mobility. Guillen indicates that "organizing is a way to bring respect and pride to the hard work that farmworkers do."[42] Suggesting to students that they consider going into majors, like agronomy or environmental science/sociology that would help us to rethink and reframe agricultural work in more sustainable ways.

Speaking Truth to Power

The slogan, SPEAK TRUTH TO POWER, is from Saul Alinsky, activist organizer during the 1960s and 1970s. The banner was displayed in huge letters across the top of the wall of the UFW office in Sunnyside in the summer of 2002, when I first began work with the organization. I was hired to work with growers to develop a fair trade product, and I would think about that motto constantly, wondering what it meant or referred to. I could not understand how speaking "truth" to people (like powerful agribusiness), who attained their power from ruthless and devious means, could be a strategy. Rosalinda explained to me that it was about always speaking the truth to those more powerful than you… that was the only weapon that poor people had. Even if you had to say it in several ways, several different times, and by different means, you never risked tripping yourself up if you always spoke the truth. She used the example of the farmworkers honestly explaining to the growers their conditions of work and living and how eventually, some of them had to listen and would eventually understand why the workers were upset.

SPEAKING TRUTH TO POWER is not just a weapon; it is a way of being, of living. You cannot be different in your personal life than in your public life to be considered an organizer with integrity.[43] This is the concept of integrating one's public life with their personal life that makes the idea of "transformation" in social justice work so extraordinary, as Rosalinda discussed earlier. During this time, President Clinton was in the spotlight for his less than honorable activities with a young intern. Although he was doing a lot of good things for the country's economy and social policies, this "disconnect" in his public life from his personal life became his political Achilles heel. This motto echoes the views of Mendez-Negrete's research on Chicana leaders, one of whom expressed it this way:

> It is not enough to exercise leadership with others; leadership begins at home… Leadership begins with the exercise of justice, fairness, and equality within the leaders' private world.[44]

Maria Gutierrez De Soldatenko urges researchers to "examine the lives of Chicana and Latina leaders" in order to "learn about their participation, commitment, and strategies… in which Latina organizers develop leadership skills in response to both Anglo and male union bureaucracy and the needs of [Latina garment] workers. In her research of organizing Latina garment workers in Los Angeles, Gutierrez De Soldatenko argues that leadership is created and embodied in the organizers, the process of organizing, and the workers in their struggle for justice. In her study, she found that all of the women she identified were leaders with similar family backgrounds and a "highly developed sense of social justice… that began in their own households or extended families."[44]

The question must then be asked, does this social justice work also translate to the attainment of egalitarian roles in the unions in which the women participate? As Margaret Rose found in her seminal work on the United Farm Workers union, the transition from a movement, where women were so vital, to the "institution" of the union "did not fundamentally alter gender relations in the family, on the job, or in the union."[45] I explore this idea in the final section below.

Organizing, Transformation, and Social Change

> It [organizing] is the feeling you get when you know that you've connected to someone to help them to help themselves so that they see how influential they've been in people's lives—so that you share power—the ability to help take it from the powerful and then to be able to walk away and leave the workers with the power they've won for themselves. That's about "as close to God as one can get"… to know that you've helped to transform someone's life.
> —Rosalinda Guillen

At one point in the CSM campaign, as they were working with the CSM management on the issues that the workers were drafting, a competitor farmworker organization from the Midwest approached the management in an attempt to win a "sweetheart deal."[46] This organization had not talked to the workers about their demands, and it was rumored that they had been brought in by one of the other local farmworker organizations to thwart the efforts of Rosalinda and her team. At this point in time, the workers and organizers had not yet affiliated with the United Farm Workers AFL-CIO in California.

The leader of this farmworkers union approached the CSM management to strike a deal that was very patronizing to the farmworkers, according to Rosalinda. He was speaking for them rather than allowing them to speak for themselves. The leader was also a born-again Christian who used his faith to proselytize and impose his beliefs on the workers. He had written into the contract that workers could be dismissed from the union if they were cited for drunk driving. To write into a contract something that first, didn't come from the workers, and second, was imposed by someone else's moral beliefs was condescending and disempowering.[47] This "style" of leadership is representative of the traditional form of leadership that I defined earlier in this essay.[48] Concern for establishing strong social relationships with the farmworkers is not a leadership "trait" in this model. The goal of achieving a union contract is first and foremost. This is accomplished by exerting "visible authority and influence" in the "political and economic affairs" of union organizing work.

> No one can become an organizer by taking classes or following a book. You can tell a good organizer by the way s/he lives their life and do their work with others—it is about living honestly, with integrity, and commitment to the cause you are working on… You can't have an ego in organizing… A lot of people call themselves organizers and what they do is organize events to bring people together… but, I'm sorry, I don't mean to disrespect their work because it is important… But that's not organizing. Real organizing is being what Cesar (Chavez) called a "servant to the people." It is not doing community service or "doing service work" because that implies doing it on your own time and doing what you think needs to get done, and maybe with their input. But when you are a servant to the community, you do the work that needs to be done as situations in the community demand.[49]

These thoughts are echoed by another former farmworker activist leader, Mily Trevino-Sauceda, Executive Director of Lideres Campesinas, a farmworker women's leadership program in California whose philosophy of promoting leadership among farmworker women "is not based on promoting single personalities, but on the creation of shared trust.[50]

The following narrative shows the significance of establishing trust among the workers through the development of secure relationships between the organizer and worker and between the workers themselves. However, the end result establishes more than worker unity; it is also about the personal transformation of the female workers' own fears about each other.

> If an organizer is imposing their values or ideas onto others, that is not organizing. But you have to have a good sense of what is right and wrong. For example, there was a woman who worked at the Chateau Ste. Michelle (CSM) winery who was extremely beautiful but unmarried; she was having affairs with the married men and had two children from these men. However, she was a good organizer—she had a good sense of timing and planning and getting the work done but the other women didn't trust her. To them, she was a whore. I hadn't known this about her; I just saw her ability to do the work and saw in her the potential power for leadership... I presumed later that she had these relationships with men to validate her worth. So I called a house meeting but the other women didn't want to invite her. I laid out all of the reasons for including her and then asked what was going on and the women told me. After listening to their concerns, I said, "Look, if we don't include her, you know that the CSM management is going to use

her against us… we have to all be in this, together, every one of us." So the women agreed, understanding the tactical need to include her. In the end, when they won the contract, this woman didn't need to have the men anymore… she could start saying "no"… she had higher wages, health benefits, a pension, vacation and sick time, and most importantly, respect from her fellow workers. She had something, she had worth. She could take care of her children by herself without the men. So organizing transforms lives in all ways… if there is unbalance in people's lives, and you are working for something that is just and right, it can't help but also bring balance into their life in other ways.[51]

Patricia Hill Collins refers to the "distinctive yet interlocking structures of oppression,"[52] that is "the macro level connections linking systems of oppression such as race, class and gender."[53] In her analysis, race, gender, and class cannot be separated from each other because they are intricately woven pieces into the larger structure of domination. To say that farmworker men and women were "sexist" by taking advantage of their *compañera* or not supporting her simplifies and overlooks the hard realities of a single, unmarried farmworker woman with children. For Martha Gimenez, this situation helps to substantiate her assertion that the basis of power rests in how social class is grounded in social interactions.[54] Of special interest is how Rosalinda's philosophy of organizing created a transformational experience for the woman but also created points of transformation for the others, both men and women in the group; in essence challenging the destructive forms of working class "machismo" preventing the attainment of complete equity in the union contract.[55]

The following example provides details of another significant instance of Rosalinda's organizing philosophy that demonstrates how lives are transformed. What becomes important to note here is the role that Rosalinda's philosophy plays in transforming the male union leaders' ideas about their female co-workers and co-organizers. This event occurred after the signing of the union contract with Chateau Ste. Michelle wineries.[56]

> After the contract had been signed, it opened up many opportunities for the workers. Now, you cannot have discrimination based on gender so all opportunities have to be available to everyone including the women. The night shift became available and there was this husband and wife team who were really poor. Well, she signed up for the night shift and passed all the tests, in particular one that dealt with operating a grape harvesting machine. If you've seen one of those machines, they are huge and intimidating; she had to learn how to operate the equipment and she passed the tests and got the position. Her husband got angry that she had gone and done that despite his protests.
>
> Apparently his wife had wanted to work the late night shift because she could make more money, which would help out their family situation. She'd worked hard to train and was proud of the fact that she'd learned to operate that heavy equipment. But her husband didn't want her to do the work because it meant that she would be the only woman out there with all these other men in the vineyards and he didn't think it was appropriate for her to be out there without him... but she did it anyway so when she returned home the next morning he beat the crap out of her and nearly put her in the hospital. Neither one of them showed up for work

that day and when the other union members found out what happened, the worker leaders came to confront me about the situation.

What this was about was the fact that they had been fighting all these years for work opportunities but in reality it was about confronting their sexism. The opportunities they fought for were assumed to be for the men only. They were upset with me that I hadn't explained this to them... the whole equality of job classification and what that meant in real life... I mean these guys really thought that women were not physically or mentally capable of doing this kind of work! The men thought that this was traditional male-only work and not appropriate for the women.

This ended up being a five-hour-long discussion with them that went late into the night. They'd come directly from the fields to talk to me about it.[57] I told the men how they could possibly think otherwise? That here were these women who had worked just as hard as they had to win this contract... they had witnessed that... So now, they are going to deny these women the right to earn the same wages as them after the work they did to bring in the contract? The men get all the reward but the women continue to get the shit work? So if that's the case, I said to them, are you saying that it is okay to let her get beat up and are you going to beat your wife up if she wants to do this work if she's qualified to do it?

The men were stunned by this question. They just had not ever been confronted like that (and by a woman) but also had not thought through the implications of their organizing work. Once it sunk in, they looked at me and said, "So, what are we going to do to fix it?" I told them, "You are the leaders and this is your contract... my question is what are YOU going to do about it? You need to show by example to everyone in the company, men and women, that this is not acceptable behavior. This has to come from you, not me, because it is worthless if it comes from me." So they went and talked to the woman who'd gotten beat up and gave her their support and assurance that she had not done anything wrong. They, as men, had to let her know that she hadn't done anything wrong. Then they went and talked to him... they actually had him suspended from work for a week to take care of his kids and wife and they went to talk to him everyday to check on him and make sure that they were all right and then they went back to work.

This was a long process to monitor... to support the woman. This is another example of the kind of transformation that occurs in people but also of having to work with what you have... the workers are human and have many problems associated with poverty and the lack of education and health care. You have to be able to let go of the need to control the situation and understand that through conflict comes the "truth" or the answer to a given situation.[58]

As it occurred here, transformation was about the workers facing the contradictions in their lives. Confronting these contradictions honestly and with integrity helps people to grow and learn from their experiences. In this instance, they had to decide if their actions were consistent with their beliefs, whether articulated or not. If they had chosen not to do anything, to support their comrade's behavior and blame Rosalinda, for example, that response could be referred to as living with one's contradictions, which I argue is representative of traditional forms of male leadership. The contradiction or inconsistency between stated beliefs and resultant actions may be understood as a sign of weakness or vulnerability that must be resolved quickly, quietly, and unobtrusively. Admitting "failure" after all of their work, that is, not recognizing the full outcome of their egalitarian goals, might possibly make them look foolish and undeserving of their newly earned leadership status. Masculinity in this patriarchal construction does not allow for mistakes, failure, or inconsistency.

That the men chose to redefine patriarchal masculinity and opt for building strong relationships with the women through honesty, integrity, trust, and power sharing attests to the model of leadership provided by Rosalinda. Years later the workers reaffirmed their trust in her leadership abilities and in her character, indicating that theirs was a life-long relationship.[59] The power of the lesson in this last narrative cannot be understated. The women workers were as much transformed by their working for equality on the job, for work opportunities, and in the home as much as the men were transformed in their liberation from their old sexist ideologies and behaviors.

Conclusion

Although gender is not made explicit in Rosalinda's leadership or organizing efforts, her emphasis on establishing trust through relationships and working to bridge the chasm between workers' public and private lives "fits" a style of leadership counter to traditional forms of leadership, as noted in the introduction. A growing body of research on women's organizing will contribute much to understanding styles and models of leadership within a broader scope than presently exists. Although I have not detailed Rosalinda's relationships with her family and significant others toward assessing this public-private gap, her present situation appears to be one of a closely knit and large extended family that claims four living, thriving generations of Guillens. Her "collectivist" philosophy derived from her early Marxist lessons at home and shaped by male mentors (her father Jesus Guillen, Cesar Chavez, her husband Joseph Moore, and young activist Kurt Peterson) seems to say as much about her mentors' philosophies as it does about how she incorporated and understood their messages and training. It is useful to understand how Guillen approaches organizing and leadership activities as Deutsch tells us that "the construction of a gendered ethnicity might help explain variations in labor strategies as shaped by her personal experiences, ideological perspectives, and the socio-cultural and political structures within which she works (labor leadership, socio-political and patriarchal environments)."[60] In Rosalinda's situation, her farmworker status gave her legitimacy as a union organizer while her gender offered the possibilities to create new ideas about women's work and worth.

Anthropologist Michelle Rosaldo writes, "....women's place in human social life is not in any direct sense a product of the things she does, but of the meaning her activities acquire through concrete social interaction.[61] In other words, understanding Rosalinda's organizing work requires an analysis of the meaning of "organizing" to Rosalinda and how others respond to her interpretation and implementation of that knowledge. Rosalinda's success in organizing the Chateau Ste. Michelle workers was a collective effort on the part of the farmworkers, the organizers, winery negotiators, and Rosalinda's efforts to maintain a successful collective. This was performed through the development and maintenance of strong relational networks forged through confrontations of personal beliefs and subsequent actions between the workers and Rosalinda, among the workers themselves, and although not discussed, between the CSM management and workers.

Rosalinda left the union in early 2004 to form her own community organization called De Comunidad a Comunidad (Community to Community), a nonprofit organization working for sustainable communities through food justice efforts. Executive

Director Rosalinda Guillen has high hopes for this fledgling organization. She is working with a cadre of women activists and grassroots leadership along with "community folk" to bring farmworker and farmer issues to the national agenda. This "women power"[62] forms the basis of a leadership model that works well with the idea that organizing is not about ego. As Josephine Mendez Negrete discovered in her research on gendered leadership "Chicanas… concluded that leadership is more than believing or speaking a certain way; it is acting out a philosophy that creates change to benefit the many over the individual. For them, it is not enough to talk about change; leaders actively work to create it."[63] And as Rosalinda commented to me, "The ultimate goal of organizing is to empower people to change their lives."[64] Indeed.

The words of Chicana scholar, writer, and feminist Ana Castillo offer a fitting closure:

Han de saber at all times that we are gente. Each of us is a valuable human being, to ourselves and to our communities.

"Mas han de saber" that we must keep attentive to the needs of our bodies, minds, and spirits. Our bodies provide a vehicle for us throughout this life and we must be attentive to their needs. Our minds must be equally nourished. The life we live is a brief one; each of our spirits has a bigger plan, but while in this incarnation, for each of us to fulfill our purpose here we must be as fit as warriors.

"Han de saber" that our actions have consequences. Xicanisma, therefore, includes an ongoing awareness of our responsibility to ourselves, to those in our personal lives, to those we make alliances with, and to the environment (with all that the word implies).[65]

MARIA CUEVAS

Endnotes

1. The extract is from a telephone interview with Rosalinda Guillen, Nov. 30, 2004. Rosalinda actually had difficulty thinking about her ethnic identity as she explained that she had always thought of herself as a "farmworker" first and "understood" her ethnic identity as secondary. The topic of my research includes interviews with Latina and Mexicana union organizers involved in the boycott against Chateau Ste. Michelle wineries in Washington State between 1989 and 1996.
2. The seven-year campaign was initiated by farmworkers at the Chateau Ste. Michelle wineries working with an independent farmworker group; discussions of unionizing began in 1987 (Zachary Pascal, Wall Street Journal, June 7, 1995). For further information on the UFW in Washington State, see the following site: United Farm Workers in Washington State. Oral History Project sponsored by the Harry Bridges Center for Labor Studies, University of Washington, Seattle, WA, http://depts.washington.edu/pcls/ufw.
3. David Martinez, contract negotiator cited by Jeff Switzer, "Chateau Ste. Michelle farmworkers sign first union contract in state history" in Northwest News: Woodinville Weekly 20, no. 5 (Nov. 6, 1995).
4. See Margaret Rose, "Women in the United Farm Workers: A Study of Chicana and Mexicana Participation in a Labor Union, 1950–1980," Ph.D. diss., UCLA, 1988; and Vicki L. Ruiz, Cannery Women/Cannery Lives: Mexican Women: Unionization, and the California Food Processing Industry, 1930–1950 (Albuquerque: University of New Mexico Press, 1987).
5. I refer to Chicana/o as those Americans of Mexican descent or Mexican nationals who are raised and socialized in the United States.
6. Dolores Delgado-Bernal, "Using a Chicana Feminist Epistemology in Educational Research," Harvard Educational Review 68, no. 4 (Winter 1998): 555–83.
7. Ibid., 555.
8. For example, see Rosaura Sanchez, "The History of Chicanas: A Proposal for a Materialist Perspective" in Between Borders: Essays on Mexican/Chicana History, ed. Adelaida del Castillo (Encino, CA: Floricanto Press, 1990).
9. Josephine Mendez-Negrete, "Awareness, Consciousness, and Resistance: Raced, Classed, and Gendered Leadership Interactions in Milagro County, California" in Chicana Leadership: The Frontiers Reader, ed. Yolanda Flores Niemann with Susan Armitage, Patricia Hart, and Karen Weathermon, (Lincoln: University of Nebraska Press, 2002), 239–58; Maria A. Gutierrez

De Soldatenko, "ILGWU Labor Organizers: Chicana and Latina Leadership in the Los Angeles Garment Industry," Frontiers 23, no. 1 (2002): 46–60.

10. See Gutierrez De Soldatenko, 46–60.
11. See Gutierrez De Soldatenko, "ILGWU Labor Organizers"; "Women in the United Farm Workers"; Sarah Deutsch, "Gender, Labor History, and Chicano/a Ethnic Identity," Frontiers: A Journal of Women Studies 14, no. 2 (1994): 1–22.
12. Ann D. Gordon, et al., "Power, Influence and Visible Authority in the World of Politics and Economic Affairs," in Between Borders: Essays on Mexican/Chicana History, cited in Rosaura Sanchez, "The History of Chicanas: A Proposal for a Materialist Perspective."
13. Popular media and literature detail the lives of many famous charismatic male leaders who excelled in their public lives yet led private lives less than honorable to their families, such as former President William Clinton, Arnold Schwarzenegger who won the 2004 California gubernatorial race despite claims of sexual harassment by former co-workers, and Illinois Republican U.S. Senate nominee Jack Ryan who fell out of the race due to the publicity of his "immoral" marital sexual exploits. This separation of public life from their private or family life is what Rosaura Sanchez defines as "categories of social significance" in traditional leadership models in "The History of Chicanas: A Proposal for a Materialist Perspective."
14. Portions of this section were taken from "Rosalinda Guillen," by Maria Cuevas, Encyclopedic entry in Latinas in the United States: An Historical Encyclopedia, ed. Vicki Ruiz and Virginia Sanchez Korrol (Oxford: Oxford University Press, forthcoming).
15. For further discussion on Rosalinda's involvement with the Rainbow Coalition, see the Harry Bridges Center for Labor Studies "History of the UFW in Washington State," http://depts.washington.edu/pcls/ufw.
16. As part of the final negotiating stages, the independent organization had to identify and affiliate with a recognized labor union; they agreed to affiliate with Cesar Chavez's United Farm Workers, AFL-CIO union based in La Paz, Calif.
17. Jeff Switzer, in Northwest News:Woodinville Weekly 20, no. 5 (Nov. 6, 1995).
18. Rosalinda Guillen interviewed by author on October 8, 2001, in Sacramento, California.
19. Ibid.
20. Ibid.
21. Patricia Zavella, Women's Work & Chicano Families: Cannery Workers of the Santa Clara Valley (Ithaca: Cornell University Press, 1987); Gutierrez De Soldatenko, "ILGWU Labor Organizers."
22. Mendez-Negrete, "Awareness, Consciousness, and Resistance."

23. Jim Wasserman, Associated Press, Sept. 30, 2002, http://www.sfgate.com/ cgibin/article.cgi?file=/news/archive/2002/09/30/state1953EDT0159.DTL
24. "Davis Inks Farm Bills," Salinas Californian, October 1, 2002, 1A.
25. The extract is taken from Cesar E. Chavez, A Union in the Community. Draft essay compiled from tapes made during a visit to Detroit in May 1967, transcribed and edited by David Leonard Cohen with assistance form Sarah Rousseau, January 1969. Also see Marilyn Edid, Farm Labor Organizing: Trends and Prospects (Ithaca, NY: ILR Press, 1994); and Erasmo Gamboa, Mexican Labor and World War II: Braceros in the Pacific Northwest, 1942–1947 (Seattle: University of Washington Press, 2000).
26. Gamboa, Mexican Labor and World War II.
27. Ibid.
28. Agricultural Workforce in Washington State 2000, prepared by Loretta Payne, Economic and Policy Analysis Unit, Labor Market and Economic Analysis Branch, Washington State Employment Security, August 2001.
29. Ibid.
30. Ibid.
31. Rosalinda Guillen interviewed by author, Nov. 30, 2004.
32. Maralyn Edid, Farm Labor Organizing: Trends and Prospects (Ithaca, NY: ILR Press, 1994).
33. Guillen interview, Nov. 30, 2004.
34. Edid, 14–16.
35. Guillen interview, Nov. 30, 2004.
36. Ibid.
37. From Saul D. Alinsky, Rules for Radicals: A Pragmatic Primer for Realistic Radicals (New York: Vintage Books, 1971).
38. Guillen interview, Nov. 30, 2004.
39. This reminds me of a quote by Archbishop Dom Helder of Racife, Brazil, who stated, "When I give food to the poor I am a saint; When I ask why the poor have no food I'm a Communist." Talking about the food production system and how it treats our least respected and valued workers can change the whole direction of the issue to one of respect and dignity.From Solidaridad Newsletter, http://www.latrobe.edu.au/ latinamerican/laics/SOLI4_99; and Catholic Agency for Overseas Development, http://www.cafod.org.uk/where_we_work/latin_america/ brazil/helder_camara.
40. Guillen interview, Nov. 30, 2004.
41. Ibid.
42. Ibid.
43. This is not to say that organizers are saints, but particularly, working with farmworkers requires a level of trust and honesty; poor people have nothing else to rely on but their integrity and hard work.

44. Chicana Leadership, 5.
45. Rose, x.
46. See Rosalinda Guillen transcript at Harry Bridges Center for Labor Studies, http://depts.washington.edu/pcls/ufw.
47. Guillen, Nov. 30.
48. Ann D. Gordon et al., "Power, Influence and Visible Authority in the World of Politics and Economic Affairs," cited in Rosaura Sanchez, "The History of Chicanas: A Proposal for a Materialist Perspective."
49. Rosalinda Guillen interviewed by author, Nov. 7, 2004.
50. From Hispanics in Philanthropy, http://www.hiponline.org/home/Resources/News/October+2004+-+HIP+Grantee+Lideres+Campesinas+Receives+Ford+Award.htm.
51. Ibid.
52. Patricia Hill Collins cited by Martha Gimenez, "Marxism and Class, Gender and Race: Rethinking the Trilogy," in Race, Gender and Class 8, no. 2 (2001): 23–33.
53. Ibid.
54. Gimenez, 27.
55. Jose Alamillo, e-mail message to author, Dec. 16, 2004.
56. The final contract was signed on Dec. 5, 1995.
57. This is an instance of being available to the workers on their time and not on Rosalinda's time; it is a learning moment and an example of relationship building that cannot be planned ahead.
58. The above comment applies here as well.
59. Ten years to be exact, according to a recent conversation between Rosalinda and the CSM workers in April 2005.
60. Deutsch, 1.
61. Michelle Rosaldo, cited by Joan Scott in "Gender: A Useful Category of Historical Analysis," American Historical Review 91, no. 5 (December 1986): 1067.
62. See Margaret Rose, "'Woman Power Will Stop Those Grapes': Chicana Organizers and Middle-Class Female Supporters in the Farm Workers Grape Boycott in Philadelphia, 1969–1970," Journal of Women's History 7, no. 4 (Winter 1995): 6–22.
63. Chicana Leadership, 242.
64. Rosalinda Guillen interviewed by author, Oct. 8, 2001.
65. Ana Castillo, Massacre of the Dreamers: Essays on Xicanisma (Albuquerque: University of New Mexico Press, 1994).

Past, Present, and Future Directions: Chicana/o Studies Research in the Pacific Northwest

Gilberto Garcia

The collection of articles in this anthology includes examples of new research on the Mexican origin population in the Northwest as well as the emergence of a new group of scholars committed to the development of Chicana and Chicano Studies scholarship in the region. Moreover, the contributions in the anthology are part of a legacy that began in the Chicano era in the Pacific Northwest. Thus, the scholarship presented in this anthology is best understood within the historical context of the beginnings of Chicana and Chicano Studies programs in the region. The first part of this essay will examine the historical origins of Chicana/o Studies in the Northwest, with a special focus on the political aspects of the creation of the programs. The second part of the essay examines the scholarship and the nature of the current research trends in the field of Chicana/o Studies. Finally, the essay concludes with an examination of the future directions in the field and its impact in the Chicano community and institutions of higher education in Washington, Oregon, and Idaho.

The Politics of Chicano Studies in the Pacific Northwest: 1968–1978

Most studies on the Chicano Movement and its impact on U.S. universities and colleges focus primarily on the experience of people of Mexican origin in the states of California, Texas, and other regions of the American Southwest. Yet, Chicanas/os in the Pacific Northwest participated in the Chicano Movement and left an important Chicano Studies historical legacy in several institutions of higher education. During the late 1960s and early 1970s, Chicana/o students protested and demanded educational

change throughout the Southwest. Early organizations such as
United Mexican American Students (UMAS) and the Mexican
American Student Association (MASA) promoted political and
educational change in California. Originally founded in Los
Angeles, California, in 1967, UMAS emerged out of a student
conference held at Loyola University, while students at East Los
Angeles College formed the Mexican American Student
Association (MASA).[1] The movement eventually reached
institutions of higher education in the Northwest with Washington
State recording the highest level of activism. Following the
example of the communities in the Southwest, students attending
the University of Washington, Washington State University, and
Yakima Valley Community College founded UMAS, MASA, and
other organizations in their quest for social change. An important
contribution of the student movement included in their list of
demands the creation of Chicano Studies programs and
departments in the universities and colleges in the region. Thus,
Chicano Studies is not a recent development in the Northwest
(see Fig. C1).

*Fig. C1. Students picketing at the University of Washington, 1968
(Irwin Nash Collection, Washington State University Libraries).*

310

The activism of the Chicano movement began at the University of Washington when students joined the California Grape Boycott in 1968. From October 1968 to October 1969, students demanded that the university stop selling California table grapes on campus. Chicana/o students played an important role in leading the grape boycott through the work of UMAS, a student organization officially recognized at the University of Washington in the fall of 1968.[2] In January 1969, UMAS publicly criticized the university's position on the grape boycott and stated, "The time has come when the University should show more concern and responsibility toward poverty than merely studying it."[3]

The boycott received the support of a broad and diverse group of student organizations such as Students for a Democratic Society (SDS) and the Black Student Union as well as from students involved in the university Associated Students organization. During the controversy, the administration wavered in its dealing with the Grape Boycott Committee. However, by Feb. 18, the administration removed California table grapes from the Husky Union Building. In protest, the Young Republicans distributed free grapes outside the building, but UMAS students still claimed victory in the boycott against grapes (see Fig. C2 and Fig. C3).[4] A report in the student-run newspaper, the *Daily*, for the first time provided information on the goals and objectives of UMAS at the University of Washington. According to the report, the number of Chicano students had increased from three to about thirty students, largely due to the recruitment efforts of the Black Student Union's minority recruitment program. The students were successful in persuading the Romance Language Department to offer a course in Mexican American history and culture in spring quarter 1969. Other issues discussed in the article included the continuation of recruitment drives in the Yakima Valley and the involvement of the student organization in the Chicano community.[5]

Fig. C3. Grape boycott, Seattle,
Safeway, Nov. 1969 (Irwin Nash
Collection, Washington State
University Libraries).

Fig. C2. Students picketing at the University
of Washington, 1968 (Irwin Nash Collection,
Washington State University Libraries).

Indeed, students from the University of Washington returned to the communities in the Yakima Valley and experimented with outreach community programs. La Escuelita, a program designed for the youth in the Yakima Valley, and El Año del Mexicano, a program involved in expanding political participation for Chicanos, attracted students from the University of Washington. For example, Chicanos from the university received a grant for Calmecac, a project focusing on the education of Chicano children in the Yakima Valley.[6] This program became a component of the project La Escuelita in Granger, Wash.

In the area of instruction, students and faculty formed a Chicano Studies Committee whose main objective was to develop a Chicano Studies proposal. This committee became involved in discussions related to the hiring of more Chicano and Chicana faculty and the eventual establishment of a Chicano Studies Program.[7] Tension and friction between the administration, the Chicano faculty/staff, and the students became evident when the university supported the rejection of Carlos Muñoz's tenured track position in the Political Science Department. In response to the administration's decision, students staged a sit-in and trashing of the Dean's office on May 13, 1974. Afterward, Dean Beckmann promised to hire a minority associate dean who would serve also as a tenured professor.[8] The sit-in set the stage for the events in 1975 that led to one of the most serious crises faced by the university.

A defining moment in the history of Chicano Studies in the University of Washington occurred in 1975 when the administration fired Juan Sanchez, Supervisor of the Chicano Division of the Educational Opportunity Program in the Office of Minority Affairs, and Gary Padilla, Director of the Chicano Studies Program.[9] Also, the administration suspended Rosa Morales, secretary of the Chicano Studies Program. Ironically, the firing of the two Chicanos took place just days after the celebration of the third annual Semana de la Raza commemorating Cinco de Mayo.[10] Newspaper accounts reported that Dean George Beckmann of the College of Arts and Sciences and Dr. Samuel E. Kelly, Vice President of Minority Affairs, recommended the dismissal of the two Chicano administrators. Apparently, in a meeting held on Apr. 29, several Chicanos confronted Dean Beckmann on the elimination of Chicano candidates for an associate dean appointment. Among the Chicanos present, Juan Sanchez and Gary Padilla participated in the discussion that later led to charges of threats against Dean Beckmann. In a statement released on the firing of the two Chicanos, Dean Beckmann argued, "Use of support of threats of violence to persons or property can not be tolerated and is not consistent with the rules of Conduct, adopted in 1973 by the Board of Regents."[11] Dr. Kelly stated that Juan Sanchez refused to abide by an administrative ruling on protests in the university; consequently, he was forced to fire him from the position for insubordination.[12] The administrative action led to an immediate response from Chicano faculty, administrators, and staff through the resignation of twenty-eight Chicanos and Chicanas from the University of Washington. However, the protesters clarified their resignation was not in response to the firings but to the administration's lack of support for the development of the Chicano Studies Program.[13]

In the statement published in the Daily, the protesters exposed the lack of support from the university, listing and citing the small number of Chicano and Chicana faculty, a deplorable record in "affirmative action," and just as important the minimal financial support for the program.[14] On May 8, the ASUW voted on a resolution to call for a strike against the university in support of the Chicano Studies Program.[15] On May 13 and May 14, the crisis reached a climax with two major demonstrations in Red Square protesting the university's position toward the Chicano Studies Program (see Fig. C4). The *Daily* reported, "The day's protest began when about 350 people marched from the Ethnic Cultural Center up University Way, through campus, past the Padelford Hall office of George Beckmann, Dean of the College of Arts and Sciences, and into Red Square."[16] At least two thousand students joined the Chicano students in the first demonstration, and around one thousand

Fig. C4. *Students picketing at the University of Washington, 1968 (Irwin Nash Collection, Washington State University Libraries).*

in the second and last demonstration heard the grievances of the protesters.[17] While demonstrators heard music, speakers, and chanted slogans, President Hogness listened to the activities outside and once in a while peered through the window. Unable to work, the president acknowledged the pressure felt from the protests and pondered the need to resolve the crisis.[18] Eventually, meetings between President Hogness and the Chicano faculty discussed the options for a resolution of the crisis; topics of discussion covered the hiring of new faculty, structural changes, and budgetary issues.[19] Finally, in a letter dated May 29 to the Chicano Concilio, President Hogness proposed several policies in support of the development of Chicano Studies at the University of Washington. The proposal made a commitment to the improvement of the Ethnic Studies programs in the university and proposed a package of reforms that contained the following commitments: the recruitment and retention of minority faculty, the establishment of a non tenured faculty scholarly program of grants, the reduction of teaching loads to improve the production of scholarship, the establishment of a visiting minority faculty program for the purpose of attracting potential candidates to the university, and the improvement of communication channels between minority and non minority faculty as well as representatives of the administration.[20]

Other areas of concern focused on Chicano Studies and other Ethnic Studies programs, especially in the area of budgets, hiring of a new director, increased opportunities for graduate students, and changes in the Equal Opportunity Program (EOP). The changes in the EOP responded to the demands of Chicanos for more autonomy in recruitment and increased budgetary support for the programs.[21] On June 3, the *Daily* reported on the faculty's retraction of the resignations, finally putting an end to one of the most serious crises in the history of the University of Washington. In the end, the administration reinstated Gary Padilla as acting director of the Chicano Studies Program and withdrew Rosa Morales' suspension.[22] Within years of the first Chicano Studies course in fall 1969, the program developed new courses in history, political science, economics, folk dance, Spanish, and theater.[23]

By 1969, students in Yakima Valley Community College began the organization of Chicana/o students with the establishment of MASA. Conferences focusing on "cultural awareness" and student organizing prepared the ground for Chicano student activism in institutions of higher education.[24] In 1971, Yakima Valley Community College approved the first Chicano Studies course in the history of that institution. Two years later, after a series of clashes and protests that included the takeover of a building, Chicano and African American students demanded an Ethnic Studies program.

In the southeastern part of Washington, Chicana/o students enrolled in Washington State University (WSU) and organized MASA. After a series of meetings and demands between a Chicano Studies committee and the administration, the university supported the establishment of Chicano Studies courses and began the discussion of minority programs in 1969. A year later, protests against U.S. involvement in Cambodia and minority issues in the university radicalized students and pressured the university to move from discussion to the actual establishment of a Chicano Studies program. Appearing in the 1970–1971 academic year, the first Chicano Studies courses covered topics on the family, education, music, and culture.[25] At WSU, the establishment of Chicano Studies was part of a larger movement that included the participation of African American Students and radical white students. Several years later, students and faculty from Washington State University provided advice and support for the establishment of a Chicano Studies program at Eastern Washington University. In September 1977, the university appointed a social work professor to carry out the duties of the director of the Chicano Education program. In spring 1978, the Department of Social Work offered the first Chicano Studies course titled "The Chicano Experience"; in spring 1979, the Chicano Studies academic unit appeared in course offerings. The first two cross-listed and required courses occurred within five years (1982).[26] An explanation for the rise in student activism in the state of Washington is partially due to a small but growing Chicana/o student population in the various institutions of higher education. According to minority student records, in 1970 Washington State University reported forty-two Chicano students enrolled in the Experimental Education Program and ten Chicano students through regular enrollment.[27] Only twenty-nine Chicano students attended Eastern Washington University during the 1975–1976 academic year; several years after the Chicano Education Program was established in 1978–1979, that number increased to eighty-seven Chicano students.[28] The early years of Chicano Studies in the state of Washington followed patterns similar to those occurring in the Southwest and offered models for communities in Oregon and Idaho. What is certain is that the historical legacy of the politics of Chicano Studies set the foundation for the future growth of Chicana/o Studies scholarship in the Northwest.

Chicana and Chicano Studies Scholarship: Emergent Perspectives and Challenges to the Dominant Paradigm

A small but growing body of literature on the Chicana/o experience emerged in the Northwest region. Early research on the Northwest region was limited to a few scholars since most of the Chicana/o scholars focused on other areas of research in their disciplines. Early Chicana/o scholars working in the region include Tomas Ybarra–Frausto, Antonia Castañeda, Carlos B. Gil, and Ybonne Yarboro-Bejarano.[29] Non Chicana/o Studies scholars also contributed to the research conducted in the region, specifically the work of Richard Slatta.[30] Washington State Chicano historian Erasmo Gamboa single-handedly contributed to much of the early research on Chicanos in the region. His seminal work reflects on the Mexican migration to the area and the role of Mexican braceros in the development of the Northwest.[31] An important contribution of the pioneers in the region was the publication of a regional Chicano Studies journal that contributed to the history of ideas and research on the Northwest. Edited and published by Chicana/o scholars from the University of Washington, *Metamorfosis* (1977–1985) recorded the Chicana/o arts and historical experience in the Northwest. Most of the contributions reflected a focus in the humanities, with articles on Chicano theater, literature, poetry, and interviews of Chicano writers.[32]

The National Association for Chicana and Chicano Studies

In 1973, a small group of Chicana and Chicano faculty under the leadership of Theresa Aragon de Shepro established a Northwest "foco" or chapter of the National Caucus of Chicano Social Scientists, the precursor organization to the National Association for Chicana and Chicano Studies (NACCS). With a very small nucleus of Chicana/o scholars in the region, the response to the establishment of the chapter was not very enthusiastic.[33] In subsequent years, Chicana/o scholars presented papers in the association, but failed to maintain an active regional "foco."[34]

In the late 1980s, a new generation of scholars entered the region and initiated a movement to place Chicano Studies in the region within the national fold. Interestingly, it was not until sixteen years later that Chicano Studies in the Northwest region became once again a participant in NACCS.[35] In 1989, the national organization accepted a resolution for the establishment of a Northwest chapter.[36] This development set the stage for the next phase of Chicana/o Studies scholarship in the region. After 1989, regional conferences organized at Central Washington University, Yakima Valley Community College, the University of Washington, Washington State University, and Eastern Washington University brought attention to the growing Latino population in the states of Washington, Oregon, and Idaho.

More significantly, the small cadre of Chicana/o scholars in the region brought the NACCS annual conference to Spokane in 1995. This was a benchmark in the history of Chicano Studies in the region and highlighted the importance of communities beyond the traditional homeland of Chicanos in the Southwest. It was only the second time the association had met outside of the Southwest. Most fitting, the organization's theme *"Expanding Raza World Views: Sexuality and Regionalism"* focused on the issue of regions and regionalism in the formation of Chicano communities in the United States.[37] During the business meeting, the organization voted to change its name and became the National Association for Chicana and Chicano Studies. At the conclusion of the Spokane conference, the Northwest chapter continued to organize and lobbied a second time for the annual conference in the region. A central idea guiding the discussion in regional meetings focused on the importance of the growth and dispersal of Mexicanos in the new millennium. In 2000, Chicana and Chicano scholars from Oregon and Washington and regional community activists brought the national conference to the Northwest a second time. Under the title of *"Sabiduria, Lucha y Liberacion: Youth, Community and Culture en el Nuevo Sol,"* the conference was held in Portland, Oregon.[38]

A closer examination of the NACCS conference programs illustrates both the formation of a cadre of Chicano Studies scholars and the growth of a body of literature on the experience of Chicanas/os beyond the Southwest. Following a similar pattern to that in the Midwest, the growth of the literature is closely related to the participation of Chicana/o Studies scholars in the association.

At the national association meetings from 1989 to 2002, presentations on the Northwest region examined the history of migration to the area, the formation of communities in the Yakima Valley and Columbia Basin, the demographic growth of Latinos in the area, and the role of women in the community.[39] In the last fifteen years, a new group of Chicana/o Studies practitioners has contributed with a small but growing body of knowledge on the communities in the states of Washington, Oregon, and Idaho. Early writers of the region joined the movement and participated in the development of the organization. In 1989, Gamboa's "The Sonoran Migration from California to the Pacific Northwest during the 1850s" and in 1995, the panel North from Southwest: Chicanas/os in Washington, Oregon, and Idaho reflect the ongoing research of the history of the region.[40] During the Los Angeles conference, Carlos Maldonado presented "The Chicano College: An Archaistic Notion, or Viable Road for Empowerment in the 21st Century." Drawing from his dissertation research, the presentation explored the issue of Chicano colleges and their relevance in contemporary society.

Several years later, this study became an important contribution to the educational history of Chicanos and to the scant body of literature on the Northwest region.[41] In this important work, Maldonado examined the establishment and decline of an alternative Chicano educational institution. Several individual presentations and panels on Chicano-Mexicano communities in the Northwest were published in journals or chapters in books. Maldonado's *Mexicanos in Spokane, 1930–1992* opened new ground by examining the emergence of a Chicano/Mexicano community in an urban area.[42] Jerry Garcia's *A Chicana in Northern Aztlan: An Oral History of Dora Sanchez Treviño*, and *Mexican Migration, Labor, and Community Formation: A Case Study of Quincy, Washington, 1943–1980*, examined gender issues and labor migration factors in the formation of communities in the Northwest region.[43] Other community studies include Gilberto Garcia's "Mexicano Communities in the State of Washington: A Case Study of Othello," which explored the social, cultural and political life of a community in the Northwest.[44]

Adding to the body of literature on the region, *The Chicano Experience in the Northwest*, a collection of original essays covered subjects on history, demographics, politics, agricultural workers, education, La Chicana, and a bibliographic essay of works in the region.[45] The significance of this publication is that all of the contributors were educators in institutions of higher learning in the region and most of them members of NACCS.[46] Maldonado contributed with "An Overview of the Mexicano/Chicano Presence in the Pacific Northwest" and "Mexicano/Chicano Agricultural Workers in the Pacific Northwest"; both studies provide historical summaries and analysis on the condition of farmworkers in the area.[47] Gilberto Garcia's "Organizational Activity and Political Empowerment: Chicano Politics in the Pacific Northwest" presents a historical and demographic analysis on the political experience of Chicanos in Washington, Oregon, and Idaho.[48] In "Latinos and Latinas in the Northwest: A Demographic Profile," Guadalupe M. Friaz examines socioeconomic and demographic variables that affect the Latina/o communities in the region.[49] Finally, Estela Elizondo Rodavancev's "Chicanos in the Pacific Northwest: A Bibliographic Essay" is an annotated bibliography covering various topics such as demographics, historical studies, bilingual education, political studies, audiovisual materials, and print media publications.[50]

A more recent publication in the study of communities beyond the Southwest, Gilberto Garcia and Jerry Garcia's "The Illusion of Borders: The Impact and Growth of the Mexican Origin Population in the New Millennium" articulates a critical perspective of the "Southwest centric" paradigm dominant in Chicana/o Studies. After an examination of recent Chicano historiography and a demographic analysis of the new reality facing Chicanos/Mexicanos in the United States, the authors conclude: "The development of a national perspective is imperative in order to examine the past and current status of Mexicans in the United States and to continue challenging the field so it moves towards full incorporation of all regions within the United States."[51] To conclude, the continued growth of Chicana and Chicano Studies scholarship in Pacific Northwest communities is shifting the paradigm dominant in Chicana/o Studies and reflects emergent perspectives that challenge old assumptions and generalizations in the formation of Mexicano-Chicano communities in the United States.

Future Directions in Chicana and Chicano Studies Scholarship in the Northwest

In spite of the small number of scholars in the Northwest and the geographical isolation from the large Mexican communities in the American Southwest, the past and present work of Chicana/o scholars established the foundations for an optimistic future in the region. The essays in this anthology reflect future directions in the field of Chicana and Chicano Studies and present a diverse and heterogeneous community. For example, while the anthology includes essays covering old topics, several of the papers explore new themes and point to new directions for research in the states of Washington, Oregon, and Idaho. Among those themes, the essays examine the comparative experience of Mexicans and other ethnic/racial groups in the Northwest, the story of the labor contractors, the role of women in the history of activism, and the history of the Catholic Church and its relationship to the community. Recent scholarship expands on the diverse experience of the Latina/o community in the region and indicates new research trends in Chicana/o Studies.

Previous studies focused on the rural and agricultural character of the population, new studies point to a more diverse experience. For example, Elizabeth Salas' "Mexican American Women Politicians in Seattle," examines the diverse participation of Mexican American women politicians in the Seattle area and illustrates the urban experience of the communities in the region.[52] Anthropologist Lynn Stephen's "Globalization, the State, and the Creation of Flexible Indigenous Workers: Mixtec Farmworkers in Oregon," directs attention to the role of Mixtec women in the farmworkers union in Oregon and illustrates the heterogeneous character of the Latino community in the Northwest.[53] Gilberto Garcia's "Beisboleros: Latin Americans and Baseball in the

Northwest, 1914–1937" explores the participation of Latino baseball players in the minor leagues in the Northwest and illuminates the diverse immigrant experience of the community.[54]

On the cultural aspects of the community, "Alfredo Arreguin: Patterns of Dreams and Nature" by Lauro Flores examines the contribution of Alfredo Arreguin in fine arts, while Jerry Garcia's "The Measure of a Cock: Mexican Cockfighting, Culture, and Masculinity" sheds light on the popular culture of Mexicanos in the region.[55] Other indications of future directions in Chicana and Chicano Studies research is found in recently completed dissertation on topics related to the Latino communities in Washington, Oregon, and Idaho. Dissertations completed in the last seven years cover topics on entrepreneurs, lawyers and civic involvement, educational institutions and Latinos, and studies on various aspects of the educational experience of Mexicans and Mexican Americans.[56] Considering the above research themes and the continuous expansion of research into different directions, the future of Chicana and Chicano Studies scholarship is bright and full of potential.

Conclusion

From the late 1960s into the new millennium, the field of Chicana/o Studies has contributed to educational reform in higher education and opened the doors to people of Latino origin. More importantly, early pioneering scholars in the region cemented the foundations for a new generation and a promising future. First of all, the establishment of programs and departments in community colleges and universities has been instrumental in the growth of students in institutions of higher education and thus the foundation for a new generation of Chicana/o scholars. Second, the field of Chicana/o Studies in the last thirty-seven years contributed with the introduction of a new curriculum that transformed the character of liberal education in the region. More significantly, Chicana/o Studies scholars produced a distinctive body of literature in the social sciences and humanities, as well as alternative interpretations of American institutions and society. These ingredients provide the foundation for the future direction of Chicana/o Studies scholarship in the Northwest.

Nevertheless, in order to guarantee a future for Chicana/o Studies scholarship, Chicanas/os in institutions of higher education must play a more active role in the mentoring, recruitment, and graduation of students. This is especially critical in the stage from the baccalaureate to the master or doctoral level. Building on the early struggles to open the doors of the university for students at the undergraduate level, it is necessary that Chicana/o faculty demand the opening of doors for Chicana/o students at the graduate level. A more active and firm position from Chicana/o faculty, administrators, staff, and students is needed to advance Chicano Studies into the future. An increase in the number of students at the graduate level will logically lead to an increase in the production of new scholarship. Currently, the status of Chicano Studies in higher education varies from institution to institution in the region. The University of Washington offers a major in American Ethnic Studies with a concentration in Chicano Studies. Chicana/o Studies faculties specialize in history, women studies, and anthropology.[57] Washington State University offers a Bachelor of Arts degree in Comparative American Cultures with an option in Ethnic Studies and specialization in Chicano-Latino Studies.[58]

Meanwhile, Eastern Washington University contains a small but relatively independent Chicano Studies program that offers a minor in Chicano Studies. Yakima Valley Community College offers an A.A. degree with a focus on Chicana/o Studies.[59] Established in 1994, the Department of Chicano Latino Studies (in reality a program) at Portland State University is a unit organized around a coordinator, chairperson, and two tenured faculty positions.[60] With the exception of Portland State

University, Chicana/o Studies is almost nonexistent in the states of Oregon and Idaho. The specific history of those institutions of higher education and the fact that Chicano student activism in those states never reached or equaled the level of intensity in the state of Washington explains the weak presence of Chicana/o Studies units in Oregon and Idaho. At the University of Oregon, the institution created an Ethnic Studies unit, but it contains no Latina/o or Chicana/o faculty. Only a Latin Americanist and a Chicano in literature are associated with the program. Oregon State University has an Ethnic Studies program composed of four faculty directed by a Chicana scholar. In comparison to Oregon and Washington, Idaho's institutions of higher education hold the worst record in regard to issues of diversity. The University of Idaho offers programs in American Indian Studies, Women's Studies, and Latin American Studies, but not in Chicana/o Studies or Ethnic Studies. The curriculum of Boise State University offers a Bilingual Education/ESL Language Program, but not Ethnic Studies or Multi-Cultural Studies. The history of Anglo-Mexican relations in Idaho partially explains the lack of Chicana/o or Latina/o Studies programs in the state. Of the three states, Idaho contains the smallest population of Latinos in the Northwest, which thus affects the strategies available for the predominant Mexican origin population. Also, the conservative climate in the region and the history of ethnic and race relations seriously affected the rise of Chicano activism that characterized the states of Oregon and Washington.

While it is too early to assess the role of Chicano Studies in the Northwest, the early foundation of these programs played an important role in the past and continues to play an important role in the growth of a group of scholars and the production of a Chicana/o Studies literature.

GILBERTO GARCIA

Endnotes

1. Rodolfo Acuña. *Occupied America: A History of Chicanos* (New York: Harper Collins Publishers, 1988), 335.
2. See the Associated Students of University of Washington for the student files on the organization, in the Special Collections, University of Washington Libraries.
3. *University of Washington Daily* (hereafter *UWD*), Jan. 22, 1969.
4. *UWD*, Feb. 18, 1969. A series of articles in the *Daily* presented a summary of the grape boycott issue on Feb. 19 and 20, 1969.
5. *UWD*, Jan. 28, 1969.
6. See letter from Franklyn L. Hruza, Director, Division of Continuing Studies Title 1 Liaison Officer, Dec. 19, 1969, and proposal on Calmecac. Located in Special Collections, University of Washington Libraries, WU Art and Sciences, Chicano Studies Program General Correspondence, 1969–1971. Accession #77-13, Box 3.
7. See files from Tomas Ybarra Frausto in the Special Collections at the University of Washington Libraries.
8. *UWD*, May 7, 1975.
9. Ibid.
10. *UWD*, Apr. 27, May 2, May 3, May 4, May 7, 1975.
11. *UWD*, May 7, 1975.
12. Ibid. See letter published in the *Daily*, May 13, 1975.
13. *UWD*, May 9, 1975.
14. Ibid.
15. Ibid.
16. *UWD*, May 14, 1975.
17. *UWD*, May 14 and May 15, 1975.
18. *UWD*, May 14, 1975.
19. *UWD*, May 23, 1975.
20. *UWD*, May 30, 1975.
21. Ibid.
22. *UWD*, June 3, 1975.
23. See the Special Collections, University of Washington Libraries, WU Arts and Sciences Dean Accession #87-28, Box 1 of 3.
24. For a discussion of the Chicano Movement in the region see, Gilberto Garcia, "Organizational Activity and Political Empowerment: Chicano Politics in the Pacific Northwest," in *The Chicano Experience in the Northwest*, ed. Carlos Maldonado and Gilberto Garcia (Dubuque, Iowa: Kendall-Hunt Publishing Company, 1995), 75–80.

25. Washington State University 1970–1971 Time Schedule, First and Second Semester.
26. Eastern Washington University Spring 1978 Course Schedule, Social Work. Eastern Washington University Spring 1982 and Fall 1982 Course Schedule.
27. Memorandum, Statistical Report on Minority Students for the Fall 1970, Oct. 23, 1970, Washington State University.
28. Memorandum, Student Enrollment, Mar. 2, 1979, Eastern Washington University.
29. See Antonia Castaneda Shular, Tomas Ybarra-Frausto, and Joseph Sommers, eds., *Chicano Literature: Text and Context* (Englewood Cliffs, NJ: Prentice Hall, Inc, 1972). The anthology included poetry from the Northwest region. Carlos B. Gil published "Washington's Hispano-American Community," in *Peoples of Washington: Perspectives on Cultural Diversity*, ed. Sid White and S E. Solberg (Pullman, WA: Washington State University Press, 1989), 159–93.
30. Richard W. Slatta, "Chicanos in the Pacific Northwest: An Historical Overview of Oregon's Chicanos," *Aztlan* 6 (fall 1973): 327–40; Richard W. Slatta and Maxine P. Atkinson, "The Spanish Origin Population of Oregon and Washington: A Demographic Profile, 1980," *Pacific Northwest Quarterly* 75 (July 1984): 109–16. Also, see the work of Richard Baker, *Los Dos Mundos: Rural Mexican Americans, Another America* (Logan, UT: Utah State University Press, 1995). On the demography of the area, see Annabel Kirschner Cook, "Diversity among Northwest Hispanics," *Social Science Journal* 23 (1986): 205–16.
31. Erasmo Gamboa, *Mexican Labor and World War II: Braceros in the Pacific Northwest, 1942–1947* (Austin: University of Texas Press, 1990).
32. Copies of *Metamorfosis* are found in the Special Collections, University of Washington Libraries.
33. See the Special Collections, University of Washington Libraries, files on Theresa Aragon Valdez, National Caucus of Chicano Social Sciences.
34. Antonia Castaneda Shular, Tomas Ybarra Frausto, Carlos B. Gil, and Yvonne Yarboro-Bejarano participated in several conferences in NACCS.
35. The National Association for Chicano Studies was established in 1972 by a group of Chicana and Chicano scholars meeting at the annual conference of the Southwestern Social Science Association. In 1995, the name was officially changed to the National Association for Chicana and Chicano Studies.
36. An organizing committee of faculty from Eastern Washington University, Washington State University, and Central Washington University made the proposal at the 1989 NACS annual conference held in Los Angeles, California.

37. Program National Association for Chicano Studies, 22nd Annual Conference. Expanding RAZA World Views: Sexuality and Regionalism. Spokane, WA, Mar. 29–Apr. 1, 1995. See the proceedings of the Spokane conference, Adaljiza Sosa-Riddell, ed, *Expanding Raza World Views: Sexuality and Regionalism Selected Proceedings from the 22nd NACCS Conference* (National Association for Chicana and Chicano Studies, 1999).
38. Program National Association for Chicana and Chicano Studies, 27th Annual Conference. Portland, Oregon, 2000. The national association met in Chicago in 1996 and 2002.
39. From 1974 to 2002, NACS annual conference programs reflect a small but growing interest in the Chicano experience in the Northwest.
40. See Erasmo Gamboa, "The Sonoran Migration from California to the Pacific Northwest during the 1950s." Paper presented in the XVII Annual Conference of the National Association for Chicano Studies, Los Angeles, California, 1989. Erasmo Gamboa, "North from Southwest: Chicanas/os in Washington, Oregon, and Idaho." Chair, panel presented in the 22nd Annual Conference of the National Association for Chicano Studies, Spokane, 1995. Gamboa published one of the first articles on the Chicano community in the Northwest. See Erasmo Gamboa, "Chicanos in the Northwest: An Historical Perspective," *El Grito* 6 (Summer 1974): 57–70. He is known for his major work on the "braceros" in the Northwest: see Erasmo Gamboa, *Mexican Labor and World War II: Braceros in the Pacific Northwest, 1942–1947* (Austin: University of Texas Press, 1990). Also, he has published articles and chapters in books ranging from topics dealing with the early Spanish explorations in the region, mule packing, the Mexican migration to the Northwest, Oregon's Chicano community, and Idaho's Chicano oral histories.
41. Carlos Maldonado, "The Chicano College: An Archaistic Notion or a Viable Road for Chicano Empowerment in the 21st Century." Paper presented in the 17th Annual Conference of the National Association for Chicano Studies, Los Angeles, California, 1989. Published later as *Colegio Cesar Chavez, 1973–1983: A Chicano Struggle for Educational Self-Determination* (New York: Garland Publishing, 2000).
42. Carlos Maldonado, "Chicano Cultural Identity in Bolillo Town." Paper presented in the 18th Annual Conference of the National Association for Chicano Studies, Albuquerque, New Mexico, 1990. Published later as "Mexicanos in Spokane, 1932–1992," *Revista Apple* 3 (1992): 118–25.
43. Jerry Garcia, "Chicanas in the Pacific Northwest: Quincy, Wash." Paper presented in the 25th Annual Conference of the National Association for Chicana and Chicano Studies, Mexico City, Mexico, 1998. Published later as "A Chicana in Northern Aztlan: An Oral History of Dora Sanchez Treviño," *Frontiers* 19, no. 2 (1998): 16–52. His research on Chicano

PAST, PRESENT, AND FUTURE DIRECTIONS

communities appeared in two presentations at the annual NACS conference, first as "Extending the Borders of Aztlan: Chicano Communities Outside the Southwest," as a panel presenter at the 21st Annual Conference of the National Association for Chicano Studies, San Jose, California, 1993; and subsequently published as "Mexican Migration, Labor, and Community Formation: A Case Study of Quincy, 1943–1980" in *The Illusion of Borders: The National Presence of Mexicanos in the United States*, ed. Gilberto Garcia and Jerry Garcia (Dubuque, IA: Kendall Hunt Publishing Company, 1995), 103–20.

44. See Gilberto Garcia, "Local Elites and Political Change in a Rural Community." Paper presented in the 18th Annual Conference of the National Association for Chicano Studies, Albuquerque, New Mexico, 1990. Published under the title of "Mexicano Communities in the State of Washington: The Case of Othello, Washington" in *The Illusion of Borders*, 121–34.
45. Carlos Maldonado and Gilberto Garcia, eds, *The Chicano Experience in the Northwest* (Dubuque, Iowa: Kendall Hunt Publishing Company, 1995).
46. Carlos Maldonado was the first regional chair of the Northwest region as well as the Director of the National Office of the National Association for Chicano Studies. Estela Rodavancev Elizondo was the regional chair of the association during 1997–1998. Gilberto Garcia served in several positions at the regional level including secretary and regional chair in 1999–2000. He served as the chair of the program committee at the national conferences held in Spokane and Portland, Oregon. Jerry Garcia was an officer in the regional chapter as well as a member of the Spokane organizing conference committee. Guadalupe Friaz served as an officer in the regional chapter of the association.
47. Carlos Maldonado, "An Overview of the Mexicano/Chicano Presence in the Pacific Northwest," in *The Chicano Experience in the Northwest*, 1–34. See also Carlos Maldonado, "Mexicano/Chicano Agricultural Workers in the Pacific Northwest" in *The Chicano Experience in the Northwest*, 99–124.
48. Gilberto Garcia, "Organizational Activity and Political Empowerment: Chicano Politics in the Pacific Northwest" in *The Chicano Experience in the Northwest*, 1–34.
49. Guadalupe Friaz, " Latinos and Latinas in the Northwest: A Demographic Profile" in *The Chicano Experience in the Northwest*, 41–69.
50. Estela Elizondo-Rodavancev, "Chicanos in the Pacific Northwest: A Bibliographic Essay" in *The Chicano Experience in the Northwest*, 193–234.
51. Jerry Garcia and Gilberto Garcia, "The Illusion of Borders: The Impact and Growth of the Mexican Origin Population in the New Millennium" *in The Illusion of Borders*, 22–24.

29

GILBERTO GARCIA

52. Elizabeth Salas, "Mexican American Women Politicians in Seattle," in *More Voices, New Stories: King County, Washington's First 150 Years*, ed. Mary C. Wright (Seattle, WA: The Pacific Northwest Historians Guild, 2003), 215–31.

53. Lynn Stephen, "Globalization, the State, and the Creation of Flexible Indigenous Workers: Mixtec Farmworkers in Oregon," *Urban Anthropology and Studies of Cultural Systems and World Economic Development* 30, no. 2–3 (2001): 189–214, 2001. Published in Spanish as "Globalización, El Estado, y la Creación de Trabajadores Indígenas 'flexibles'" Trabajadores Agrícolas Mixtecos en Oregon. *Relaciones* 90, no. 3 (primavera 2002): 89–114.

54. Gilberto Garcia, "Beisboleros: Latin Americans and Baseball in the Northwest, 1914–1937," *Columbia: The Magazine of Northwest History* 16, no. 3 (Fall 2002): 8–13.

55. Lauro Flores, *Alfredo Arreguin: Patterns of Dreams and Nature, Diseños, Sueños y Naturaleza* (Seattle, WA: University of Washington Press, 2002); Jerry Garcia, "The Measure of a Cock: Mexican Cockfighting, Culture, and Masculinity," in *I am Aztlán: The Personal Essay in Chicano Studies*, ed. Chon A. Noriega and Wendy Belcher (Los Angeles: UCLA Chicano Studies Research Center Press, 2004).

56. The following list of dissertations was completed through a search in the Dissertations Abstracts. I would like to thank Raul Garcia for assisting me in the initial stages of the research on the dissertations as well as in the Special Collections and Archives at the University of Washington. For the dissertations written by Spanish surnamed students, see Eduardo J. Armijo. "Head Start Performance Standards and Their Relationship to Key Early Head Start Programs Aims," Ph.D. diss., University of Washington, 2004.; Gerardo Diaz Canul, "The Influence of Acculturation and Racial Identity Attitudes on Mexican Americans' MMPI-2 Performance," Ph.D. diss., Washington State University, 1993; Maria Chavez-Pringle, "Latino Lawyers and Civic Engagement in Washington State," Ph.D. diss., Washington State University, 2002; Roberto Clenente, "Interdependent Perspective of Functions and Relations Perceived by School Counselors, ESL teachers, European-American, and Latino students," Ph.D. diss., Oregon State University, 1998; Gabriel E. Gallardo, "The Socio-spatial Dimensions of Ethnic Entrepreneurship: Business Activities among African-American, Chinese, Korean, and Mexican Persons in the Seattle Metropolitan Area ," Ph.D. diss., University of Washington, 2000; Erasmo Gamboa, "Under the Thumb of Agriculture: Bracero and Mexican American Workers in the Pacific Northwest, 1940–1950," Ph.D. diss., University of Washington, 1984; Tobias Marcelino Gonzales, "Locus of Control and Study Habits-Attitudes Scales as Predictors of Academic Achievement of Specially Admitted (EOP) Hispanic University Students," Ph.D. diss., University of

Washington, 1984; Luz E. Maria Villaroel, "A Study of Self-Concept among Mexican-American/Chicano(a) Students Attending Community Colleges and Four-Year Institutions of Higher Education in Oregon. Ph.D. diss., Oregon State University, 1986; Carlos Saldivar Maldonado, "The Longest Running Death in History: A History of Colegio Cesar Chavez, 1973–1983," Ph.D. diss., University of Oregon, 1986; Socorro Martinez, "A Comparative Study of Attitudes of Mexican-American Students in Third Grade Bilingual and Non-Bilingual Classrooms," Ph.D. diss., University of Oregon, 1983; Carmen Cecilia Ramirez, "A Study of the Value Orientation of Lane County, Oregon, Mexican American Mothers with a Special Focus on Family/School Relationships," Ph.D. diss., University of Oregon, 1981; Albert Alonzo Sanchez, "A Comparative Analysis of Acculturation and Learning Styles of Mexican-American Adults," Ph.D. diss., University of Idaho, 1998; Daniel Lawrence Trujillo y Casias, "Differential Perceptions of the Chicano Student Counseling Center at Washington State University: An Evaluative Study," Ph.D. diss., Washington State University, Pullman, 1978; Senon Monreal Valadez, "An Exploratory Study of Chicano Parent Perceptions of School and the Education of Their Children in Two Oregon Community Settings," Ph.D. diss., University of Oregon, 1974.

57. http://depts.washington.edu/aes/reqs.html
58. http://www.catalog.wsu.edu/Academics/CAC/descriptions.asp
59. Yakima Valley Community College Catalogue, 2002–2003. Chicano Studies, 102.
60. http://www.meromero.com/chicano program_3.html

CONTRIBUTORS

MARIO C. COMPEAN is an independent scholar based in San Antonio, Texas. He holds an M.A. in Educational Policy Studies with emphasis in the historical and social foundations of education from the University of Wisconsin-Madison, and has done graduate studies in history at Washington State University. He has held faculty appointments in Chicano Studies at several colleges and universities. The Crewport oral history research cited in this essay was conducted while he was Chicana/o Studies instructor and coordinator at Yakima Valley Community College in Yakima, Wash. Compean was an activist and leader in the Chicano Movement in Texas, cofounder and State Chair of the Mexican American Youth Organization (MAYO), and the founding State Chair of La Raza Unida Party.

MARIA CUEVAS is currently a doctoral candidate in Sociology from Washington State University in Pullman. She also holds a Bachelor of Arts degree from the University of California, San Diego, in Urban and Rural Studies (1981), a Master's in Public Health (1984), and a Master's in Social Welfare (1993), both earned at the University of California, Los Angeles. During (2002–2004) she worked with the United Farm Workers (UFW) union nonprofit organization called La Union del Pueblo Entero (LUPE) in Sunnyside, Wash. At present she holds an appointment with the Department of Liberal Arts at Washington State University in Tri-Cities where she teaches courses in Sociology, Rural Sociology, and Women's Studies.

DANIEL DESIGA was born in Walla Walla, Wash., and currently resides in Yakima, Wash. He earned a Bachelor of Fine Art degree from the University of Washington. A widely recognized Northwest Chicano artist, he is best known as a producer of murals and other works of art expressing farmworker themes. Daniel DeSiga's works have appeared in such diverse institutions as the Denver Art Museum, the San Francisco Museum of Modern Art, and the Wight Art Gallery at the University of California in Los Angeles. His murals appear in Shifra Goldman's book, *Walls of Fire*. DeSiga's publications also include the bookcover for *Culture Y Cultura: Consequences of the U. S -Mexican war, 1846–1848* published in 1998 by the Autry Museum of Western Heritage. The bookcover and Chapter Six of *Memory, Community, and Activism: Mexican Migration and Labor in the Pacific Northwest* includes portions of the *El Sarape* mural of Toppenish, Wash., *El Veterano*, *La Campesina*, and *Quintando la Sizaña*.

CONTRIBUTORS

GILBERTO GARCIA is a Professor of Chicano Studies at Eastern Washington University, and holds a Ph.D. in Political Science from the University of California at Riverside. He is coeditor with Carlos Maldonado of *The Chicano Experience in the Northwest* and coeditor with Jerry Garcia of *The Illusion of Borders: The National Presence of Mexicanos in the United States*. He is also the recent author of "Beisboleros: Latin Americans and Baseball in the Northwest, 1914–1937" in *Columbia: The Magazine of Northwest History* (Fall 2002).

JERRY GARCIA is an Assistant Professor of history and Chicano/Latino Studies and an Associate Research Scholar with the Julian Samora Research Institute at Michigan State University. He holds a Ph.D. from Washington State University. He is the coeditor with Gilberto Garcia of *Illusion of Borders: The National Presence of Mexicanos in the United States*. He is also the author of "A Measure of a Cock: Mexican Cockfighting, Culture, and Masculinity" in *I AM AZTLAN: The Personal Essay in Chicano Studies* edited by Chon Noriega and Wendy Belcher, and a number of other articles. He writes on the history and culture of Chicanas/os in the United States and is currently preparing a manuscript on domestic and foreign labor in the Pacific Northwest during World War II.

KATHLEEN RUBINOW HODGES works as a Reference Librarian at the Library and Archives of the Idaho State Historical Society. She and Dr. Errol D. Jones have coauthored "Writing the History of Latinos in Idaho," in *Latinos in Idaho: Celebrando Cultura*, ed. Robert McCarl (Boise: Idaho Humanities Council, 2003); and *The Hispanic Experience in Idaho: Papers Written for A Research Seminar at Boise State University* (Boise: Boise State University, Dept. of History, 1998).

ERROL D. JONES is a Professor of Latin American History at Boise State University and specializes in Mexican history. He is the editor, with David LaFrance, of *Latin American Military History: An Annotated Bibliography*, and the author of numerous articles on Latin American and Mexican historical topics. His most recent article, "The Shooting of Pedro Rodriguez," appeared in *Idaho Yesterdays*, Spring/Summer 2005.

334

CONTRIBUTORS

CARLOS MALDONADO holds a Ph.D. from the University of Oregon and is currently an Associate Professor of Chicano Studies and Director of the Chicano Education Program at Eastern Washington University. He is the author of *Colegio Cesar Chavez, 1973–1983: A Chicano Struggle for Educational Self-Determination* (Garland Publishing, 2000); *The Chicano Experience in the Northwest* edited by Carlos S. Maldonado and Gilberto García (Dubuque, Iowa: Kendall/Hunt Publishing Company, 1995); and "Mexicanos in Spokane, 1930–1992," *Revista Apple* 3, no. 1–2 (Spring 1992).

JOHANNA OGDEN, a Portland State University graduate, is coauthor of "Camp 56: An Oral History Project, World War II Conscientious Objectors and the Waldport, Oregon Civilian Public Service Camp," copublished by the U.S. Forest Service and Portland State University, forthcoming. She helped research "Voices of Oregon: Twenty-Five Years of Professional Oral History at the Oregon Historical Society," *Oregon Historical Quarterly, Summer 2002*. She has also investigated, documented, and arranged Spanish language transcription of the holdings of Latino oral histories in Pacific Northwest historical institutions.

RAMON SANCHEZ holds a Ph.D. in American Studies from the University of New Mexico, an M.F.A. from Bowling Green State University, and a B.A. from the University of Texas at El Paso. His dissertation, "Hispanic Themes of Redemption, Renewal, and Regeneration," is a critical evaluation of these themes in álvar Núñez Cabeza de Vaca's 1542 *La Relación* with specific attention to the development of Mexican American themes of redemption, renewal, and regeneration. Among his publications are entries in the Chicano Writers series of the *Dictionary of Literary Biography* Vols. 122 and 209. In addition, a collection of short stories titled *How to Meet the Devil and Other Stories* was published in 1995. Currently, Dr. Ramon Sanchez teaches at Central Oregon Community College.

MARGARITA VILLANUEVA holds a Ph.D. from the University of California at Santa Cruz and is an Associate Professor of Community Studies at St. Cloud State University in Minnesota. Her areas of interest include Latina/o Studies; Race, Ethnicity, Gender; Women's Studies; Cultural Studies; Environment and Community; and Historical/Comparative Sociology and Anthropology. Her publications include "Improving Communications: Latina Immigrants and Service Providers In Central Minnesota," for the Center for Rural Development and Policy Studies; "Racialization and the Latina Experience: Economic Implications," *Feminist Economics* 8, no.2 (July 2002): 145–61; and "TransForm/and Women's Studies: Latina Theory Re-Imagines *América*," in *Exclusions in Feminist Thought: Challenging the Boundaries of Womanhood*, ed. Mary Brewer (Brighton,UK/Portland, OR: Sussex Academic Press, 2002).